PELICAN BOOKS

STONEHENGE

R. J. C. Atkinson was born in 1920 and educated at Sherborne and Magdalen College, Oxford. From 1944 to 1949 he was Assistant Keeper of Antiquities at the Ashmolean Museum, Oxford, and then became Lecturer in Prehistory in the University of Edinburgh. In 1958 he was appointed to the Chair of Archaeology at University College, Cardiff, of which he was Deputy Principal from 1970 to 1974. He retired as Professor Emeritus in 1985. He served for ten years on the University Grants Committee, and is currently the chairman of the Royal Commission on Ancient and Historical Monuments in Wales and the senior Commissioner of the Royal Commission on the Historical Monuments of England. He has been a member of the Ancient Monuments Board for Wales since 1958 and of the Science-Based Archaeology Committee of the Science and Engineering Research Council since 1975, and is the chairman of the York Minster Excavation Committee. He has directed numerous excavations on prehistoric sites in England, Wales and Scotland, and since 1950 has collaborated with Professor Stuart Piggott and the late Dr J. F. S. Stone in excavations at Stonehenge and in advising the Department of the Environment on the restoration of fallen and leaning stones. Apart from Stonehenge his principal interests are in the application of scientific and mathematical methods to the solution of archaeological problems.

R. J. C. Atkinson

STONEHENGE

PENGUIN BOOKS

in association with Hamish Hamilton

Penguin Books Ltd, Harmondsworth, Middlesex, England
Viking Penguin Inc., 40 West 23rd Street, New York, New York 10010, U.S.A.
Penguin Books Australia Ltd, Ringwood, Victoria, Australia
Penguin Books Canada Limited, 2801 John Street, Markham, Ontario, Canada L3R 1B4
Penguin Books (N.Z.) Ltd, 182–190 Wairau Road, Auckland 10, New Zealand

—

First published by Hamish Hamilton 1956
Published in Pelican Books 1960
Reprinted with revisions 1979
Reprinted 1986

—

—

Printed and bound in Great Britain by
Cox & Wyman Ltd, Reading
Set in Monotype Garamond

Dedicated to my wife
amoris causa

Contents

CONTENTS

List of Plates

List of Figures

Acknowledgements

FOR permission to carry out the excavations described in this book my colleagues and I are indebted to the Inspectorate of Ancient Monuments in the Ministry of Works, and in particular to the late Chief Inspector, Mr B. H. St J. O'Neil, whose untimely death while this book was in preparation has robbed me of a friend and British Archaeology of one of its leading figures.

For leave to excavate a portion of the Stonehenge Avenue we are equally indebted to the National Trust.

The map of the Stonehenge region (fig. 8) is based on an unpublished original kindly placed at my disposal by Professor Stuart Piggott, and the drawing in fig. 7 on a sketch and description by Mr G. A. Gauld communicated to my colleague the late Dr J. F. S. Stone.

Permission to reproduce photographs has kindly been given by Professor Stuart Piggott (Plate 17a), Dr J. F. S. Stone (Plates 16a, 19b, and 21) and the late Dr O. G. S. Crawford (Plate 23a). Plates 1 and 2a are published by permission of Aerofilms Ltd, and Plate 3 by permission of Gateway Film Productions Ltd. The remaining plates are from prints made from my own negatives by Mr Malcolm Murray, technician in the Department of Prehistoric Archaeology, University of Edinburgh.

For reading the text before publication I am particularly grateful to Professor Piggott, Dr Stone, Mr Antony Snelling, Mr Brian Hope-Taylor, and my wife, all of whom have made valuable suggestions for its improvement.

Preface

I MAKE no apology for adding yet one more item to the extensive literature of Stonehenge. No full account of this, our leading prehistoric antiquity, has been written for more than twenty years, a period which has witnessed a lively quickening of public interest in archaeology and a renewed onslaught on the problems of Stonehenge itself. The intermission of a year in the current series of excavations at Stonehenge has given me the opportunity of setting down the main results which have been achieved so far, together with a more general sketch of the archaeological perspective against which they must be viewed. I do not for a moment pretend that the conclusions here put forward are final, for an archaeologist would be rash indeed who was not prepared for even his most cherished theories to be rudely controverted by subsequent research. None the less, I am rash enough to believe that the interpretation of Stonehenge given in this book is sufficiently coherent and firmly based to warrant publication, even though the current work on the site is not yet complete. Future events will show whether this confidence is misplaced.

One of the principal occupations of my colleagues and myself during our recent excavations at Stonehenge has been the answering of innumerable questions put by visitors. Among the busy preoccupations of an excavation undertaken in full view of a numerous and by no means inhibited audience, such questions are not always greeted with the warmth, or answered at the length, that they would frequently deserve under less harassing circumstances. I hope that this book will answer some of those questions; it cannot hope to answer them all.

This is not a book for archaeologists, or at least for those in whose studies Stonehenge must play a significant part; though I trust that even for them it may serve as an account of the results of our recent work, until the publication of the final report under the imprint of the Society of Antiquaries. Here I have written primarily for the ordinary visitor to Stone-

henge, in whom I have assumed an inquiring interest in the
history and purpose of the monument, but no knowledge
either of the details of its structure or of its archaeological
background in terms of British prehistory. But I have not
tried to write merely a hand-book to Stonehenge, to be used
by the inquiring visitor on the spot, as a supplement to the
concise Guide published by the Ministry of Works. Though
it will, I hope, be used in that way too, I have tried to give a
sufficiently full account of Stonehenge and its problems to
enable them to be understood by the reader who has never
seen the monument itself. If I succeed in this purpose, it will
be largely owing to the generous attitude of my publishers in
the matter of illustrations.

In writing a popular book on an archaeological subject
there is an ever-present temptation to simplify, to avoid controversial points, and to present the results of research in a
far more positive and confident manner than one would dare
to assume in addressing professional colleagues. While I cannot claim to be guiltless, I am at least aware of this temptation
and have tried to resist it. Where the evidence is ambiguous, I
have tried to make its ambiguity plain; and where there is no
sensible answer to a question I have not attempted to conceal
our ignorance. At the same time I have not scrupled to indulge in certain speculations, of a kind which my more
austere colleagues may well reprehend, upon the possible
significance and interpretation of many aspects of Stonehenge
where the evidence will not bear the full weight of certainty.
Silence upon such questions is too frequently justified by an
appeal to the strict canons of archaeological evidence, when
in fact it merely serves to conceal a lack of imagination.

I hope, therefore, that this account of Stonehenge in the
light of the most recent research will do something to dispel
the fog of doubt and misconception which still enshrouds our
foremost antiquity. I hope too that it may provide some illustration of the sort of evidence that archaeologists use, of the
ways in which they handle it, and not least of the limitations
to which their methods are subject. For though there can be
no doubt about the very great public interest in the *results* of

archaeological research, there is still much ignorance of how
those results are obtained, an ignorance for which archaeologists themselves are chiefly responsible.

Finally and above all, I must stress that the recent work at
Stonehenge has been a work of collaboration, and that it is to
my friends and colleagues Professor Stuart Piggott and Dr
J. F. S. Stone that are largely due such merits as this book
may possess. For its inadequacies, however, no one but myself is responsible.

Preface to the Pelican Edition

SINCE this book was first published, there have been two more seasons of excavation at Stonehenge, in 1956 and 1958. Happily the results of this new work have not made it necessary to alter in any important respect the account of the monument given in the original edition. Indeed, in many cases it has been possible to confirm suggestions which earlier could be put forward only as guesses.

For this reason I have not had to make any radical changes in the original text, beyond what is required to bring up to date the description of the monument, whose appearance has been strikingly altered and improved by the re-erection of some of the fallen stones. For this admirable piece of skilled and judicious restoration the Ministry of Works has earned the gratitude of every visitor to Stonehenge.

The main results of this recent work are described in the Postscript at the end of the book (p. 203). As in earlier years, our researches at Stonehenge have been made possible by the most generous and enlightened support from the Ancient Monuments Branch of the Ministry of Works. I am also delighted once more to acknowledge most gratefully the debt which I owe to my friends Professor Stuart Piggott and the late Dr J. F. S. Stone. It is melancholy to record that by Dr Stone's unexpected death in 1957 our happy collaboration at Stonehenge has been brought to an untimely end.

Preface to the 1979 Reprint

THIS edition is reprinted from the text of the Pelican edition of 1960, pending the publication of a fully revised version of this book. The preparation of this is well advanced; but its completion has been hindered by my involvement in university administration, and latterly by ill-health. I apologize to my would-be readers for the delay.

Since the first printing of this edition there have been two further seasons of work at Stonehenge, in 1959 and 1964. During the same period additional radiocarbon dates have been obtained for Stonehenge and the Avenue, the latest of these in January 1978. Meanwhile it has become clear that radiocarbon dates cannot be accepted at their face value, and have to be corrected to give the best estimate of the real date. For these reasons the time-scale for the building history of Stonehenge has altered in a radical way.

To take account of the results of later excavations, and of the new chronology, I have added a second Appendix (pp. 213–16). This should be read carefully in conjunction with chapter 3. The chronological table on pp. 215–16 replaces that on p. 101. The Bibliography has been brought up to date, and rearranged alphabetically by author.

When this Preface was already in draft, the death was announced of Robert Newall, who for half a century was the doyen of Stonehenge studies. He collaborated with Colonel Hawley in the extensive series of excavations from 1919 to 1926, and most of the line-illustrations in Hawley's interim reports are from his hand, though this has never previously been acknowledged in print. Many of his own invaluable observations of those excavations are gratefully incorporated in this book.

R. J. C. A.

CHAPTER ONE

Approach to Stonehenge

STONEHENGE stands on Salisbury Plain, about eight miles north of Salisbury and a little more than two miles west of Amesbury. To the visitor who approaches the monument for the first time, particularly from the direction of Amesbury, the first glimpse is often keenly disappointing, for the stones, vast though they are, seem entirely dwarfed by the even vaster background of rolling Wiltshire downland. It is not until one approaches more closely, so that the stones are silhouetted against the sky, that the true size of the place becomes apparent, and begins to communicate to even the most casual and unfeeling visitor something of the awe and wonder with which it has for so many centuries been invested.

The monument stands on a slight eminence of the chalk downs, but its position was evidently not chosen to command a particularly wide view. To the west the ground rises slightly; in all other directions it falls, though gently, the steepest slope being on the east, where the surface declines to the floor of a dry valley. In the immediate neighbourhood of the stones the ground is almost level.

The details of the surrounding landscape are almost wholly man-made: the buildings of Larkhill Camp to the north; the sunlit hangers of Boscombe Down aerodrome on the eastern skyline; the massed birch trees of Fargo Plantation to the north-west; the long wind-break of conifers north-eastwards towards Durrington; and the two plantations of beeches, north of the Amesbury road, which conceal the cemetery of Bronze Age burials known as the Old and New King Barrows. Only to the south does something of the primitive landscape remain, where the skyline of Normanton Down is punctuated by the barrows of another cemetery. Happily, however, all the more obtrusively modern elements in the landscape lie at a moderate distance, so that even today the visitor, especially if he is fortunate enough to have the place to himself, can still

sense something of that wild and treeless isolation which even
the least sensitive observer must feel to be the proper setting
for Stonehenge.

Of the nature of the original landscape of Stonehenge, at
the time the monument was erected, we know nothing
directly. We can be fairly sure, admittedly, that the actual
conformation of the ground, the shapes of the skylines, the
hills, and the valleys, have not changed appreciably. But of the
vegetation, the grass, the bushes, the kinds and disposition of
the trees, which clothe the bare bones of a landscape and give
it its essential character, we have no evidence. The most one
can say is that probably the ground was a good deal less bare
than today, broken by at least occasional thickets of thorn,
juniper, and gorse, and possibly by scattered but isolated
trees. Even then, however, the effects of human occupation
may have been apparent, though in a form less obtrusive than
bricks and mortar. For nothing is more effective in clearing
and keeping in check the natural vegetation than the continuous browsing of sheep and cattle; and it may well be that
Stonehenge was originally set not in a thorny wilderness, but
amid a carpet of short springy turf, even as it is today, created
and maintained by the ceaseless wandering of prehistoric
herdsmen and their flocks.

Of the stones themselves no words of mine can properly
describe the subtle varieties of texture and colour, or the un-
countable effects of shifting light and shade. From a distance,
they have a silvery grey colour in sunlight, which lightens to
an almost metallic bluish-white against a background of storm
clouds, an effect so notably recorded by Constable in his well-
known water-colour. When the ground is covered in snow in
midwinter, with a dull leaden sky threatening further falls,
they seem nearly black; and at sunset in midsummer their
surfaces glow, as if from within, with a soft warm pinkish-
orange light.

At a nearer view, each stone takes on its own individual
pattern of colour and texture. Some are almost white, like
coarse marble, with the sparkling grain of white lump sugar,
and so hard that even thirty-five centuries of weathering has
not dimmed the irregular patches of polishing executed so

laboriously by the original builders. Others are a dull matt
grey, streaked and lined by close-set vertical cracks and fis-
sures, like the grain of some vast stump of a petrified tree;
and others again are soft, buff or even pink in colour, and
deeply eroded into hollows and overhangs in which a man
may crouch, the compact curves of his limbs and the rounded
thrust of shoulder and hip matching the time-smoothed protuberances of the stone around him. Here and there, the fine
smooth grain of the stone is broken by small nodules of
creamy or pinkish flint. And in places patches of a natural
siliceous cement, like a thick weathered layer of amber lacquer,
marks where the rock has split along a natural plane of
cleavage.

On many of the surfaces, particularly on the lee side protected from the scouring force of wind and rain, there is a
light growth of fluffy grey-green lichen, accented here and
there by vivid patches of scaly yellow, which softens the con-
tours of the stone, and half conceals, like a growth of fur, the
scars left by those who have sought a little squalid immortality
by the laborious incision of name or initials.

The huge mass of the stones, their upward taper, and the
uncompromising four-squareness of the lintels which they
support, together give an impression of forceful upward
growth combined with an immense solidity and security.
There is no top-heaviness, no feeling of impending ruin, even
where an upright now leans from the perpendicular. Nor do
the many stones which have fallen, and now lie half buried in
the soil, give one any sense of cataclysmic destruction. Even
their fall seems to have had a ponderous and purposeful de-
liberation.

To the inquiring observer the signs of man's handiwork are
everywhere apparent: the squared and tapering forms of the
stones; the severely functional shapes of the mortice and
tenon joints on uprights and lintels; and the delicate rippled
fluting of their tooled surfaces, like wave-patterns left on the
sand by an ebbing tide. Yet these things, though they betray
the hand of the mason, and alone allow us to confer upon
Stonehenge the dignity of architecture, are nowhere obtrusive.
Everywhere these specifically man-made forms are being

etched and gnawed by remorseless time, so that the stone, having once yielded itself to the builders and suffered shaping to their purpose, now seems to be reasserting its own essential nature by the gradual obliteration of their handiwork. To me at least this stubborn yet imperceptible battle between the works of man and of nature, in which nature must inevitably triumph in the end, gives to Stonehenge a quality of immemorial antiquity and, at the same moment, of timeless permanence, that is lacking from all our other early prehistoric monuments, whose stones have only been chosen, but not shaped, by man.

All this, admittedly, is a private and personal vision, and some at least of my more austere colleagues would say that it has nothing whatever to do with the archaeology of Stonehenge. True enough, each man's vision of Stonehenge is particular, and none, perhaps, will much resemble my own. Yet even the archaeologist (perhaps, indeed, the archaeologist more than others) must look at his monuments not merely with a professional eye (an eye which too often is buried, ostrich-like, below the ground), but also with that wandering and passively receptive regard which, with practice, can penetrate beyond the surface to an inwardness which is none the less real or significant for being personal and, in part at least, incommunicable. For who is to say that for the ultimate understanding of Stonehenge, not in terms of the categories of archaeological research, but as part of our human inheritance, and to that degree as part of ourselves, the aesthetic experience must play a lesser part than the precise and academic dissection of the evidence we recover from its soil?

CHAPTER TWO

The Structure of Stonehenge

To understand the history of Stonehenge, one must first know the various structures of which it is composed. Many of these are immediately apparent to the eye, but others can be seen only when one knows where to look, and others again, no less important, are now invisible on the surface, having been obliterated by time or by the deliberate intention of later builders. For the most part, these various structures, visible and hidden, are arranged in concentric circles, and they may most conveniently be described in approximate order from the outside inwards. The reader will find that the description which follows will be the more easily understood by constant reference to figs. 1 and 2, and to Plates 1 and 2a.

The Ditch

The outermost feature of Stonehenge, which forms the boundary of the site, is one which is frequently overlooked by the visitor, who having paid his sixpence walks eagerly across it with his eyes fixed on the stones in the centre. This feature is a circular earthwork (Plate 1) consisting of a broad ditch, now almost wholly silted up, with the remains of a bank on its inner edge, and traces of a smaller bank on its outer margin. The earthwork is broken by two original gaps. One, the main entrance, is on the north-east side. The other, much narrower, is on the south. The other apparent breaks in the bank and ditch, including that through which the visitor usually walks from the road, are of modern origin.

One half of the circumference of the ditch, measured clockwise from its entrance, is now deeper than the remainder, as is also a short stretch immediately to the north of the entrance. This is the part which was completely excavated by Colonel Hawley (p. 195) in the 1920s, and was afterwards only partially refilled and returfed. The rest of the ditch is untouched by the excavator. At present it appears as a shallow depression, with a fairly regular width of about 20 ft, the grass-grown surface being at the most only a foot below the level of the surrounding turf. Originally, however, the ditch was

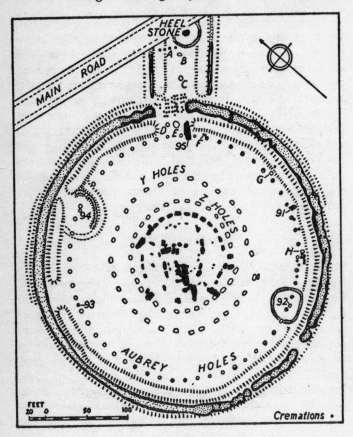

FIG. 1. Plan of Stonehenge

extremely irregular, both in width and in depth. Its sides were steep, and towards the bottom nearly vertical. The bottom itself was usually flat, but the level varied suddenly from place to place, the changes often corresponding to sudden constrictions of the sides. The maximum depth recorded in the excavated parts is about 7 ft from the surface, and the minimum 4½ ft. Indeed the ditch is not really a continuous excavation, but a series of quarry-pits dug separately, and to varying depths, which were afterwards joined up more or less

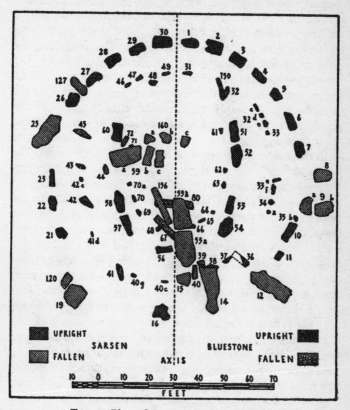

FIG. 2. Plan of the stones of Stonehenge

by breaking down the intervening barriers of unexcavated chalk rock. But occasionally these barriers were left, and the gap in the ditch on the south side is probably one of them.

Irregular ditches of this kind, like the outline of a string of very badly made sausages, are characteristic of neolithic earthworks in southern England. Their apparently unfinished state does not mean that the work was abandoned before it was completed, but that the builders regarded the ditch merely as a quarry for material to build the bank. It was the bank which was the important element of the earthwork, and the ditch had no meaning, in itself, as a structural or symbolic feature.

The material which now fills the ditch consists almost entirely of chalk rubble, coarse and loose at the bottom but becoming finer and more earthy above. This is entirely the product of natural weathering, initially through the breaking up of the exposed sides of the ditch in winter frosts, and later, more slowly, through the washing in of the material of the bank by rain. Probably the ditch was already silted up very nearly to its present level within a couple of centuries from the date of digging.

In this early silting very few objects have been found. The only common ones are the tools used by the original excavators, pick-axes made from red deer antler and shovels from the shoulder-blades of oxen, which lay at intervals on the bottom, where they had been abandoned when the digging was finished. Apart from these, the finds consisted of scattered animal bones (presumably the remains of food), a very few fragments of pottery (p. 88), and a handful of scraps of bluestone (pp. 70, 90). These last are of the greatest importance, since they show that the bluestones must already have been on the site when the ditch was only partially silted, and hence at an early stage in the sequence of construction.

It is only in the topmost foot or so of silting, consisting of earthy mould, that objects occur in any quantity. Here every kind of rubbish, from neolithic pottery to car headlight-bulbs, and from Roman coins to beer-bottle tops, is mingled with fragments of the stones and with a vast number of small chips of natural flint, the latter derived by weathering from the adjacent banks. Unfortunately this great mass of objects of known date yields little reliable information, because it is clear, from the distribution of the natural flint chips, that even when the ditch was silted up almost level with the surrounding surface, lateral movement of material from the banks was still taking place. Thus objects of known date dropped on the banks can still have found their way into the upper filling of the ditch centuries, and even millennia, after they were originally dropped; and their position in the filling consequently gives no reliable guide to the date at which the silting had reached the level at which they occur.

The Bank

The bank stands immediately on the inner edge of the ditch. When allowance is made for its denuded condition, it is evident that it was originally built with considerable accuracy in a true circle, with a mean diameter of 320 ft. Such accuracy is easily obtainable, of course, merely by the rotation of a suitable measuring-cord fastened to a peg in the centre, provided that there are no obstructions, such as upright posts or stones, in the area to be enclosed.

Very little now remains of the bank, which is nowhere more than 2 ft high. Indeed, its actual height is even less than appears, for excavation in 1954 revealed the surprising fact that the surface of the natural chalk is nearly a foot higher beneath the centre of the bank than it is elsewhere. This is due to the gradual dissolution of the chalk by the acidity of percolating rain-water during the course of centuries, the soluble constituents being removed and the insoluble residue incorporated in the overlying soil. Only where the surface has been protected by the bank above it has this process of weathering been prevented, or at least slowed down.

The present width of the bank is about 20 ft, and its original width was probably much the same. But its original height must have been at least 6 ft, and possibly more, if account is taken of the size of the ditch from which its material came. Very probably, however, it was rapidly reduced in size by slipping and being washed back into the ditch within a century or two of its construction, and its appearance during at least the last two thousand years has doubtless been much as it is today.

Besides the main bank on the inner side, there are slight but indubitable traces of an outer, or counterscarp, bank as well, which can best be seen immediately north (that is, anticlockwise) from the entrance of the earthwork. Curiously enough, this feature has seldom previously been recorded, and has otherwise passed unnoticed, although it must once have been substantial, with a width of perhaps 8 ft and a height of 30 in., since excavation has shown that here, as under the main bank, the surface of the natural chalk has been protected from weathering.

The purpose and significance of the bank is discussed below (p. 170).

The Entrance Causeway

Probably the only intentional gap in the circular earthwork is the entrance causeway on the north-east side. Here the digging of the ditch and the throwing up of the bank has been interrupted for a space of 35 ft to provide an entrance of sufficiently imposing dimensions. The visitor will note that the width of this entrance is much less than the width between the ditches of the Avenue which runs towards it (fig. 1), a fact whose significance for the relative dates of earthwork and Avenue is discussed below (p. 72).

The uncovering of the chalk surface on the causeway by Colonel Hawley revealed a number of circular holes between the ends of the ditch, evidently dug to support the bases of wooden posts about a foot in diameter, or a little less. These post-holes can no longer be seen, but their positions are shown in fig. 1. They were set in a more or less regular pattern, 4 to 5 ft apart, forming rows running both across and parallel to the axis of the causeway. Their purpose is entirely unknown. From their disposition it seems certain that they are contemporary with the digging of the ditch, and earlier than the construction of the Avenue (p. 71).

Rather further inwards, on a line with the ends of the bank, are two large holes which evidently once held upright stones (fig. 1, D, E). These holes are roughly symmetrical to the axis of the causeway, and the stones they held may have formed a pair of entrance pillars, a kind of symbolic door to the original monument (p. 71).

The Aubrey Holes

There are fifty-six Aubrey Holes, set in an accurate circle 288 ft in diameter, immediately within the inner margin of the bank. The average distance between them, measured round the circumference, is 16 ft. Thirty-four of them have been excavated (nos. 1–32, 55, 56) and their positions have been marked on the ground by patches of white chalk (Plate 1). The locations of the unexcavated holes have been found by probing and 'bosing'.*

The holes are in the form of roughly circular pits, varying in width from 30 to 70 in., and from 24 to 45 in. in depth. The sides are steep and the bottoms flat. Their contents were extremely mixed. In general, however, the filling consisted of the chalk rubble originally dug out of the hole, which had apparently been deliberately shovelled back soon afterwards, some of it having been disturbed by the digging of later holes into it, often right down to the bottom, which were filled with burnt soil containing fragments of charred wood. In most of the holes there were deposits of cremated human bones, either in compact masses or scattered throughout a large volume of filling. Sometimes these cremations were in the primary filling, but more often in the later disturbances. Several of them were accompanied by long bone pins, resembling meat-skewers or short headless knitting-needles, which were probably hairpins;† and by rod-like instruments of chipped flint about the size and shape of a little finger, whose archaeological name of 'fabricator' merely serves to conceal our ignorance of their real purpose.‡

The Aubrey Holes owe their rediscovery and their name to

* 'Bosing' consists of ramming the surface of the turf with a weighted hammer, and listening for the change in the sound so produced which indicates a disturbance beneath. The method can be used with considerable precision, but only, as at Stonehenge, where the underlying rock is close to the surface.

† Not used, of course, like the modern hair-pin, but thrust through a large and probably greasy bun or coiled plait at the back of the head.

‡ Though some fabricators may have been used as strike-a-lights with a lump of iron pyrites, the forerunner of the later flint and steel, or, for that matter, of the petrol lighter.

Mr R. S. Newall, who collaborated with Colonel Hawley in parts of his excavations and persuaded him to pursue a clue given by John Aubrey, the Wiltshire antiquary of the seventeenth century (p. 187), who in his unpublished account of Stonehenge refers to 'cavities'* visible just within the bank. They form one of the most puzzling and controversial features of Stonehenge, and even now it is difficult to give an entirely satisfactory explanation of them. But at least it can be said that they were never intended to hold any kind of upright, either the bluestones, as was supposed soon after their discovery, or wooden posts, a suggestion prompted by the later excavation of the near-by timber sanctuary of Woodhenge (p. 156). Their possible purpose and significance is discussed below (p. 171) in the light of similar rings of pits excavated elsewhere in Britain.

The Cremation Cemetery

In addition to the cremated burials found in the filling of the Aubrey Holes, a number of others were found in the silting of the ditch and beneath the turf on the bank and just within it. The exact number and position of these burials was unfortunately never recorded by Colonel Hawley, but an approximate idea of their distribution can be gained from his diary, and is illustrated in fig. 1. The main concentration is near Aubrey Holes 14 and 15, with smaller groups in the ditch to the east of the south causeway and to the north-west of the main entrance. None was found between the line of the Aubrey Holes and the stones in the centre, but some may yet remain in the bank, little of which has so far been excavated. The total number of cremations found hitherto, including twenty-five from the Aubrey Holes, is about fifty-five. One of those in the ditch rested right on the floor, with no sign of disturbance of the overlying silt, and must therefore be contemporary with the digging of the ditch; while the position

*Mr Newall tells me that it was a misreading of this word in Aubrey's somewhat illegible hand that led Colonel Hawley to adopt the rather inappropriate term 'crater' for any irregular hole that he found in his excavations.

of others in the middle and higher levels of the silting suggests that they, and probably all the cremations, were deposited within two centuries at the most from the inception of the cemetery, which seems to belong as a whole to the neolithic period and to the first phase of the monument (p. 172).

It has sometimes been suggested that not all these cremations are of prehistoric date, because well within living memory the latterday Order of Druids buried portions of the cremated remains of their deceased members within the Stonehenge enclosure (a practice now forbidden). The possibility of confusion is less than might be supposed, however, since apart from the greater degree of calcination in modern cremations the recent Druidical deposits are said to have been very small ('no more than would go into a waistcoat pocket'*), whereas the bones of an average prehistoric cremation will fill a man's hat.

The Outlying Stones and the 'Barrows'

Apart from the stones at the centre of Stonehenge, there are four outlying stones, and the sites of two others, now vanished, are marked on the north and south sides of the earthwork by the two ditched enclosures known as the 'Barrows'.

The Heel Stone (no. 96) is a single large block of sarsen stone (p. 36) standing within the Avenue outside the entrance of the Stonehenge earthwork, close to the main road. In section it is sub-rectangular, with a minimum thickness of 8 ft, rising to a bluntly pointed top about 16 ft high. Excavation has shown that a further 4 ft is buried in the ground. It now leans noticeably towards the centre of Stonehenge, but was presumably upright originally. It is an entirely natural boulder, doubtless deliberately selected for its size and shape, but unlike all the other sarsen stones of the monument it shows no sign of deliberate shaping or tooling of its surface (Plate 3).

Round the Heel Stone,† some 12 ft from its base, is a narrow

---

*The words are those of Mr Gorry, formerly one of the custodians of Stonehenge, to whom I am indebted for much curious and colourful information concerning the habits and predilections of modern visitors.

† The spelling 'Hele Stone' is an archaizing affectation of earlier antiquaries, and is better forgotten. The full name is the *Friar's Heel*, from

circular ditch, half of which now lies beneath the grass verge of the road. This ditch must be more or less contemporary with the erection of the Heel Stone, and seems to have been a symbolic rather than a physical barrier, as it was refilled with rammed chalk rubble very shortly after it was dug, before any silt had had time to collect on the bottom. The finding of a fragment of freshly fractured bluestone in this deliberate filling, in the excavations of 1953, gives an additional proof of the early presence of the bluestones on the site, for it can be shown (pp. 70, 75) that both the Heel Stone and its ditch belong to early phases of the monument's history. The same excavations showed that the inner edge of the eastern bank of the Avenue overlies the filling of the Heel Stone's ditch, so that the latter must have been refilled before the Avenue was built.

The Heel Stone is the subject of one of the most popular and persistent misconceptions concerning Stonehenge, namely that it marks the point of sunrise on Midsummer Day for an observer stationed at the centre of Stonehenge, or on the Altar Stone (p. 56). Actually, it does nothing of the sort. It is true, admittedly, that at the present day the midsummer sun, in its eastward-slanting climb, does pass over the Heel Stone, with a little less than half its disc showing above the horizon. But it does this only some appreciable time after true sunrise, that is, the moment at which the first gleam of light appears on the horizon as the upper margin of the sun creeps above it. True sunrise, in this sense, will not take place over the point of the Heel Stone until about the year A.D. 3260. Nor is it generally realized that *when Stonehenge was built* the point of midsummer sunrise was appreciably further to the west (that is, to the left of the observer), so that by the time the sun had climbed to a position directly over the Heel Stone it already stood clear of the horizon by a space equal to about half its apparent diameter.

The Slaughter Stone (no. 95) is a large elongated block of

---

the legend that the Devil threw the stone at a friar, striking him on the heel, whose imprint can still be seen on the outer face of the stone. In fact, the legend may well have been invented to explain the name, for which there is no other known derivation.

sarsen stone (p. 36), some 21 ft long, 7 ft wide, and 3 ft thick, which now lies prostrate on the east side of the entrance causeway, immediately beyond the end of the bank. Its upper surface is now level with the surrounding turf, and Colonel Hawley found in 1920 that at some time the stone had been deliberately buried in a rough pit cut in the natural chalk.* It is possible, though not certain, that as late as the mid seventeenth century, when John Aubrey made his sketch-plan of Stonehenge (p. 187), the stone stood upright on its outer end.

Like the rest of the sarsens at Stonehenge, the Slaughter Stone has been dressed to shape, and has its lower (now the outer) end roughly pointed (p. 133). The line of small holes running obliquely across the toe of the stone marks an abortive attempt, in relatively modern times, to split off a fragment of the extreme end by means of wedges. The tooling of the stone is best seen on the sides, now vertical, and on the top, now the inner end. The delicate rippled fluting on the upper surface is only revealed late on a summer evening, when the reddening light of the setting sun strikes obliquely across it.

It is almost certain that the Slaughter Stone is the survivor of a pair of upright pillars which formed a gateway to the monument. The other pillar seems to have stood in a large adjacent stone-hole (fig. 1, E) which may already have served to support a stone in an earlier phase of construction (p. 71). Of this second stone nothing remains; but the original existence of a pair of stones, rather than one only, is confirmed by the fact that the Slaughter Stone and stone-hole E lie symmetrically on either side of the axis of Stonehenge (p. 62). The absence of any trace of a projecting tenon on the top of the Slaughter Stone makes it unlikely that this suggested pair of uprights supported a lintel.

The name of the Slaughter Stone is nothing more than a too-fanciful invention of earlier antiquaries, and the visitor

*Part of the disturbance round the stone is due to excavations by William Cunnington, the coadjutor of Sir Richard Colt Hoare (p. 190), in 1801. Cunnington considerately laid down beneath the stone a bottle of port, later disinterred by Colonel Hawley; but unfortunately the cork had decayed. The possibility that Cunnington made similar provision for posterity elsewhere at Stonehenge has added a minor spice of expectation to the recent excavations.

will listen in vain for the ghostly shrieks of expiring victims spreadeagled on its bloodstained surface, unless he allows his imagination to run well ahead of the facts.

The two *Station Stones* (nos. 91 and 93) are blocks of sarsen stone of unequal size which stand just within the bank, approximately on the line of the Aubrey Holes, on the southeast and north-west. The former (no. 91) is a rather rough boulder about 9 ft long which has fallen outwards and now lies against the inner slope of the bank, probably as the result of treasure-digging round its base. Its inclination was much less in the eighteenth century. Its surface shows very little sign of deliberate tooling. Its fellow, no. 93, is a much smaller stone, only 4 ft high, which still stands upright. Tooled patches are visible on its north and south sides.

The two so-called *Barrows* evidently mark the sites of a similar pair of stones, which have disappeared. The South Barrow can be seen as an area enclosed by a slight ditch, roughly circular but flattened on the side towards the bank, immediately east of the south causeway (Plate 1). It includes two Aubrey Holes (17 and 18), and its ditch cuts through no. 19. At its centre Colonel Hawley found a large hole which from its shape had apparently once held a stone, though this had already disappeared before the eighteenth century.

The North Barrow is diametrically opposite, at the point where the visitor usually passes through the earthwork on his way to the stones. It is difficult to see, as its western half has been obliterated by the track which formerly passed over it. Like its fellow, it consists of an approximately circular area bounded by a small ditch with a low bank outside it;* and though there is now no visible sign of a central hole, its presence was recorded in the eighteenth century, and can still be detected by probing.

The term 'barrows' for these structures is misapplied, since neither appears to have had any central mound, the slight apparent elevation of the interior being an optical illusion due to the slope of the inner sides of the surrounding ditches.

---

*The presence of a similar outer bank in the South Barrow has not been recorded, and cannot now be confirmed, as the whole area was excavated by Colonel Hawley.

If lines are drawn between the two Station Stones, and between the two stone-holes in the Barrows, they will be found to cross at the centre of the main stone structure at an angle of 45°, and to lie symmetrically in relation to the axis of Stonehenge; and similar lines drawn from the South Barrow to stone 91, and from stone 93 to the North Barrow, will be found to be parallel to the axis. This precision and symmetry cannot be fortuitous, and one must assume that the four Stations are connected in some way with the process of locating the centre from which the main stone structure was to be laid out. One need not suppose, of course, that the existing Station Stones, or their vanished fellows, were actually used as surveyor's reference-points, for which purpose they are far too large and imprecise; but rather that they form permanent and symbolic memorials of an operation of field geometry which, if it were to be repeated today, would tax the skill of many a professional surveyor.

Several writers on Stonehenge in the eighteenth and nineteenth centuries express a belief in the former existence of a stone just inside the bank on the south-west side, in the neighbourhood of Aubrey Hole 28, which would have marked the prolongation of the axis, and incidentally the approximate point of midwinter sunset (p. 96). No one has ever seen this stone, though Mr W. A. Judd, one of the leading nineteenth-century authorities on the lithology of Stonehenge, reported that he had found its stump 'still in the earth, about a foot under the surface'. A later search made with a sword and an auger by the then owner of Stonehenge failed to confirm this claim, and the existence of this stone must remain problematical.

Some of the problems connected with the four Stations are discussed below (p. 78).

The Y and Z Holes

The next structural features, working inwards towards the centre, are the two rings of pits known as the Y and Z Holes.*

---

*The Aubrey Holes, when first discovered, were given the designation X appropriate to an unknown quantity. The choice of the letters Y and Z

Their existence was entirely unsuspected until they were revealed during the excavations of 1923–4. Half of each ring (nos. 1–15, 29, 30) was then uncovered, and two more holes (Y16, Z16) were examined in 1953. The position of a few of these excavated holes can now be detected as slight depressions in which the grass grows rather darker in colour,* but of the untouched holes on the west side no trace is visible on the surface, which explains why they have been passed over by all the earlier writers on Stonehenge. The positions of the unexcavated holes, marked in fig. 1, have been found by probing.

Both rings are noticeably irregular, both in the spacing of the holes and in their distance from the outer circle of sarsen stones. The mean distance of the Z Holes from the latter is 12 ft, and that of the Y Holes 36 ft, but individual holes may vary from this mean line by as much as 4 ft and 8 ft respectively. This irregularity, and the fact that the number of holes in each ring matches the original number of stones in the sarsen circle, suggest very strongly that the Y and Z Holes were laid out only after the erection of the sarsens, when the latter would have prevented accurate measurement from the centre. This has been confirmed positively by the observation that hole Z7 had been cut through the filling of the ramp which forms an outward extension of the stone-hole of stone 7.

The circle of Z Holes is incomplete, since Z8 is missing. As its position coincides approximately with the fallen fragment of stone 8, it has often been supposed (for this reason among others) that the Z Holes (and presumably the Y Holes also) were dug only at a late date in the monument's history, when the fall of stone 8 would have prevented the digging of the corresponding Z Hole. A more recent assessment of the evidence suggests, however, that the absence of hole Z8 may be explained otherwise (p. 83), and need not be taken as evidence for the late date of the Z and Y rings as a whole.

---

for the subsequent discoveries was an obvious one. A suggestion that they should be known as the Newall and Hawley Holes, after their discoverers and excavators, has not found general acceptance.

*It is to be hoped that the excavated holes will before long be marked by white patches, as are the Aubrey Holes, for the better guidance of the inquiring visitor.

The holes themselves, though showing some variation in size, are almost all of a common shape and character (Plate 4a). In plan they are oblong or sub-rectangular, the long axis following the circumference of the circle in which they are set. Their average dimensions at the top are 6 ft by 4 ft, and their depth is fairly uniform, averaging 41 in. in the Z Holes and 36 in. in the Y Holes. The sides are steep, and the bottom flat. Only two holes, Y2 and Y7, were shallower than 30 in., and the latter was regarded by Colonel Hawley as unfinished.

The filling of the holes was also uniform, and consisted almost entirely of fine brown soil, free from stones except at the bottom, where there was a concentration of natural flints. Below this, covering the sides and bottom of the hole, was a thin layer of coarse chalk rubble, the product of the weathering of the sides of the hole in the first few winter frosts.

The filling of the holes yielded a large quantity of finds. Except for a number of bluestone fragments (almost all of rhyolite, p. 47) on the bottom, usually no more than one fragment in each hole, all the objects recovered came from the earth filling. They consisted of numerous chips of the stones, both bluestone and sarsen (the latter for the most part in the upper levels of the filling), and broken scraps of Iron Age and Romano-British pottery of the third century B.C. and onwards.

The occurrence of this late pottery has formed the basis for the theory, universally accepted until recently, that the Y and Z Holes were dug, at the earliest, in the pre-Roman Iron Age, and formed an addition to Stonehenge long after its original construction, and indeed when it was already in part a ruin (it being supposed that stone 8 had already fallen). But the excavation of the two holes in 1953 has shown that the date of the holes cannot necessarily be equated with the date of the pottery found in their filling (p. 98), and that in fact they almost certainly belong to a much earlier stage in the monument's history, though one admittedly later than the erection of the sarsen stones. The probable place of the Y and Z Holes in the sequence of construction is discussed in detail below (pp. 80, 97). All that need be said here is that they seem to have been dug as stone-holes to contain the bluestones in the form of a double circle, but that for some reason unknown this plan was abandoned before it was put into effect. The nature of the filling and the absence of any impressions of the bases of stones on the floor of the holes makes it quite certain that no stones were ever in fact erected in them.

The Sarsen Circle

The next structure to be described is the one which first strikes the eye of the visitor, namely the remains of the great outer circle of stone uprights, which originally supported on their tops a continuous ring of stone lintels. The material of these uprights and lintels, like that of the trilithons (p. 40) and of the outlying stones (p. 29), is sarsen,* a kind of natural sandstone. The principal area where this stone now occurs on the surface, and the nearest to Stonehenge, is on the chalk downs a few miles north-west of Marlborough in North Wiltshire. Here, even though much stone has been removed in modern times for building or to bring the land under cultivation, the boulders lie in places so thickly on the ground that one can travel across them, by stepping or jumping from one to another, for long distances without ever setting foot on the turf. It is undoubtedly from here that the sarsens were chosen and transported to Stonehenge, a distance, even as the crow flies, of about eighteen miles. The problems of engineering and man-power involved in this astonishing feat may be the better appreciated by realizing that some of the heavier stones of the monument weigh in the region of fifty tons, and had to be moved with only the simplest forms of rope, lever, roller, and sledge (p. 119).

Sarsen appears to have been formed by the natural cementing together of a bed of sand laid down in Tertiary times, many millions of years ago, on the sea-bed. This sand originally rested on the chalk, itself an earlier marine deposit. With the subsequent elevation of the land, and the gradual weathering away of uncemented sands, and of the softer chalk rock

* The derivation of this word is uncertain, though it is usually regarded as a corruption of *Saracen*, meaning a foreigner.

beneath them, this more resistant layer of sarsen has been left exposed on the surface, not, of course, in a continuous sheet, but as scattered and fragmented boulders, all more or less of uniform thickness in any one region.

The original number of uprights in the circle was thirty, but of these only seventeen remain in position (1–7, 10, 11, 16, 21–23, 27–30), while eight others are either fallen (12, 14, 25), or represented by fragments only (8, 9, 15, 19, 26). The remaining five stones (13, 17, 18, 20, 24) are missing altogether. It may be observed that the main concentration of missing and fallen stones is in the south-western half of the monument, whereas on the opposite side no less than eleven stones successively are intact.

The surviving stones vary in their dimensions, as is only to be expected from the variation of the natural raw material and the extreme difficulty of dressing it to shape (p. 124). All of them, however, are approximately rectangular in cross-section, with an average width of 7 ft and a thickness of 3–4 ft. In every case the better (i.e. the flatter) of the two broad surfaces has been set facing inwards. To avoid confusion, the circumferential surfaces are referred to hereafter as the *faces*, and the radial surfaces as the *sides*. Seen in elevation the stones taper towards the top, the amount of taper, for any one surface, averaging 5 in. In many cases (for instance, stone 10, Plate 4b, and stone 16, Plate 5) this taper is not straight, but convexly curved, a device known under the name of *entasis* from the columns of Greek temples and later buildings in the classical style. Its purpose there is to create an optical illusion of straightness (since a taper which really was straight would appear, paradoxically, as concave), and it is not impossible that the entasis of the Stonehenge uprights, though ruder and exaggerated in form, may be a deliberate attempt to create this illusion by the same means.

The average height of the stones in the circle is 13½ ft, and shows much less variation than their widths and thicknesses, as might be expected since they had to support a ring of lintels which for the sake of appearance alone had to be at least approximately level (p. 40). Excavation has shown that the stones are buried to a depth of between 3 and 5 ft, so that their average overall length is 18 ft. Their average weight is in the region of twenty-six tons.

One stone in the circle, no. 11, is much smaller than the rest, measuring only 4 ft wide by 2 ft thick. It now stands only 8 ft out of the ground, but presumably at some time the upper part has been broken off and removed from the site. The use of this markedly undersized stone (there can be no question of its width or thickness having been reduced since its erection) suggests that the builders were hard put to it to find sufficient blocks of the requisite size to complete the circle.

The uprights have been positioned with considerable care and accuracy, with their inner faces at ground level as tangents to a circle 97⅓ ft in diameter. The mean error from the line of this circle is only just over 3 in. To allow for the varying widths of the stones, and to prevent the accumulation of errors from this source, their centres are equally spaced round the circle at intervals of 10½ ft, any variations of width being taken up in the spaces between them, which average 3½ ft, or half the width of the stones. The two uprights forming the entrance to the circle (nos. 1 and 30) have been deliberately spaced one foot wider than the rest, and the gaps between the adjacent pairs (29–30, 1–2) reduced correspondingly.

Of the sarsen lintels, of which there must originally have been a continuous ring of thirty, only six remain in position (130, 101, 102, 105, 107, 122).* Fragments of two other lintels (120, 127) now lie partly buried in the ground. The remainder, numbering twenty-two, are missing. Their absence can be accounted for by their relatively smaller weight (about a quarter of that of the uprights), which would facilitate their removal by the medieval and later stone-masons and builders of the district, to whom, in an otherwise stoneless region, Stonehenge must have formed a useful and convenient quarry.

The lintels measure, on the average, 10½ ft in length, 3½ ft in width, and 2⅓ ft in thickness. In cross-section they are rectangular, but in plan they exhibit an architectural refinement which is not usually appreciated by the casual visitor, unless

---

*The numbers of the lintels are 100 more than the second stone, measured clockwise, on which they rest, or once rested.

his attention is drawn to it. This refinement takes the form of curving the inner and outer faces of the lintels, so that they follow the curve of the circle on which they lie. This can best be seen by standing against the inner face of stone 27 and looking along the inner face of the three lintels over the entrance (130, 101, 102) (Plate 6a), or by crouching or lying flat between stones 6 and 7, and looking up at the silhouette of their lintel against the sky, which shows this curvature particularly well on its outer face.

The lintels do not simply rest on the tops of the uprights, but are held in place by mortice-and-tenon joints, a device which is a woodworker's rather than a mason's technique (p. 177). Each upright has a pair of small projecting knobs or tenons on its upper surface (Plate 6b), one for each of the two lintels it supported. They are generally round, about 6 in. in diameter at the base and 3 in. high, though one at least, the western tenon on stone 16, is oval.

Each lintel has a corresponding pair of round pits, or mortices, on its underside, usually rather larger in size than the tenons over which they fitted. In places, however, the clearance between tenon and mortice is very small.

The upper surface of the uprights has been very carefully dressed smooth and level, and as an additional safeguard against lateral movement the edges on the inner and outer faces have been left slightly raised, the lower edges of the lintels being chamfered to correspond. The ends of the lintels thus rest in dished beds, which have much the form of a tea-tray with an inverted pudding-basin in the middle (Plate 7a).

Furthermore, each lintel is jointed to its neighbour by tongue-and-groove (or toggle) joints (Plate 6a), another device borrowed from carpentry. The distribution of the two kinds of joint is not uniform. Lintels 101 and 102, for instance, each have a groove at the west and a tongue at the east end; whereas nos. 122 and 130 both have a pair of tongues. Other lintels, now vanished, must thus necessarily have had a pair of grooves.

Evidently great care was taken to get the upper surfaces of the lintels horizontal, and level with each other. There can be no doubt that this object was achieved with considerable accuracy (Plate 7b), in spite of the size and weight of the stones and the primitive equipment of the builders. The maximum error from a mean horizontal plane of the tops of the surviving uprights (there are too few stones left to get reliable figures for the lintels themselves) is less than 7 in., and it is quite possible that the major part, at least, of such errors was compensated in the final shaping and fitting of the lintels themselves. Certainly this has been done in the case of the entrance lintel (101), on the underside of which the visitor can see quite clearly a rebate worked about an inch deep on the end of the stone, to lower it by that amount upon its supporter no. 1 (Plate 10a).

The uprights and lintels of the sarsen circle have all been dressed to shape by the extremely laborious process of pounding their surfaces with heavy stone mauls (hammer-stones held in the hands). The details of this operation are discussed below (p. 122). In some cases the surfaces, particularly the inner faces (Plate 4b), were reduced to a smooth even plane, though often the original finish has been degraded by subsequent weathering. Elsewhere, however, the process has been carried only to an intermediate stage, leaving the surface marked by shallow rippling or grooving. Excellent examples of this unfinished tooling can be seen when the sun strikes obliquely across them on the north-west sides of stone 16 (Plate 5) and stone 2.

The Horseshoe of Sarsen Trilithons

The rest of the sarsen structure at Stonehenge consists of the remains of five trilithons* set in a horseshoe open towards the north-east. The first and second of these (51-4), counting clockwise, are intact (Plate 8). Of the third, one stone (55) has fallen inwards, and the other (56) though now upright was leaning inwards, until re-erected in 1901 (p. 192), resting on the tall bluestone in front of it (no. 68), which is still out of the perpendicular as a consequence. The lintel, stone 156,

---

*A term invented by William Stukeley in 1740, from the Greek *tris*, three, and *lithos*, a stone.

now lies on its side askew in front of no. 56. The date of the collapse of this trilithon is unknown, but must have been earlier than A.D. 1574, since an illustration of that date shows stone 56 as already leaning.

The fourth trilithon was restored in 1958. It fell outwards all of a piece with 'a very sensible concussion, or jarring of the ground' on 3 January 1797, probably as the result of the softening of the soil in a sudden thaw after a heavy frost. It had evidently been out of the perpendicular long before that date. A contemporary account records that in its fall it 'levelled with the ground a stone also of the second circle that stood in the line of their precipitation'. This must refer to bluestone 42; but earlier engravings show that this stone had already collapsed before the trilithon fell.

The fifth trilithon is also partly ruined. Stone 59 has fallen inwards (this also must have happened before 1574), breaking into three pieces, and the three fragments of the lintel (160) lie in front of the surviving upright, stone 60. The latter leans inwards slightly, a circumstance which gives cause for some alarm, as the whole of the lower part of the outer face of the stone is deeply eroded (Plate 9) and a horizontal crack is developing some three feet from the ground.

The heights of the trilithons increase towards the central one. The first and fifth have (or had) an overall height, including the lintel, of 20 ft; the corresponding measurement for the second and fourth is 21½ ft; and for the great central trilithon 24 ft. The depth of the uprights in the ground varies from about 3 ft for nos. 57 and 58 to nearly 8 ft for no. 56.

There seems no doubt that the builders were anxious to display above ground the maximum height of stone that was compatible with apparent stability and safety. This is well illustrated by the two uprights of the central trilithon, whose overall lengths are 24 ft for stone 55 and 29 ft 8 in. for stone 56. To obtain the maximum height the shorter stone was set in the ground to a depth of only 4 ft, and to lessen the obvious dangers of this proceeding a pronounced projection or foot was left on the outer side of the base of the stone (Plate 10b). To bring the top of its fellow, stone 56, to the same height no less than 8 ft had to be buried in the ground. This stone is

by far the largest at Stonehenge, and is indeed the largest
worked monolith in Britain (excepting Cleopatra's Needle on
the Embankment in London, which can hardly be considered
a serious competitor).*

As in the sarsen circle, the lintels of the trilithons are fixed
to their uprights by mortice-and-tenon joints, though in this
case there is only a single tenon on each upright, for obvious
reasons. These tenons are much bigger than those of the outer
circle, the largest, on stone 56 (Plate 7a), measuring 9 in. in
height. Here also the tops of the uprights are dished to give
additional security against sideways movement. The mortices
in the lintels are correspondingly large. Good examples can
be seen on the fallen lintel 156 (Plate 12b). The fit of mortice
and tenon was evidently not always very close, as there is
room for a bird to nest between the tenon and mortice on
stone 52.

John Aubrey, the antiquary of the seventeenth century,
makes a characteristic and delightful comment on the starlings
which then, as now, nested in this hole. 'The high stones of
Stonehenge are honeycombed so deep, that the Stares doe
make their Nests in the holes. Whether those holes are naturall
or artificiall I cannot say. The holes are towards the tops of
the jambe-stones. This did put me in mind, that in Wales
they doe call Stares Adar y Drudwy, sc. Aves Druidum. The
Druids might make these Holes purposely for their Birds to
nest in. They are loquacious birds and Pliny tells us of a Stare
that could speake Greeke. Why not?'

The trilithons have the same architectural refinements as
the stones of the outer circle. The uprights taper towards the
top with a slight convexity, an effect best shown by stone 56
(Plate 13), which is undoubtedly the most carefully wrought
of all the sarsens. The lintels are cut to a curve on both faces,
the outer curve being the more pronounced (Plate 15a and b).
In addition they show a very subtle refinement, in that they

*Enormous though it is, however, stone 56 by no means represents
the limit of prehistoric man's capabilities in Europe. The great stone at
Locmariaquer in Brittany, the Pierre de la Fée, is 66½ ft long, and though
it is now prostrate and broken into four pieces must certainly have stood
upright originally.

are some 6 in. wider on the top than on the bottom (Plate 15b). This means that the sides are inclined slightly towards the ground, probably with the intention of creating the illusion that they are vertical. If they were in fact vertical, their height would make them appear to recede. It was evidently not considered necessary to repeat this device on the lintels of the sarsen circle, where the illusion of recession would be much less marked, since they are thinner and stand at a lower height from the ground.

The lintel of the great trilithon, no. 156, has a pair of shallow irregular depressions towards the ends of its original upper surface (now the western side). Though the form of these depressions has doubtless been much altered by weathering, the coincidence of their positions with those of the two deep mortices on the other side of the stone makes it difficult to attribute their formation to weathering alone. In the past they have sometimes been taken for evidence that the great trilithon was originally surmounted by a smaller version of itself, for the uprights of which these depressions were the emplacements. But there is no other evidence to support this bizarre conjecture, and the depressions are best regarded as unfinished mortice holes, the builders having preferred, for some unknown reason, to invert the ultimate position of the lintel while its dressing was still in progress.

Like the stones of the sarsen circle, the trilithons have all been dressed to shape. Particular care has been taken to give a smooth and even finish to the inner faces, and to the lintels. But in some cases (in particular the north-east side of stone 52, Plate 14) the sides have been left in the intermediate stage of rippled tooling, while the outer faces, except those of the central trilithon, have been left relatively rough, with large bulges and discontinuous areas of dressing (Plate 8).

The Carvings on the Sarsen Stones

There is hardly a single sarsen stone at Stonehenge which does not bear at least one inscription of a personal name or initials. One of the most deeply engraved, and probably also the earliest, is on the inner face of stone 53 (Plate 11a), a little

above eye height. It reads IOH:LVD:DEFERRE.* It was
while I was preparing to photograph this inscription one
afternoon in July 1953 that I had the good fortune to notice
the prehistoric carvings immediately beneath it.

The principal carvings in this stone consist of a hilted
dagger, point downwards, and four axe-heads, cutting-edge
upwards. In addition there are a number of other axe-heads,
less deeply cut or more severely weathered, and several vaguer
markings, almost certainly artificial but too much eroded for
even the most conjectural identification.

A few days after this initial discovery David Booth, the
ten-year-old son of one of our helpers at Stonehenge, discovered the first of an even larger group of axe-carvings on
the outer face of stone 4 (Plate 11b); and during the succeeding weeks Mr R. S. Newall, while engaged in taking casts of
these, found a number of shallower and more weathered axes
on the same stone, and three quite well defined axes on the
lower part of the adjacent stone 3.

During the same season Mr Newall also made a rubbing of
the rather vague sub-rectangular marking on the inner (then
the upper) face of stone 57 (Plate 12a). Its existence had long
been recognized, but until the discovery of the dagger and
axes no particular attention had been paid to it, and it had
usually been assumed to be of recent date. The rubbing, however, revealed a feature of the carving which had not previously been observed, since it is very shallow, and has in any
case been largely obliterated by the shoes (and not infrequently
the hob-nailed boots) of generations of visitors. This feature
is a rounded extension of the upper margin of the design. As
soon as its presence was realized, Mr Newall at once saw the
close similarity of the design to certain carvings which occur
in Brittany in chambered tombs and on standing stones of
neolithic date. French archaeologists have termed these sym-

---

*That is, Johannes Ludovicus (or John Louis) de Ferre. I have not
been able to trace anyone bearing this name in the seventeenth century,
the period to which the style of lettering and the degree of weathering
are appropriate. The letter E is executed in the form of a Greek Σ, an
academic affectation which has misled more than one visitor into supposing that the whole inscription is in Greek.

bols 'shield-escutcheons' (*boucliers-écussons*), but this is merely
a conventional name which should not be taken literally, particularly as there is no other evidence for the use of rectangular
shields in Europe at the period when these carvings were
made. It is much more probable that they, and the Stonehenge
specimen, are conventional representations of a cult-figure,
possibly a mother-goddess. This possibility is discussed in
greater detail below (p. 179). Whatever its precise significance,
however, there is no reason to doubt that the carving on stone
57 is of prehistoric origin. As the visitor can see for himself,
it has already been seriously damaged by the feet of visitors
in the century and a half since the stone fell, and its future
preservation was a matter of some concern. Indeed, the only
satisfactory way of ensuring its safety was to re-erect the stone
on which it is carved, or for that matter the whole of the fallen
trilithon; and it is gratifying that this has been done so successfully by the Ministry of Works in the restoration of 1958.

The observant visitor will notice that below the base of the
main carving on stone 57 there are traces of another rectilinear
design of much smaller proportions. The significance of this
is unknown, though there is every reason to think that it is
contemporary with the larger carving above it.

Three more prehistoric carvings on the sarsens remain to
be mentioned. In August 1953 Mr Brian Hope-Taylor found
an additional carving on the west side of stone 53, about 3½ ft
above the ground. It appears to represent a second hilted
dagger, only about half the length of that on the inner face of
the same stone. Certain peculiarities of its form suggest that it
was originally carved as an axe-head, and was later converted
to a dagger by adding a hilt and pommel and by lengthening
the tapering butt of the axe to form a pointed blade.

On New Year's Day 1954 the late Dr O. G. S. Crawford
made two further discoveries* while examining the carvings
described above. The first is the grooved outline of what
seems to be a stumpy knife or dagger, with a short hilt, on the
south side of stone 23. Unlike the other carvings, the area
within the outline has not been lowered below the level of the

*Described by him, with a number of admirable photographs, in
Antiquity, XXVIII (1954), 25–31.

surrounding surface. The second carving is on the south-east side of stone 29, about 6 ft above the ground, and consists of a depressed area whose shape resembles approximately that of a headless and limbless human torso, with broad shoulders and narrow waist. Its height is 16 in. Neither of these new discoveries of Dr Crawford's is as easy to see as some of the carvings already described; and in the opinion of some archaeologists both marks are of doubtful human origin.

The techniques used in making the carvings, and their implications for the date of the sarsen stones, are discussed below (pp. 92, 139). But quite apart from these archaeological considerations, the carvings present us with a remarkable object-lesson in the fallibility of human observation. Few people who have seen the Stonehenge dagger will deny that, once one knows where to look, it is perfectly obvious; indeed when the sun is shining across the face of the stone, it can be seen from the gate of the Stonehenge enclosure, over 100 yards away. Yet during the past three centuries hundreds of thousands of visitors must have looked at the dagger (to say nothing of the other carvings) without actually *seeing* it. Nothing could demonstrate better that one sees only what one is expecting to see. I do not pretend for a moment, of course, that I was expecting to see the dagger at the time that I found it. But I am convinced that I should not have seen it, had not my attention been engaged at the time upon *carvings*, though admittedly modern ones. If these remarkable carvings can have escaped notice for so long in the most frequented of all British antiquities, archaeologists may well ruefully ask themselves how many similar surprises may lie in wait for them in less celebrated monuments.

One final carving at Stonehenge deserves to be mentioned, if only because it forms a trap for those who care to search (and may there be many of them) for further carved symbols. On the east side (originally the under side) of the fallen lintel of the great trilithon (stone 156) is a deeply incised outline in the form of a question-mark, the upper loop of which encloses the letters LV. On more than one occasion in the past this has been claimed to be of prehistoric date, and the sickle-like form of the main outline has invited the inevitable attribution to the Druids. It has been conclusively proved, however, that this design was cut by an itinerant workman, probably a stone-mason, about the year 1829.

Having described the carvings, I must add an appeal to the visitor *not to finger them*. Admittedly the stone is exceptionally hard, and fingers are soft. But one need look no further than the recumbent effigies in Salisbury Cathedral to see what constant fingering can do; and there is no need to add wilfully to the effacement already wrought by time.

The Bluestones

The bluestones at Stonehenge form two settings which repeat the plan of the sarsens: a circle of uprights within the sarsen circle and a horseshoe of uprights within the horseshoe of sarsen trilithons. They are so called from their colour, which in dry weather is a bluish-grey. But when they are wet after rain they acquire a noticeably blue tinge, especially where the constant abrasion of the feet and hands of visitors has smooth-ed and even polished their surfaces.

The term 'bluestones' is a common and convenient one, but it conceals the fact that the stones so named comprise a variety of rocks which, petrologically speaking, are entirely different. The one most commonly represented is a dolerite, a coarse-grained crystalline rock of greenish-blue colour, speckled with irregular white or pinkish nodules, about the size of a pea or smaller, of a form of felspar. These nodules give the rock a highly characteristic appearance, and have led to the positive identification of its source. For this reason the material is normally referred to by archaeologists as *spotted dolerite*. There are also at Stonehenge three stones (44, 45, 62) composed of the same material, except that the characteristic white spots appear to be absent. These may conveniently be called *unspotted dolerite*.

The next variety is represented only by one buried stump (32e) and four stones of the bluestone circle (38, 40, 46, 48). It is a *rhyolite*, a form of volcanic lava of dark blue-grey colour with a hard flinty texture and a sharp fracture. It often ex-hibits a delicate flow-structure of thin white parallel lines, or

more rarely of bands of small white globular masses, as if a
stream of stony sago had been trapped within the solidifying
siliceous matrix. This latter type is known as *spherulitic rhyolite*.

The third main variety is represented only by four stumps
buried beneath the surface (32c, 33e, 33f, and 41d), and by
chips in the top-soil. This is an altered *volcanic ash*, dark olive-
green in colour when unweathered, with a laminated fracture
and a noticeably softer texture than the other bluestones. This
softness doubtless accounts for the fact that no specimens
survive above ground at Stonehenge.

Two further varieties of bluestone have also been identified,
though only below ground. The *calcareous ash*, a laminated
blue rock, is represented by the single stump 40c; while there
are two stumps of *Cosheston sandstone*, a blue-grey rock spangled
with mica (40g and 42c).

It has long been recognized that these igneous rocks were
entirely foreign to the Stonehenge region, and must have
originated somewhere in the zone of geologically older for-
mations in the west and north of Britain, or even in Brittany.
Many of the geologists of the nineteenth and early twentieth
centuries who considered the problem of the bluestones be-
lieved that the transport of the stones might have been effected
naturally by the movement of ice-sheets in the Pleistocene
period (the so-called Ice Age), the stones being left stranded,
and ready to hand for the builders of Stonehenge, somewhere
on Salisbury Plain. But later analysis of the directions of
Pleistocene ice movements has shown conclusively that this
could not have happened, and that the bluestones, whatever
their origin, must have been transported *by man* for a considerable distance.

Their origin was finally localized for good by Dr H. H.
Thomas of the Geological Survey in 1923.* He was able to
show that the three main varieties of bluestone could be
matched exactly with outcrops of igneous rocks in the Prescelly Mountains of north Pembrokeshire, and that the only
locality in which all three occurred in close physical proximity
was an area about a mile square at the extreme eastern end of
the range, between the summits of Carn Meini and Foel

Antiquaries Journal, III (1923), 239–60.

Trigarn. From my own observations on Prescelly Mountain I have been able to confirm that the unspotted dolerite (which was not recognized by Dr Thomas) also occurs there as outcrops. There can thus be no doubt now that it was from this very restricted region that the bluestones were chosen and brought to Stonehenge. The technological implications of this extraordinary undertaking are discussed below (p. 105).

The Bluestone Circle

The bluestone circle, or what remains of it, lies between the sarsen circle and the horseshoe of sarsen trilithons. It is now very incomplete and much ruined. Only six of its stones still stand upright, more or less intact (31, 33, 34, 46, 47, 49); another five are leaning (32, 37, 38, 39, 48); eight have fallen flat or are fragmentary (36, 40, 41, 42, 43, 44, 45, 150); and ten survive only as stumps either just above the ground (35) or wholly beneath the surface (32c, 32d, 32e, 33e, 33f, 40c, 40g, 41d, 42c). With the exceptions noted above, they are of spotted dolerite. It is noticeable that of the five rhyolites, four form two diametrically opposite pairs, and it may well be that if we knew the material of some of the missing stones, or could find more stumps beneath the turf, a number of other diametric correspondences would appear.

The setting of the stones is irregular, and approximates to a circle far less closely than that of the much more massive and unwieldy sarsens outside them, the mean error being more than four times as great. The circle which is the best fit to the surviving stones has a diameter of 75 ft. The irregularity suggests, and other evidence confirms (p. 56), that the bluestone circle was erected later than the sarsen trilithons within it, which thus prevented the describing of an accurate circle from the centre of the monument.

The original number of stones in the circle has been variously estimated at different times. Some writers assumed that there were thirty, to correspond with the thirty uprights of the sarsen circle; though in fact the spacing of the surviving stones, even before the excavations of the present century, must have indicated a higher total. Others, to circumvent this difficulty, while still retaining a total of thirty, have assumed that the spacing of the stones was unequal, with a closer setting on the south-west side of the circle. The majority of writers, however, and especially the more recent ones, have agreed that the original number was forty.

This estimate seems reasonable enough, if one considers the spacing only of those stones which survive above ground. But excavation has shown that the actual spacing of the stones in the circle must have been much closer than anyone had previously supposed. Colonel Hawley, for instance, found the sockets for four stones, and two stumps, between stones 33 and 34; and our own excavations have shown that there were five stones between nos. 32 and 33 (Plate 19a), and probably eight between nos. 40 and 41.

These results, when plotted on a large-scale plan in combination with the surviving stones, enable a new and far more accurate estimate to be made, of 60 stones with a possible error of one stone more or less. The spacing of this original circle does not seem to have been uniform, the stones on the north-east side being rather further apart than elsewhere. In particular, there is a wide gap between the two stones flanking the entrance (31, 49), which have also been set intentionally a little within the circumference of the circle on which the remainder stand.

The size and shape of the stones in the circle is very variable. Some, like stones 32 and 33, are columnar, with a sub-rectangular section. Others, such as stones 31 and 38, are slab-like, with their broad faces set circumferentially. There is an equal variation in their heights and in the depths to which they are set in the ground. Altogether, even when allowance is made for natural weathering and wilful damage, they present a much less artificial and finished appearance than the stones of the bluestone horseshoe (p. 53) or the sarsens.

It is commonly said that apart from the Heel Stone (p. 29) *all* the stones of Stonehenge, bluestone and sarsen alike, have been dressed to shape. A merely superficial examination of the bluestones in the circle tends to confirm this statement, for many of them have an apparently artificial columnar shape, while the surfaces, particularly of the slab-like stones, have a rounded smoothness suggestive of deliberate tooling.

However, a more critical inspection, combined with a close comparison with the stones of the bluestone horseshoe (all of which have undoubtedly been tooled), makes it quite clear that this impression is false. With the two exceptions mentioned below, *all* the bluestones of the circle are in their natural state (Plate 16b), and none shows any sign of deliberate tooling or dressing. Their columnar shapes and their relatively smooth surfaces are the product of natural fracture and weathering, a fact which can be confirmed by anyone who has visited their source on the Prescelly Mountains. There, on the southern crest of Carn Meini, are great bare jagged outcrops of spotted dolerite (Plate 17a), from which the winter frosts are still detaching columnar and slab-like boulders, which tumble down to join the wide scree on the slope beneath. It needs only a brief search of these screes to match very closely, in size, shape, and surface appearance, almost any of the intact stones in the bluestone circle at Stonehenge. One or two earlier writers have drawn attention to this circumstance, but in general it has been ignored. It is only now, in the light of the new evidence for the earlier history of the bluestones at Stonehenge (p. 58), that its significance can be appreciated.

There are two stones in the circle, however, which have certainly been dressed to shape. Both have fallen down, and both evidently once served as lintels for small trilithons, and were only later set up in their present positions as pillars in the circle. Stone 150, of spotted dolerite, now lies flat on the ground (Plate 17b), revealing on its upper surface the two well-made mortices which betray its former use as a lintel. It is about 8 ft long, slightly curved in plan, like the much larger lintels of the sarsen trilithons (p. 42). The mortices are 41 in. apart, centre to centre, and except in size exactly resemble those of the sarsen lintels. All the visible surfaces have been tooled (the stone has not been lifted, so that the condition of the hidden surfaces is unknown), and on the outer end a close inspection, and still better an examination with the fingers, reveals the same rippled tooling which occurs on the sarsen stones (p. 40). The position of this stone, on which stone 32 now leans (Plate 17b), makes it quite clear that before its fall it formed part of the bluestone circle, standing upright on its outer end, with the mortice holes facing outwards so that they were hidden from an observer at the centre of the monument.

Stone 36, also of spotted dolerite, was recognized as a former lintel only in 1929, when Mr Newall and the Rev. George Engleheart removed sufficient of the surrounding soil to enable the mortices on its underside to be felt (though not seen or photographed, as the permission given by the Office of Works did not extend to the lifting of the stone).

In 1954 we felt that a more complete examination and record of this remarkable stone was required, and it was accordingly lifted by means of a chain-block secured to the apex of a tripod erected over it, and turned over on its side, supported on timbers, so that its underside could be examined at leisure (Plate 18a). After measured drawings and photographs had been taken, it was returned to its former position, half buried beneath the surface.

The exhumation of this stone allowed for the first time a full appreciation of the manual skill, no less than the feeling for form and design, possessed by those who dressed the bluestones to shape. Its basic form is that of a prism, just over 6 ft long, whose sides taper upwards from a flat base, in which the two mortices have been hollowed out slightly askew. But it is not a true prism, for all the edges are slightly curved, and all the surfaces except the base gently rounded, so that the outlines are softened, and the stone takes on a cushioned quality which belies the unyielding hardness of its material.

The two mortices are slightly oval in plan, with interior surfaces ground smooth and almost polished. Around the inner one (to the left in Plate 18a), and extending from it towards the end of the stone, is a shallow kidney-shaped depression, evidently a carefully worked seating for the top of the upright which here supported it. The base of this seating is marked, a little above and below the edges of the mortice, by two narrow and very shallow longitudinal grooves, whose surface is highly polished (Plate 18b). The appearance of these grooves makes it quite certain that they have not been worked by hand, but have been produced by frictional wear of the lower surface of the lintel upon two narrow ridges on which it rested. When one examines the uprights of the bluestone horseshoe (two of which are known to have had tenons on the top, and to have served as the uprights of a trilithon, p. 55), one finds that in some cases their upper surfaces have sharply ridged margins (Plate 20a). These ridges, if a lintel rested upon them, would undoubtedly have produced in time precisely the type of wear and polish which occurs in stone 36. The amount of relative movement has clearly been very small, probably no more than would be caused by thermal expansion and contraction of the stones and, possibly, by the slight rocking of the lintel on its uprights in gales of exceptional force. In any case, these worn grooves provide positive evidence that stone 36 was not only intended to serve as a lintel, but that it was actually so used, and for a period long enough for this wear to have taken place. This is the chief piece of evidence for the former existence of a structure of *tooled* bluestones, which must have included at least two trilithons, since there are two bluestone lintels (p. 51).

Like its fellow, stone 36 was finally set up as a pillar in the bluestone circle, with its mortices facing outwards. It was evidently buried in the ground only deep enough just to cover the lower mortice, for the stone below this level is completely unweathered.

The significance of the incorporation of these two dressed lintels in the circle of otherwise undressed stones is discussed below (p. 80). It is improbable that any of the remaining stones in the circle are also lintels re-used, as none of them shows any sign of tooling, and all the more likely candidates have been examined by Mr Newall with negative results.

The Bluestone Horseshoe

The bluestones in the horseshoe, which stand a few feet within the sarsen trilithons, present a marked contrast to those of the circle, just described. Not only are they all in the form of tall pillars, some 2 ft square in section and upwards of 6 ft high, but they have also all been very carefully and skilfully dressed to shape. All of them are of dolerite, no. 62 of the unspotted and the rest of the spotted variety.

The spacing of the surviving stones makes it clear that the horseshoe originally contained nineteen pillars, set at intervals of 5½ ft centre to centre. Those at the south-west end (stones 62–70) stand with their inner faces touching the circumference of a semicircle 39½ ft in diameter. The outer ends of the horseshoe appear to coincide with the north-eastern ends of the first and fifth trilithons (stones 51 and 60). There is no reason to suppose that it extended any further, and indeed there is some positive evidence that it did not (p. 82).

Only six stones survive as uprights (61–3, 68–70). Two more are stumps projecting a few inches above the ground (64, 65), while there is one buried stump (66, Plate 19b) beneath stone 55, apparently already shattered before the fall of the latter. The central pillar of the horseshoe (67) has fallen obliquely inwards, but is unbroken. Stones 71 and 72 (Plate 16a) are really the broken halves of a single pillar, shattered by the fall of stone 59.

Measurements of the surviving uprights suggest that the stones were set so that their heights above ground increased from the two ends of the horseshoe towards the centre, thus matching the increasing heights of the sarsen trilithons (p. 41). The height of stone 61 is 6 ft 2 in., and that of the central stone (67) may be estimated at 8 ft. Their overall lengths, however, are in some cases considerably greater, that of stones 67 and 68 being about 13 ft, and their weight about 4 tons.

The tooling of the surfaces of the stones has been carried out with great care, the standard of workmanship and finish being far higher than that exhibited by the sarsens, and matched only by the two former lintels in the bluestone circle (p. 51). In general the pillars are roughly square or rectangular in section, sometimes markedly so, as in the case of stones 71–2 (Plate 16a). There is usually a slight upward taper, and the faces and sides are slightly rounded or cushioned, an effect already seen on stone 36 (p. 52). In most instances the dressing has been carried to its final stage, leaving the surface smooth and even, but in places there are traces of the intermediate stage of parallel rippled tooling, as on the sarsen stones. This is best seen on the outer face of stone 70 in oblique lighting, and on the upper surface of the fallen stone 67, where the transverse rippling has been accentuated by the polishing action of the feet of visitors.

In every case where the upper part of a pillar survives intact, its top surface has been dressed flat and level. There are signs, however, that two pillars at least once terminated in a tenon, and must therefore have been uprights in a trilithon. On stone 70 the lower part of this tenon is still visible as a slightly raised circular platform (Plate 20b), the main part of the projection having been deliberately dressed away. On the inner end of stone 67 the removal of the tenon has been even more thorough, but its former presence is shown by a slight but still detectable bulge in the centre of its otherwise flat surface. It is quite probable also that the adjoining pillar 69 (Plate 20a) was once the upright of a trilithon. No trace of a tenon is visible on its top; but the inner and outer edges of the top are raised in slight ridges, exactly as on the sarsen uprights (pp. 39, 42), and the upper extremity of the stone is noticeably shouldered, as if to reduce its size to fit a seating worked on the underside of the lintel, as on stone 36 (p. 52). The same ridging of the edge can be detected on the outer face of stone 70.

Two other bluestones in the horseshoe require special mention. The broken stump, no. 66 (Plate 19b), has a projecting tongue worked on its eastern face, which may well have extended originally right to the top of the stone, nearly 8 ft from the ground. Confirmation of this may be seen in the corresponding stone on the other side of the axis, no. 68 (Plate 21), which has a well-made groove of similar dimensions all the way up its west side. These two remarkable features must surely be associated, and it may be accepted that at one time these two stones stood side by side, the tongue on the one fitting into the groove on the other, just as match-boarding is fixed together today. This kind of joint is one which is more proper to timber than to stone; but its immediate prototype is probably the tongue-and-groove joint employed on the sarsen lintels (p. 39).

It is quite clear, therefore, that among the dressed bluestones there are six, possibly seven (36, 66, 67, 68, 69, 70, 150), which were formerly part of a structure which included at least two trilithons. This structure was afterwards dismantled, and its components set up as separate pillars in the present horseshoe and circle, the evidence for their earlier use, in the form of tenons and mortices, being obliterated or concealed as far as possible. Obviously, therefore, neither the horseshoe nor the circle (since the latter contains the two dressed lintels) represents the original setting of the bluestones, and traces of an earlier setting may be expected to be found, either at Stonehenge or elsewhere. In fact, as is shown below, there is evidence at Stonehenge itself for *two* such earlier settings (pp. 58, 80).

It is known that the final setting of the bluestones in their present arrangement took place *after* the erection of the sarsen trilithons, since it was found in 1901 that stone 68 stands in the filling of the sloping ramp which forms an extension of the stone-hole of stone 56.

The Altar Stone

The naming of the Altar Stone is due, apparently, to Inigo Jones, who made the first 'plan' of Stonehenge in 1620 (p. 186). Though it has long since become established, it should not be taken to imply any knowledge of the real purpose of the stone, which is entirely unknown.

The Altar Stone (80) is the largest of all the 'foreign stones' at Stonehenge. It is a rectangular recumbent block of sandstone, 16 ft long by 3½ ft wide by 1¾ ft deep, embedded in the earth about 15 ft within the central sarsen trilithon. Two fallen members of this trilithon now lie across it (stones 55 and 156), and their weight has probably pressed it down to its present position. Like the adjoining bluestones, it has been carefully dressed to shape, but its exposed surface is now considerably abraded by the feet of visitors.

The Altar Stone is not symmetrical to the axis, nor does it lie at right-angles to its line, though this lack of symmetry is small enough to be appreciated better on a plan than by casual inspection on the ground. Nevertheless, the amount of discrepancy appears to be more than can be accounted for by movement when the two sarsens fell upon it. It cannot be assumed, therefore, that the Altar Stone was ever placed intentionally in the position it now occupies. Indeed, it has been suggested that it formerly stood upright on one end, on the axis, and has fallen on top of its own stone-hole, as the neighbouring stone 55 has certainly done. Some support for this suggestion comes from the report by Colt Hoare, the patron of William Cunnington (p. 31n.), that the latter found a disturbance 6 ft deep 'close to the altar'. Though it is not certain exactly where this was, the description of the filling of the hole makes it sound much more like a genuine stone-hole than the site of some treasure-hunter's excavation.

The material of the Altar Stone is a fine-grained pale green sandstone, with a high content of tiny fragments of mica, which glisten brightly on the surface of a fresh fracture. It also contains minute grains of garnet, and this has enabled the probable source of the rock to be identified. This, interestingly enough, is not in the Prescelly Mountains of Pembrokeshire, the source of the rest of the foreign stones (p. 48), but in the Cosheston Beds (a division of the Old Red Sandstone of South Wales) which crop out on the shores of Milford Haven, further south in the same county. This identification, though not so certain as that of the bluestones proper, is of great interest in supporting the view that the foreign stones were transported by sea (p. 105), for Milford Haven is the first stage of the most likely sea route from Prescelly.

No other stone composed of this rock is known at Stonehenge, though occasional fragments of it, very probably detached from the Altar Stone itself, have been found in the soil of the site. Significantly, chips of an entirely different micaceous sandstone have also been collected on the site, and have been identified with a particular outcrop of the Cosheston Beds at Mill Bay on the south shore of Milford Haven, about 2½ miles above the ferry at Pembroke Dock.

The Q and R Holes

This series of holes, which is entirely invisible on the surface, is perhaps the most important discovery made during the recent excavations. In 1954 a segment of the bluestone circle was examined between stones 32 and 33 (fig. 3). The positions of five additional stones of the circle were identified in their expected positions (32a–e) (Plate 19a). But outside these we also discovered a series of rather irregular holes, between the bluestone circle and the sarsen circle, which were filled with tightly rammed dirty chalk rubble. These were named, for convenience, the Q Holes.* Soon afterwards we found the first of a corresponding series of R Holes, with identical filling, just *inside* the present bluestone circle, between it and the adjacent first trilithon. And before long it became apparent that each pair of Q and R Holes, measured radially, formed the enlarged ends of a dumb-bell-shaped trench, the centre portion of which was filled with very tightly packed clean chalk rubble. These structures are referred to below, for convenience, as the 'dumb-bells'.

The careful excavation of these Q and R Holes revealed on their bottoms the impressions left in the relatively soft chalk by the bases of heavy stones; and the occurrence of minute chips of dolerite embedded in some of these impressions showed conclusively that the Q and R Holes had once been the sockets for bluestones, presumably the same stones that are still at Stonehenge. Here then was the evidence for one of the earlier bluestone structures already mentioned (p. 56).

Once this small series of 'dumb-bells' had been discovered, it became possible to make sense of some earlier discoveries made by Colonel Hawley, whose significance had up to then been obscure. When excavating a rectangular area within the bluestones flanking the entrance (nos. 46–9, 31) Hawley found the inner ends of five elongated holes in the chalk, extending inwards radially from the existing bluestones, but not

---

*In choosing this designation, I had in mind John Aubrey's frequent use, as a marginal note in his unpublished MS. *Monumenta Britannica*, of the phrase 'quaere quot' – 'inquire how many' – which seemed appropriate to the occasion.

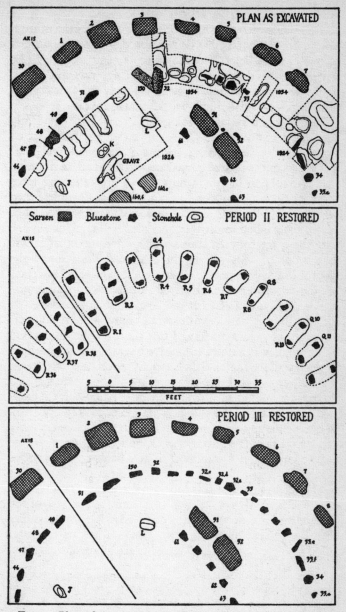

FIG. 3. Plan of the eastern part of Stonehenge, with division
into periods

corresponding exactly with their positions. It is evident from his published sections that he had also dug into the *outer* end of one of these holes, between stones 30 and 49, though he did not realize that he had done so. There can now be no doubt that these elongated holes are simply the continuation of the series of radial 'dumb-bells' found in 1954.

Further round the circle, going clockwise, Hawley evidently also dug into two more Q Holes, within the fallen sarsen stones 8 and 9; and in 1954 one more complete 'dumb-bell' was found and excavated immediately to the south of stone 33.

It is thus possible to identify, in an arc extending from stone 46 clockwise to stone 34, the positions of no less than twelve radial pairs of Q and R Holes, and to infer the presence of two more filling the gaps in the excavated series, one in line with the space between stones 2 and 3 and the other in line with stone 7. This spacing, if continued right round the circle,* would give a total of thirty-eight pairs of holes, repre-senting two concentric circles of bluestones with mean dia-meters of 74 ft and 86 ft. It can be calculated, however, that the 'dumb-bells' in line with stones 31 and 49 have an over-all length of at least 17 ft, and that those adjoining them on either side are at least 11 ft long; whereas the average length of the rest of the 'dumb-bells', each of which held two stones, is a little over 6 ft. From this it follows almost certainly that there were additional in-lying stones flanking the entrance, two extra in each of the longest 'dumb-bells' and one extra in each of the adjacent ones. This means that the total number of bluestones in this setting was 82, 76 forming the two con-centric circles and 6 additional in-liers flanking the entrance (fig. 3).

The relative date of this bluestone structure (now known as Stonehenge II, pp. 72, 90) in relation to the rest of the monument is fortunately known. Clearly, it must be earlier than the present bluestone circle, since stones of the latter stood in some cases in the rammed chalk filling of the central

*When the bluestone lintel 36 was lifted in 1954, the presence of a 'dumb-bell' could be detected in the chalk beneath it by probing, but its excavation could not be undertaken, owing to the necessity of replacing the bluestone lintel exactly in its original position.

part of a 'dumb-bell'. We also know that it is earlier than the erection of the sarsen circle, because the inner margin of the stone-hole of stone 3 was found to have been cut through the tightly packed filling of Q Hole 4. The bluestones must therefore have been removed from the Q Holes (and presumably from the R Holes also), and the holes themselves refilled and obliterated, before preparations were made for the erection of the sarsens.

This conclusion is of the greatest importance for the question of the orientation of Stonehenge (p. 174). It will have been observed that the entrance to this double bluestone circle, marked by the additional in-lying stones, corresponds very closely with the axis of the later sarsen structure. It thus follows that the orientation of Stonehenge towards the midsummer sunrise was an accomplished fact before the sarsen monument ever existed.

The Post-Holes

In addition to the post-holes on the entrance causeway, already described (p. 26), Colonel Hawley found a large number of others. Most of these occurred in the central area, among the stones and a short distance outside the sarsen circle. They make no recognizable* pattern but it must be remembered that except between the Z Holes and the bank (an area in which relatively few post-holes occurred) excavation was confined to small and discontinuous cuttings. Doubtless many of these holes were dug to support whatever form of scaffolding or other construction was used in the erection of the sarsen uprights and the lifting of their lintels into position (pp. 132, 134). Others may be of much more recent date, and represent temporary wooden stalls or other buildings erected for the fairs which used to be held at Stonehenge. Others again, in the area within the sarsen circle, may possibly belong to some early setting of wooden posts associated with the first phase of the monument's history (p. 170). Today, nothing more can be done than to record the fact that these post-holes exist. Upon the evidence available, it is useless to try to interpret them.

*For that reason and for the sake of clarity they have been omitted from the plans, figs. 1 and 8.

The Graves

During his excavations Colonel Hawley found two graves
containing human remains. One of these lay immediately outside Y Hole 9 (fig. 1); it was 5½ ft long, and dug only deep
enough just to contain the body below the level of the chalk.
It contained the skeleton of an adult man, the body evidently
having been forced into a space that was too short for it, as
the thorax was crushed. From Hawley's description it may be
inferred (though there is no specific statement to this effect)
that the body was lying on its back, with legs extended. In the
absence of any finds, not even stone chips (a point of some
importance, p. 99), in the filling of the grave, its date is unknown. It may be said, however, that the extended attitude
(if such it was) and the somewhat perfunctory disposal of the
body point to a date not earlier than the Romano-British period.

The second grave lies athwart the axis of the monument,
between the shattered fragments of stone 160 and stones 49
and 31 (fig. 3). When found by Colonel Hawley it had already
been disturbed, and the bones were mixed up with an extraordinary collection of objects of various dates, from Bronze
Age pottery to clay pipe-stems, which reads like an odd lot in
an auctioneer's catalogue. Its date is consequently unknown,
but there is no reason to suppose that it is not prehistoric.

The Axis

The literature of Stonehenge, including this book, contains
constant references to the axis. This is the axis of symmetry
of the monument, or strictly speaking of the sarsen monument only, comprising the five trilithons, the outer circle, the
four Stations, and the Slaughter Stone with its hypothetical
companion (p. 77).

It should be made clear from the outset that the *exact* line
of this axis can no longer be recovered. To do this requires at
least *two* points on its line to be known. In fact, only *one* such
point is known, namely the mid-point of the space between
stones 1 and 30. Its line cannot be fixed at the centre of the
monument, since there is no one point which can be claimed
as such, owing to the errors in the positioning of the stones of

the outer circle. It cannot be fixed where it passes through the central trilithon, since stone 55 has fallen, and stone 56 has been re-erected (p. 192), not necessarily in exactly its original position. And it cannot be fixed on the south-west side of the circle, where it passed between stones 15 and 16, because stone 15 no longer survives in position; nor at the Slaughter Stone, for the same reason.

Admittedly at all these points the line of the axis can be estimated to an inch or two either way, and most people would think this good enough. There is a reason, however, for emphasizing that the *exact* line of the axis can never now be known. It seems clear that the axis, as laid out by the original builders, was intended to coincide with the direction of sunrise on Midsummer Day. That it did so *approximately* we may be sure. But many writers on Stonehenge have assumed that the coincidence was *exact*, and from there have gone on to deduce the date of the erection of the sarsens from the known rate of change, over the course of centuries, of the direction of midsummer sunrise. It is the impossibility of fixing the axis *exactly* which renders all such attempts unreliable, particularly when it is realized that a difference of one inch at one or other end of the axis (on the line of the sarsen circle)* makes a difference of over two centuries in the calculated date (p. 95).

It will be noticed that if the axis is prolonged north-eastwards it does not bisect the original entrance of the earthwork, but it does *approximately* coincide with the mean centre line of the Avenue. The implications of these facts are discussed below (pp. 72, 94).

The 'Stonehenge Layer'

Wherever one digs within the Stonehenge earthworks, and indeed on the bank and ditch and for some little way outside them, there is found beneath the turf a rubbly layer composed of fragments of natural flint, chips of the Stonehenge stones, both bluestone and sarsen, and miscellaneous rubbish representing the whole span of the site's history, from late neolithic

*Corresponding to an angular difference of 3 minutes of arc, or one-twentieth of a degree.

pottery to pieces of modern beer-bottles. This layer lies immediately beneath the turf and mould, and on undisturbed ground rests directly upon the natural chalk. It normally passes over the top of disturbances, such as empty stone and post-holes, especially if the latter contain a fair proportion of chalk rubble in their filling. But where the filling is predominantly of soil, as in the Y and Z Holes (p. 35), the layer dips somewhat below its usual horizontal level.

Colonel Hawley called this the 'Stonehenge layer', and attributed great importance to it as an index of date. He assumed that the very large numbers of stone chips in the layer (among which bluestone always predominates) were the products of the actual tooling and dressing of the stones on the site, and that the formation of the layer containing them was thus contemporary with the erection of the stones. He therefore concluded (and the conclusion is perfectly valid, *provided that* his initial assumption is accepted) that the Stonehenge layer could be treated as a chronological horizon, everything beneath it being earlier than the erection of the stones.

So much has been based on this argument in the past that it requires very careful examination. To begin with, it is by no means certain that the stone chips *are* the product of the dressing of the stones. As is pointed out below (p. 125), the nature of sarsen stone is such that the waste produced in the process of dressing it to shape is likely to have been in the form of sand rather than of solid chips. And though the shaping of the bluestones would certainly produce waste in the form of chips, the distribution of the chips in the Stonehenge layer does not favour this theory of their origin. For the dressing of stones within the Stonehenge earthwork would produce a number of isolated and localized concentrations of chips, confined in each case to an area of a few feet around the actual spot where the stone was dressed. Whereas in fact such localized concentrations do not occur and the distribution of stone chips is remarkably uniform.* Moreover,

* Colonel Hawley numbered each of his trenches, and counted the various kinds of stone chips in each trench. But unfortunately he made no plan of his trenches, or at least none survives, so that the position of individual trenches can now be fixed only very roughly, if at all. It is known, however, that most of his cuttings in the area between the bank and the Z

there is some evidence that the dressing of the bluestone took place at some distance from Stonehenge.

A further consideration (and this is much more damaging to Hawley's theory) is that there is no reason to regard the 'Stonehenge layer' as a true layer at all, that is to say, as a single deposit laid down at any one period. Indeed, the wide range in time of the objects found in it shows that it is nothing of the sort. It is a well-attested fact (though one which is too often ignored, sometimes wilfully, by field archaeologists) that any object dropped on the surface of the ground, if there is a depth of more than an inch or two of soil, will become buried below the surface within the space of a few years. This burial is due to the natural activity of earthworms* which bring up soil from below and deposit it on the surface as worm-casts, and at the same time cause the undermining of objects on the surface by the formation of hollow burrows, which gradually collapse.† It is clear that the Stonehenge layer is nothing more than the accumulation of all the objects dropped on the surface of the ground, which have travelled slowly downwards until their movement was arrested either by solid chalk or chalk rubble, or by earlier accumulations in which the activity of earthworms was at a minimum, owing to the small constituent proportion of actual earth.

It is thus quite obvious that the so-called Stonehenge layer cannot be used as a chronological index, since its formation has been continuous and is still continuing today. The uniform scattering of stone chips all over the site, however, still requires explanation, and is discussed below.

Holes were of uniform size (20 ft by 5 ft), so that it is possible to state with some confidence that, on the basis of his counts per cutting, the distribution of chips was uniform within the normal statistical limits of variation, and that there were no marked local concentrations in this area.

*The classic account of these fascinating creatures, which includes a number of specific observations of their effect upon archaeological sites, is Charles Darwin's monograph *The Formation of Vegetable Mould through the Action of Worms with Observations on their Habits*, first published in 1881 and many times reprinted.

† This process has been demonstrated at Stonehenge itself in the recent excavations. The scatter of chalk crumbs left on the surface on the sites of Colonel Hawley's dumps was seen to form a thin horizontal layer at a depth of 2–2½ in. The present rate of burial is thus 6–8 in. per century.

The Avenue

The last feature of the Stonehenge complex which remains to be described is the Avenue. This begins at the entrance of Stonehenge as a broad processional way, bounded by a low bank and a shallow ditch on either side. The present width inside the banks is about 40 ft, and the distance between the ditches, centre to centre, is 75 ft.

On the centre line of the Avenue, between the entrance of the Stonehenge ditch and the Heel Stone, Colonel Hawley found two empty stone-holes (fig. 1, B, C) from which the stones must have been removed before the eighteenth century. Nothing is known of the date of their erection, but their axial position suggests that this was not before the construction of the Avenue itself.

A little further out there was a line of four large post-holes, some 3 ft in diameter and 4 ft deep (fig. 1, A), whose purpose is likewise unknown. They must be of earlier date than the Avenue, as the most westerly of them was buried beneath its western bank; and they may well be connected in some way with the earliest monument at Stonehenge, since a line drawn from the centre of the circular earthwork through the centre of its entrance appears to bisect this line of post-holes at right-angles.

The relationship of the Heel Stone and its ditch to the Avenue has already been discussed (p. 30).

After crossing the modern road, the Avenue continues in a straight line down a gentle slope, its ditches usually discernible by an increased growth of thistles. The end of this first straight alignment coincides with a sharp fall of the ground to the floor of a dry valley (fig. 8). Here, according to William Stukeley in the eighteenth century, the Avenue split into two branches, one swinging northwards to meet the Cursus (p. 150) and the other eastwards to climb the slope to the gap between the Old and New King Barrows. These two branches were also recorded by Colt Hoare in 1812, and by the late Sir Flinders Petrie in 1880. Since then the eastern branch, and a continuation of it beyond the further point observed by

Stukeley, has been dramatically rediscovered by air-photography, but no one has seen the northern one.

Excavations in 1953 showed that Stukeley's northern branch has no real existence, and that he allowed his too enthusiastic and not over-critical imagination to work upon portions of two ditches, neither of them connected with the Avenue or with each other, which here run parallel for a short distance, and do in fact point in the direction of the Cursus to the north. One of these ditches is certainly, and the other probably, of much later date than the Avenue itself.

From this point onwards, where the Avenue swings through a gentle curve eastwards to cross the floor of the dry valley and mount the slope beyond, it has been obliterated by cultivation, and the line of its ditches can be traced only from the air (or on the ground under very favourable conditions) by the darker green tone of the crops growing over them. It was this that led to the discovery of the remainder of their course by Dr O. G. S. Crawford on photographs of the district taken in 1921 by the Royal Air Force. These showed that after passing the crest of the hill between the Old and New King Barrows, the Avenue swung gradually south-eastwards, taking up a new straight alignment which crosses the Amesbury road, passes beneath West Amesbury House, and comes to an end on the bank of the River Avon in the paddock in front of the house. All but the last 230 yards of this course has been checked by probing and by excavation, which has shown that the width of the avenue, though variable, increases on the average from 75 ft at Stonehenge to 110 ft just north of West Amesbury House. Its termination on the river bank still remains to be proved.

The purpose of the Avenue and its date are discussed more fully below (pp. 75, 151). It is enough to say here that it appears to be a processional way linking Stonehenge with the River Avon, and that its inception may have had something to do with the hauling of the bluestones from the river to the monument. It may be for this reason that it follows a rather roundabout route instead of the direct line from the river, so as to avoid the steeper slopes which would have taxed the strength of the hauling-parties.

CHAPTER THREE

The Sequence of Construction

In this chapter I set out the arguments for the sequence of construction at Stonehenge. I do not pretend that these arguments make easy reading, but I offer no apology for their complexity. The unravelling of the evidence for the Stonehenge sequence is extremely difficult in itself, and even more difficult to communicate clearly and coherently to the reader who lacks the advantage of close acquaintance with the site. It would be wrong to pretend otherwise, or to attempt to simplify the matter by the suppression of relevant facts, even if their precise significance is in doubt. Moreover, I am rash enough to suppose that the presentation of these arguments in detailed form may have some value in illustrating the kind of evidence which archaeologists use and the way in which they handle it.

It will have been realized that not all the numerous structures described in the previous chapter are of the same date. Like so many of our English cathedrals and churches, Stonehenge is a composite monument with a long history of construction, during which grandiose additions have been made to earlier and simpler structures, and old work has been torn down to make way for new. Just as a great church may reveal in its stones, for those who can read it, the story of the changing tastes, and in some measure the changing beliefs, of successive generations of builders, so also the stones of Stonehenge, ruder certainly but by no means mute, bear witness to the growing aspirations and the diverse religious beliefs of a prehistoric age.

The component structures of Stonehenge can be assigned to three main periods of building, the last of which is further subdivided into three phases. These are summarized below, and the evidence for the sequence is then considered in detail.

Stonehenge I comprises the Heel Stone, the ditch, the bank, and the Aubrey Holes, together with the two stone-holes in the entrance, the post-holes on the causeway and near the Heel Stone, and possibly some wooden structure at the centre of the circle.

Stonehenge II is the double circle of 82 bluestones in the Q and R Holes, the Avenue, the Heel Stone ditch, and possibly the two axial stone-holes on the Avenue.

Stonehenge IIIa includes the Four Stations, the Slaughter Stone and its former companion, the sarsen circle, and the horseshoe of sarsen trilithons.

Stonehenge IIIb comprises the setting of dressed bluestones, and the Y and Z Holes.

Stonehenge IIIc is represented by the existing setting of the bluestones in the circle and horseshoe.

Stonehenge I

Even a superficial examination of the plan of Stonehenge suggests that the ditch, bank, and Aubrey Holes belong to one and the same period of construction. The ditch and bank, of course, are necessarily contemporary, since the one is derived from the other; and the Aubrey Holes share with them the common centre from which the circles of all three were laid out.

A closer examination shows that this centre differs from that of the circle of sarsen stones, and lies about 3 ft south-south-west of the latter. This suggests that there is a difference of date between the two groups of structures. Since the circles of the ditch, bank, and Aubrey Holes (which are close approximations to true circles) could have been laid out only if the area between them and their centre was free from obstructions, it follows that they must belong to a period earlier than the erection of the sarsen stones.

Now it has already been shown that the sarsen circle and trilithons were preceded (p. 61) by the double bluestone circle of Stonehenge II, whose axis coincides closely with that of the later sarsen structure. But this axis differs by about 5° east-wards from that of the circular earthwork, which is accordingly also likely to be of different date from Stonehenge II. That it is in fact earlier than Stonehenge II is shown by the position of the lowest bluestone chips in the silting of the ditch, which do not occur on or near the bottom, but only at about half the total depth of silt. From this it follows that the ditch had already been open for some time before the movement of bluestones on to the site. The ditch and bank (and therefore the Aubrey Holes also) must thus be earlier than Stonehenge II, and accordingly belong to period I.

This is confirmed by the relationship of the original entrance of the earthwork to the Avenue. This axis of the Avenue coincides fairly exactly with that of the sarsen structure (Stonehenge IIIa) and that of the double bluestone circle (Stonehenge II). It is therefore unlikely that the Avenue is earlier than period II at the earliest. But, as is shown below (p. 73), the eastern end of the circular ditch at the entrance appears to have been filled up deliberately, when it was already partly silted, in order to enlarge the entrance to match the width of the Avenue. The earthwork must thus be earlier than the Avenue, which is itself not earlier than Stonehenge II.

The Heel Stone must belong to the first period for the following reasons. The ditch which surrounds it can be shown (p. 75) to belong to period II. Therefore the Heel Stone itself must belong either to period II, or to period I. If it belonged to period II, it would be contemporary with the Avenue. In this case, one might expect that it would have occupied an axial position on the Avenue, which it does not. Its eccentric position suggests, therefore, that it is earlier than the Avenue, and belongs to period I.

This is confirmed by an excavation made up to the base of the stone in 1953, which produced fragments of late neolithic Beaker pottery (p. 157) from the fine earthy filling which occupied the space between the side of the stone and its stone-hole. This earthy filling could only be accounted for by the decay of the anti-friction stakes which originally lined the side of the stone-hole, and prevented the toe of the stone from digging in to the side when it was hauled upright (p. 131). The level at which the pottery was found made it clear that it could only have reached that position some appreciable time *after* the erection of the stone. Fragments of identical pottery have also been found in the silting of the Stonehenge ditch at a level corresponding with that of the earliest fragments of bluestone, but no lower. These latter represent Stonehenge II. It thus follows that the erection of the Heel Stone preceded period II, and it must therefore belong to period I.

The four post-holes which extend half-way across the Avenue close to the Heel Stone (fig. 1, A) must also belong to the first period, for they are symmetrical to the axis of the circular earthwork, but not to that of Stonehenge II and IIIa. Moreover, one of them is covered by the bank of the Avenue, so that they must necessarily be earlier than period II.

The same argument from symmetry applies to the post-holes on the entrance causeway, and to the pair of stones which must have stood in holes D and E. These stones were presumably of sarsen, like the Heel Stone, and to judge from the size of the holes were similar to stone 93, though possibly taller.

The earliest monument at Stonehenge thus appears to have been a circular enclosure bounded by the earthwork, with the ring of Aubrey Holes just inside it. As these holes appear to have been ritual pits, dug for some religious or ceremonial purpose and refilled almost immediately (p. 27), the presence of two of them on the entrance causeway itself (nos. 55, 56) need not be taken to imply that they are of different date from the earthwork. For once refilled they would cause no obstruction, and in any case there is a clear space of 16 ft between them.

The only stones present at this period seem to be the Heel Stone and the pair of stones in the entrance. The only timber structures identified are the four post-holes near the Heel Stone (A) and the rows of post-holes on the causeway. The first of these may perhaps have held the uprights of a triple gateway, surmounted by wooden lintels, much like the gateways of temples made familiar to us in Japanese prints. And if this were so (though it must be made quite clear that this is entirely speculative), such a structure could well provide the ultimate prototype for the lintelled sarsens of later date, and for the carpenter's joints used in fixing them together.

Of the post-holes on the causeway little can be said, except that their numbers seem to be too great, and their arrangement too haphazard, for them to represent any kind of fence or barrier restricting access to the enclosure.

Reference has already been made (p. 61) to the possibility that some timber structure, in the form of a setting of posts, or even a small roofed building, may have existed at this period in the centre of the monument. Admittedly there is no positive evidence for such a structure. But there is none against it either, for the greater part of the central area within the present bluestone circle remains unexcavated. Moreover, it is reasonable to suppose that so large a sanctuary would have had something at its focal point. But what this was it is doubtful that we shall ever know.

Stonehenge II

The structures added in the second period consist of the double bluestone circle in the Q and R Holes, the Avenue, the Heel Stone ditch, and perhaps the two stones that stood in holes B and C.

The double circle must be later than period I, since bluestone chips begin to occur very sparsely in the middle levels of the ditch, but not lower. There are far too few of these to regard them as the waste products of dressing the stones to shape, and indeed there is no reason to suppose that any of the bluestones were artificially shaped at this period. But it is understandable enough that in the process of hauling them on to the site and setting them upright fragments would occasionally be detached accidentally, and would be thrown into the partially silted ditch.

We know also that the double circle had already been dismantled before the erection of the sarsens of period IIIa since in one case (p. 61) a sarsen stone-hole had been cut through the filled-up socket of a bluestone. The double circle is thus later than period I, but earlier than period IIIa.

That the Avenue is contemporary with the double bluestone circle can be shown as follows. The end of the Avenue is wider than the entrance of the earthwork of period I, so that the two cannot be part of the same plan, and the Avenue must accordingly be either earlier or later than the bank and ditch. That it is earlier is unlikely, since in the absence of any structure on the site of Stonehenge it would lead nowhere. That it is in fact later is proved by Colonel Hawley's observation that the last 25 ft of the ditch of the circular earthwork, east of the original causeway, had been deliberately filled up, in order to bring the width of the earthwork entrance into line with the width of the Avenue. This means that the Avenue must have been built *after* the circular earthwork was already in existence.

It follows, therefore, that the Avenue must belong either to period II or to period III, and this is confirmed by the coincidence of the Avenue with the common axis shared by the structures of these two periods. A more detailed consideration of the deliberate filling recorded by Colonel Hawley shows that in fact the Avenue belongs to period II.

This filling was of clean chalk rubble (that is, without admixed earth), extending to a depth of about 3 ft from the present surface of the silting. Where this rubble came from is uncertain, but the obvious source is the bank adjoining the ditch at this point. It may be objected that if this portion of the bank had been thrown back into the ditch, the remainder of the bank ought *now* to be much lower than elsewhere; whereas in fact it is only slightly lower. But it must be remembered that throughout the circuit of the earthwork almost the whole of the original bank has slipped or been washed back into the ditch through natural processes of weathering. In the short stretch now in question this natural process has merely been anticipated by the deliberate throwing of part of the bank into the ditch; but the ultimate effect on the surviving height of the bank has been the same.

The important and significant point is the condition of the material in the ditch itself. Where this is the result of entirely natural silting the upper filling is fine in texture, and dirtied by the admixture of surface soil; whereas Colonel Hawley records that the filling in the end of the ditch was clean chalk of a much coarser texture.

The fact that the filling extended to a depth of 3 ft means that the ditch must have been open to that depth when it was thrown in. This level corresponds with that at which the earliest bluestone chips and fragments of Beaker pottery have been found, and is thus contemporary with Stonehenge II. Further confirmation of this came from an excavation of the ditch in 1954, about 30 ft west of the entrance. Here the total depth of silt was 6 ft. The lower half of this was coarse loose chalk rubble, representing the rapid weathering of the exposed sides of the ditch in the first few years after it was dug. Above this was a thin earthy layer, composed of soil from the lips of the ditch which had fallen in through the undermining, by weathering, of the upper part of the sides. This layer represents a rest-level, at which the process of silting was sharply arrested, because the sides of the ditch were now completely covered by silt and no longer exposed to the direct action of rain and frost. At the same time the deposition of soil in the surface of the silt would allow the rapid establishment of a protective growth of vegetation.

Resting on this temporary surface was a fragment of unweathered bluestone, showing that the ditch must have been open to this depth at the time the bluestones first arrived at Stonehenge.

Above this rest-level the chalky silt extended to a total height of $4\frac{1}{2}$ ft from the floor of the ditch, becoming progressively finer and dirtier towards the top. At this level there was a sharp transition from chalky rainwash to earth containing innumerable stone chips and rubbish of all periods (the so-called Stonehenge layer, p. 63), which in turn was covered by a few inches of mould and turf containing only the most recent objects.

Resting on the surface of the chalky rainwash were two large sarsen mauls, identical with the many specimens found by Colonel Hawley in the sarsen stone-holes, where they had been used as packing-stones (p. 133). There can be no doubt that these mauls are the tools used in dressing the sarsens in period IIIa, and the two present specimens may well have been used in the tooling of the adjacent Slaughter Stone or its vanished companion. Their presence at this level means that the ditch must have been silted up at least to that level (or higher, since the action of earthworms would have caused the mauls to sink through the upper soil layer until they reached the chalk silt) by period IIIa. Since it is known that the deliberate filling on the other side of the causeway took place at a time when the ditch was still open at a *lower* level than that of these two mauls, it must necessarily have taken place before period IIIa, to which they belong. And since the filling can be associated with the building of the Avenue, it follows that the Avenue, since it cannot be of period III, must be of period II, and therefore contemporary with the double bluestone circle.

Once this is established the purpose and layout of the Avenue become clearer. It seems very probable that the bluestones were brought from Pembrokeshire mainly by water (p. 105), the last stage of their journey being up the River Avon to the neighbourhood of Stonehenge. It is thus understandable that the builders should have made a processional way up which the stones could be hauled from the river to the site, and that the final stretch of this way should be aligned on the intended axis of the monument. However, this axis points well away from the landing-place on the river bank, so that the Avenue had necessarily to be laid out in more than one alignment, so that eventually it joined the river to Stonehenge without too many abrupt changes of direction, and without forcing the hauling-parties to negotiate unnecessary steep slopes.

It should be added that the width of the Avenue appears to have been determined by the position of the existing entrance of the earlier earthwork. The centre-line was fixed, as the prolongation of the axis of the double circle; and the western ditch was aligned, naturally enough, on the west end of the existing causeway. The other ditch therefore had to be at an equal distance from the centre-line, giving a total width of just over 70 ft. This arrangement is the one which involved the least alteration to the existing earthwork.

The reasons for placing the ditch of the Heel Stone in period II are easily understood. The ditch is very narrow and steep-sided, and if left open for more than a week or two, especially in the winter, would silt up very rapidly. But excavation shows that in fact there is no natural silt on the bottom of the ditch. On the contrary, it appears to have been filled up with tightly rammed chalk rubble almost as soon as it was dug. This rubble contained a fragment of unweathered bluestone (rhyolite), which cannot be earlier than period II. This, then, is the period of the filling of the ditch, and hence also of its digging, since the two operations can be separated by an interval only of weeks.

The purpose of this ditch can only be conjectured. Once the course of the Avenue had been decided, it would be clear that the Heel Stone would stand within it, though not symmetrically. As part of the earlier sanctuary of period I the Heel Stone was doubtless hedged round, for the new builders, with all kinds of taboos and restrictions; and the digging of the ditch round it may well be interpreted as an expression, in physical form, of a ritual prohibition by which the sacred stone was cut off from the more profane activities with which the Avenue was associated. Even so, however, there seems to have been some compromise between the requirements of ritual and of expediency, for the ditch was filled up almost at once, so that thereafter it formed a symbolic rather than a physical barrier.

Of the two stones which seem to have stood in holes B and C nothing is known (though one of them, C, may possibly have survived until the seventeenth century, when a stone which may tentatively be identified with this position was recorded by John Aubrey). They are axial to the Avenue, and are thus unlikely to be earlier than period II; but they could equally well have been part of the grandiose reorganization of phase IIIa, when the same axis continued in use.

Stonehenge II thus consisted of the addition to the existing structures of period I of the double circle of bluestones in the centre, and the Avenue outside, together with the ditch round the Heel Stone, and possibly stones B and C. How many of the earlier features were then dismantled it is impossible to be sure. If there was any central timber construction in period I, it was probably destroyed and replaced by the double circle. The wooden 'gateway' near the Heel Stone was probably removed as well, since it would no longer be symmetrical to the new axis; and the two stones in holes D and E may have been taken away for the same reason. Probably also the deposition of cremations in the cemetery and the Aubrey Holes now came to an end, for there is reason to think that the new builders of period II had a religious and cultural tradition very different from that of their predecessors, and that cremation-burial played no part in it (p. 157).

Stonehenge IIIa

The work of the third period includes the five sarsen trilithons, the outer circle of thirty sarsen uprights and their lintels, the four Stations, and the Slaughter Stone and its companion. Together these represent a complete rebuilding of the monument, which involved the transport of no less than eighty-one stones, some of them of vast size, for a distance of over twenty miles.

It has already been noted that the number of bluestones in the double circle of period II was eighty-two. The close correspondence with this figure of the number of sarsen stones* can hardly be a simple coincidence, and suggests that in spite of the radical differences in the scale, plan, and workmanship of the new monument, some continuity with the earlier and simpler structure had nevertheless to be symbolized in this way.

This continuity did not extend, however, to the incorporation of the old double circle in the plan of the new work. As we have seen, the bluestones of Stonehenge II were removed from their sockets, and the cavities filled with tightly rammed chalk rubble, before the stone-holes were dug for the sarsen circle (p. 61). Indeed it is probable that this preliminary would have been necessary, even if it had been intended afterwards to re-erect the bluestones, for the size and weight of the sarsens is such that it would have been most difficult, if not impossible, to raise them and their lintels unless the surrounding surface had been entirely cleared of obstructions.

After the dismantling of the bluestones and their removal to some place of safety, the first operation must have been the erection of the five sarsen trilithons, for they are far too

*Indeed, if one allows the existence of the fifth Station Stone on the south-west side of the earthwork (p. 33), the correspondence would be exact.

big to have been manoeuvred once the outer circle was in place. The building of the outer circle presumably came next, followed by the erection of the four Station Stones and the Slaughter Stone and its companion.

It must be admitted that if one subjects this proposed sequence to a really critical analysis, there is no compelling reason for insisting that all the sarsen stones are components of a single and united plan, conceived and executed as a whole. But in archaeology, as in other academic disciplines, one must avoid the unnecessary multiplication of hypotheses. In the absence of any positive evidence that the sarsen structures are of different dates, one must accept their symmetry about a common axis and the similarity of their shaping and jointing as sufficient reasons for treating them all as parts of one and the same design.

The only possible exceptions are the four Station Stones, of which only two survive (nos. 91, 93). These stones are apparently linked geometrically to the rest of the sarsen structure (p. 33). But it must be remembered that the axis, and possibly the centre, of the double circle of period II is substantially identical with that of the sarsens, so that it is conceivable that the Station Stones really belong to period II. This notion is to some degree supported by the great difference in surface finish between stones 91 and 93 on the one hand, and the rest of the sarsens (apart from the Heel Stone) on the other. Admittedly there are small patches of tooling on these two stones, but this could have been done after their original erection; and apart from this tooling they are much more like the Heel Stone, in that they are substantially natural boulders. Moreover, it could be significant that the ditches of the two Barrows, surrounding the sites of Station Stones now vanished, are very similar to the ditch round the Heel Stone, though not so deep. These ditches must be later than period I, since they are flattened in plan on the outer side, to avoid running over the bank into the ditch, while that of the South Barrow cuts through an Aubrey Hole. But though later than period I, there is nothing in the ditches themselves to show whether they belong to period II or later.

For these reasons my colleagues and I have toyed more than

once with the idea that the four Station Stones formed part of an earlier circle of widely spaced sarsens, lying just outside the Aubrey Holes, and contemporary, broadly speaking, with Stonehenge II.

Some apparent support for this speculation may be seen in the three large and irregular holes found by Colonel Hawley just outside the line of the Aubrey circle, between Aubrey Holes 1 and 2, 7 and 8, and 13 and 14 (fig. 1, F, G, H). Holes G and H are equidistant, to within a couple of feet, from Station Stone 91, while hole F is twice the same distance from hole G. It might thus be supposed that these, and the stone-hole 92, represent the sockets for part of this hypothetical early sarsen circle.

Unfortunately, however, the interval from hole H to stone-hole 92 is greater than the other intervals. Furthermore, if those intervals are significant, there ought to be a corresponding hole between Aubrey Holes 4 and 5. Search has been made for this hole by probing, bosing (p. 27n.), and by an electrical resistivity survey, all with uniformly negative results; and it may safely be assumed that this hole does not exist. One cannot exclude an alternative hypothesis, that there was a circle of even wider spacing, of which holes F, G, and H are representatives, from which the stones were later removed, some of them being slightly tooled and re-erected, as the Station Stones, in period IIIa. It must be recorded, however, that although the spacing of these holes looks intentional, their shapes are said by Colonel Hawley to have been very irregular; and he himself regarded them as natural holes made by the growth of bushes.

There can be no certainty on this question, at least until there has been further excavation in the appropriate places. In the meantime it seems preferable to regard the four Stations as an integral part of the plan of Stonehenge IIIa while bearing in mind the difficulties raised by their relatively unfinished surfaces, and the bare possibility that they once formed part of an earlier setting of sarsens within the bank.

The possible purpose of the four Stations has already been discussed (p. 33). If they do in fact belong with the rest of the sarsen structure, their apparent function of surveyor's marks would imply that the axis and the centre were calculated afresh for the new building; and in view of the care and skill which have been devoted to the setting-out of the sarsen stones it seems very probable that this was done. It is supported, for what it is worth, by the fact that the best estimate of the axis of the sarsen structure of period IIIa differs from the mean axis of the Avenue of Stonehenge II by about 12′ or one-fifth of a degree. Too much weight should not be given to this, however, in view of the impossibility of now determining the exact line of the later axis (p. 62).

Stonehenge IIIb

The structures added in phase IIIb appear to be the setting of dressed bluestones and the Y and Z Holes. The reasons for regarding these as associated with each other, and as a separate phase of construction, are set out below.

The elements of the Stonehenge complex which remain to be assigned to their place in the sequence are four in number: the present bluestone circle, the present bluestone horseshoe, the Y and Z Holes, and the earlier structure of dressed bluestones. How are these four elements related to each other?

The present circle and horseshoe of bluestones must be of the same date, and part of the same plan, since both contain components of the dismantled setting of dressed bluestones. They must be later than the sarsen setting of phase IIIa, since stone 68 of the horseshoe stands in the filling of the ramp of stone-hole 56; and the irregularity of the present circle shows that it was erected *after* the sarsen trilithons were in position.

The Y and Z Holes are also later than the sarsens, as is shown by the irregularity of their plan, and the fact that Hole Z7 was cut through the external ramp of stone-hole 7.

The setting of dressed bluestones is necessarily earlier than the present setting of the bluestones in a circle and horseshoe, but its relationship in time to the sarsen structure is not known directly. The argument formerly used to support a later date for the bluestones as a whole, namely that bluestone chips never occur in the filling of the sarsen sockets, is not even correct and must obviously be abandoned; for we now know that there were bluestones at Stonehenge long before any sarsens were erected.

Though there are thus no positive indications of the date of the dressed bluestone setting, there are some grounds for associating it with the Y and Z Holes. These latter, though unfinished and never used, were obviously intended as the sockets for a double circle of bluestones, numbering sixty in all (there are actually only fifty-nine holes, since Z8 is missing). We know that the number of bluestones available from the dismantled double circle of period II was eighty-two. If sixty are subtracted from these, twenty-two remain, which is precisely the apparent number of the stones in the dressed bluestone setting (nineteen in the present horseshoe, the two lintels in the circle, and the Altar Stone). This correspondence cannot be dismissed as a chance coincidence; and it may accordingly be accepted (as a working hypothesis which covers the observed facts in the simplest way) that the dressed bluestone setting and the Y and Z Holes are associated with each other, and form parts of one and the same phase of construction.

If this is accepted, then the four elements mentioned above fall into two pairs, the dressed bluestones and the Y and Z holes as the earlier (phase IIIb), and the present circle and horseshoe of bluestones as the later (phase IIIc).

It may be argued, of course, that the Y and Z Holes are *later* than the present setting of bluestones, since there is no physical connection to show that they are not. But to suggest this is to introduce an unnecessary hypothesis, and to ignore the very striking arithmetical relationship between their number and that of the dressed bluestones.

The dressed bluestone setting of phase IIIb is the only structure at Stonehenge for whose nature and location the evidence is almost wholly inferential, for all the other periods are represented either as surviving constructions above ground, or by empty sockets beneath the surface. So far as its location is concerned, it is clear that this setting must have stood *either* somewhere within the sarsen trilithons (for excavation outside that line has not revealed any empty sockets which could belong to such a setting), *or* away from Stonehenge altogether. In view of the apparent numerical association with the Y and Z Holes and the fact that the setting included two small-scale copies of the sarsen trilithons, a location in the central area of Stonehenge itself is by far the more probable.

There is indeed some concrete evidence for this. When excavating within the bluestone circle on the north-east side, Colonel Hawley found three holes (fig. 3, J, K, L) which he regarded as a possible extension of the bluestone horseshoe.* Of these J and L are obviously stone-holes and were so regarded by their excavator. They measure 4 ft by 2 ft and 4 ft by 3 ft respectively. The central hole, K, measured 3 ft by 2½ ft, and was said by Hawley to be a double post-hole. This it may well have been, though the dimensions of its two halves are greater than those of the other post-holes in the area.

Although the stone-holes J and L appear to continue the line of the present bluestone horseshoe, it is very doubtful whether they do in fact belong to it. For the average spacing of the stones in the horseshoe, centre to centre, is 5½ ft, the amount of variation being a few inches at the most; whereas the spacing from stone 61 to stone-hole L is just over 9 ft. It seems more probable, therefore, that holes J and L (and possibly hole K, though this is less certain) are the survivors of an entirely different setting of stones. And this setting may be identified tentatively with that inferred from the existence of re-used dressed bluestones in the present circle and horseshoe. It may thus be assumed, as a working hypothesis which remains to be confirmed or disproved by subsequent excavation, that the dressed bluestones originally stood in a horseshoe or oval approximately on the line of the present horseshoe, though at a different spacing.

The nature of this structure is even more uncertain than its position. We know that it must have contained the tongued-and-grooved pair (66, 68, p. 55), presumably standing in actual contact.† Unless we assume the existence of a second

*He also found a number of scattered post-holes. These make no recognizable or significant pattern, and have been omitted from the plan for the sake of clarity.

†It is tempting at first sight to suggest that this pair of stones stood on the axis in hole K, but unfortunately the latter is far too small to accept their bases, even in close contact.

such pair (for which there is no evidence), it is likely that it stood in an axial position. For the care with which the stones have been dressed implies an equal concern for the symmetry of their plan. Again, we know that there must have been at least two trilithons, of which the lintels survive (36, 150, p. 51). The setting presumably included the Altar Stone as well, since it too has been dressed to shape. And as it is by far the largest of the foreign stones, and of a different rock from the remainder, it too may have occupied a position of special importance somewhere on the axis. However, there is quite insufficient evidence for selecting any one plan rather than another for this setting of dressed bluestones.

The second part of the work of phase IIIb consists, as has already been argued, of the Y and Z Holes. The size and shape of these leaves little doubt that they are stone-holes, presumably intended for the sixty bluestones that remained from the original total of eighty-two, after the twenty-two best specimens (that is, the longest) had been selected to be dressed for the structure discussed above. But it is clear that the intention of the builders was never carried out, for the floors of these stone-holes are unmarked by any impression of the base of a stone, such as has been found in the Q and R Holes and in stone-holes of the present bluestone circle. Indeed it looks as if the holes themselves were never completed, for Y7 was very shallow and irregular and Z8 is missing altogether. The difference in the regularity of spacing of the holes on either side of a radial line passing between stones 8 and 9 is very striking. One gets the impression that the work started with holes Z9 and Y9, and continued from there clockwise round the circle. As far as Z3 and Y3 the spacing is fairly uniform, allowing for the fact that no radial measurements could be made directly from the centre of the circle. From here onwards, however, there is a marked deterioration, and one feels that for some reason the builders suddenly lost their sense of purpose, struggled on for a little in a half-hearted way, and finally abandoned their work without even completing the full number of holes.

We shall never know what it was that induced this state of apathy or despair, whether it was some natural calamity such as the collapse of some of the stones, the death of a priest or chieftain, or some portent presaging disaster and the wrath of the gods. But clearly it was something considerable, if it could lead to the abandonment of a plan projected on so large a scale. And this abandonment was complete, for the excavated holes not only did not receive the bluestones destined for them, but were never even filled up. This is evident from the nature of their silting, which is entirely the product of slow natural weathering and the deposition of fine soil by wind and rain.

Attention has already been drawn to the occurrence in most of the excavated Y and Z Holes of a fragment or two of bluestone (almost always of rhyolite) on the very bottom. These fragments seem to be deliberate deposits, and perhaps it is not too fanciful to see them as propitiatory token offerings, made as symbolic substitutes for the bluestones themselves, to ward off any evil consequences that might result, so to speak, from depriving the gaping holes of their rightful and expected contents.

If this interpretation of the Y and Z Holes is correct (and it must be emphasized again that it is no more than the working hypothesis which best fits the facts available at present), it follows that phase IIIb must be divided into two stages of activity, of which the abortive plan of the Y and Z Holes was the later. For it is clear that, from the evidence of the frictional wear on the bluestone lintel 36 (p. 53), the dressed bluestone setting was not only projected, but was actually put up, and stood long enough (the period must be measured in years, not in months) for this wear to have taken place. The reason for dismantling this structure was doubtless the abandonment, at a later stage, of the second part of the work, that is the Y and Z Holes.

Stonehenge IIIc

The final reconstruction of the stones is represented by the present setting of the bluestones in the circle and horseshoe. This must necessarily be later than the dressed setting of the stones, whose dismantled elements it incorporates; and it is reasonable to suppose that it followed fairly closely upon the calamitous abandonment of the previous phase. The dressed bluestones were dismantled, and so far as possible the evidence for their earlier use was obliterated. The tenons on the uprights were battered away, and where complete obliteration was impossible, as in the case of the lintels, the stones were relegated to the outer circle, where they would least betray their earlier function.

One cannot help feeling that whatever it was that led to the sudden abandoning of the work of the previous phase, whether a natural catastrophe or some shameful act of gross impiety, it demanded nothing less than the complete remodelling of the plan of the bluestones, even if this involved the undoing of the many months of patient and devoted skill lavished upon the dressing and fitting of the stones.

The Later History of Stonehenge

The present setting of bluestones constitutes the final phase of *construction* at Stonehenge. There remains the question of *destruction*. It has already been pointed out that the distribution of fallen and missing stones is curiously uneven, and looks like the result of deliberate destruction rather than chance collapse. The probability of stones falling of their own accord at Stonehenge is much less than might be supposed, for the uprights are set far deeper in the ground than is common in other British stone circles. At Avebury, for instance, where a number of the stones rival those of Stonehenge in mass, the stone-holes are exceedingly shallow, often no more than 16 in. deep, so that the stones stand upright only in virtue of the skill with which they have been balanced on their bases. Yet many of these stones are still standing, whereas a number of those at Stonehenge, which are less top-heavy in shape and stand up to 5 ft deep in the ground, are now prostrate.

If the present ruin of Stonehenge is due, at least in part, to deliberate destruction, when is this likely to have happened? There seem to be two main periods when circumstances favouring such destruction, as an act of policy, could have existed. The first is the period of the Roman occupation of

Britain, when it is conceivable that Stonehenge was regarded by the occupying power as a dangerous focus for resurgent nationalism, particularly perhaps during the early years of the occupation, when the flourishing cult of Druidism was stamped out with unusual ferocity. There is indeed some evidence for the breaking up of stones during the Roman period (p. 99). But it must also be remembered first, that there is no evidence whatever for connecting Stonehenge with the Druids, whose ceremonies and observances took place, we are told, in natural groves of trees rather than in artificial temples; and secondly that it was the policy of the Roman authorities to absorb and modify for their own purposes the native religious cults (Druidism apart), rather than to invite their persistence in a clandestine and hostile form by overtly suppressing them.

The other most probable occasion for the deliberate overthrowing of the stones is during the Middle Ages, when it is known that certain prehistoric monuments in some parts of Europe at least served as the centres of pagan rituals which were both an offence and a threat to the spiritual power of the Church. There is nothing that compels one to insist that the destruction of Stonehenge took place in one rather than the other of these two periods (or, for that matter, in either); though if the relative quantity of rubbish of the two periods is any guide, it suggests that visitors to the site, whether as devotees or as destroyers, were very much more numerous during the Roman period than in medieval times.

The Dating of the Sequence

So far I have been dealing with the various structures at Stonehenge merely as a relative sequence. It remains to assign actual dates to the periods and phases distinguished above. The evidence for this is of three kinds. First, there are fragments of pottery and other datable objects, including the carvings, which occur in association with one or other of the constructional features, and allow the approximate period of their erection, or some other event in their history, to be deduced. Secondly, there is the evidence for the *duration* of particular phases, provided for instance by the accumulation of silt in the ditch or in the Y and Z Holes, or by the wear on the bearing surface of stone 36. And finally there is evidence for the date of one period only (the first), which is quite independent of archaeological judgements, and is based upon the known rate of decay of radio-active carbon in dead organic matter.

Until recently archaeologists have been in the habit of dating their prehistoric material by *periods*, to which names are given such as 'Late Neolithic' or 'Middle Bronze Age' or 'Early Iron Age'. This practice is symptomatic, of course, of the relative vagueness of archaeological chronologies; and though it has the merit of honesty, in that it does not claim to be more precise than the nature of the evidence warrants, it has the disadvantage that except to the expert it conveys very little about the actual periods involved, measured in years. Moreover, it must be realized that names like 'Early Bronze Age' are not really labels for periods of past time, but names for stages in the technological development of human societies. And since such development does not take place uniformly, even in an area as small as Britain, it is inevitable that at one and the same time there will be a community, say, in Wessex which, in virtue of the possession of certain diagnostic types of bronze weapon, must be assigned to the Middle Bronze Age, while another in northern England, less advanced, belongs to the Early Bronze Age, and a third in northern Scotland, retarded through geographical isolation, will still be in the Late Stone Age.

Our increased understanding of the regional differences in the rate of technological progress has made this kind of absurdity a commonplace. For this reason archaeologists are now beginning to abandon the use of terms like 'Middle Bronze Age', at any rate to distinguish *periods of time*, and are being driven to give dates in actual years, or at any rate in centuries B.C. This is all to the good, if only because the use of a common system of chronology emphasizes that prehistory is nothing more than the backwards extension of history, and that the aims of the archaeologist and the historian are ultimately identical. Moreover, the use of absolute dates is becoming increasingly justified by the dates in actual years now being provided by techniques such as the radio-active carbon estimations mentioned above.

But it must not be assumed, of course, that the use of a common system of dating implies a common standard of accuracy. To say that St Paul's Cathedral was built in the seventeenth century A.D. means something very different, in terms of accuracy of statement, from saying that Stonehenge II was built in the seventeenth century B.C. So long as the archaeologist has to deal with societies that are neither literate themselves, nor are in close contact with literate communities elsewhere, there must inevitably be a sizeable margin of uncertainty in his dates; and the size of this margin will increase, roughly speaking, in proportion to the distance, measured in time and in space, of the community in question from other communities whose chronologies are either recorded directly, or can be reconstructed with the aid of documents, coins, or inscriptions.

The reader is therefore warned that in what follows the dates are very rough ones, and cannot be treated as if they were dates A.D. For the earlier of them at least, the margin of uncertainty may be as much as two centuries either way.

The date of *period I* is given by pottery fragments found close to the bottom of the ditch; by the bone pins and flint 'fabricators' which accompanied cremations in the Aubrey Holes and elsewhere; and, within wide limits, by a radio-active carbon estimation carried out on charcoal from an Aubrey Hole.

The pottery consisted of four or five fragments found by Colonel Hawley close to the south causeway, in the primary silting of the ditch on its east side. Most of these fragments were badly decayed, and all but two had lost their outer surface. These two, however, could be joined together and identified as a piece of the same type of Secondary Neolithic pottery that occurs commonly at the neighbouring sanctuary of Woodhenge (pp. 156, 177). It may be dated to the period 1900–1700 B.C.

This date is confirmed by the objects found with the cremations, which again are typical of the Secondary Neolithic

cultures of Britain, and indeed occur also with similar cremations in cemeteries and in circular sanctuaries whose main
internal feature is a ring of pits generically similar to the
Aubrey Holes at Stonehenge (p. 156).

The date given by the radio-active carbon estimation of
samples of charcoal from Aubrey Hole 32 (excavated in 1950)
is 1848 B.C. ±275 years. At first sight this looks surprisingly
close to the date suggested on purely archaeological grounds,
but this impression is false.

The basis of the method may be explained briefly as follows.
The atmosphere and all living matter contain carbon combined in gaseous or solid form, of which a very small proportion is a radio-active isotope, carbon 14. During life this
proportion remains constant in organic matter, owing to the
normal physiological exchange of carbon through breathing,
eating, and excretion. When the plant or animal dies, this
exchange ceases, and the proportion in its tissues of radio-active
carbon (^{14}C) to ordinary carbon (^{12}C) begins to decrease,
owing to the disintegration of the radio-active component. As
the rate of disintegration is known, it is possible to calculate
how long must elapse before the proportion of ^{14}C to ^{12}C in
a sample falls to any given level. Thus the age of a particular
specimen can be estimated by determining the proportion of
the two kinds of carbon in it at the present day, using techniques of analysis and measurement which have been developed for this purpose.

Owing to the random nature of radio-active disintegration,
and the difficulty of excluding from the apparatus the effects
of penetrating cosmic radiation, the estimates given by this
method have a sensible margin of uncertainty, and it is this
which is expressed, for the date of Stonehenge I, by the figure
'±275 years'. Translated into everyday terms, this means
that the odds are about 2 to 1 that the date of Stonehenge I
lies *somewhere* between 2125 and 1575 B.C., and about 20 to 1
that it lies *somewhere* between 2400 and 1300 B.C. The ^{14}C
estin.ation thus supports the date arrived at on archaeological
grounds, but in no way increases its precision. It should be
added, however, that since this estimation was made in 1950,
a number of improvements have been made in the method,

and it is hoped that in the near future new dates will be obtained in which the margin of uncertainty will be very much smaller, perhaps of the order of ±60 years.

Stonehenge II corresponds, as we have seen (p. 73), to a level of the ditch silting at which fragments of late neolithic Beaker pottery occur. The period covered by such pottery in Britain is from about 1750 B.C. to about 1550 B.C., and it is accordingly somewhere within these two centuries that the building of Stonehenge II should be placed.

The level at which this pottery and the earliest fragments of bluestone occur is slightly above the rest-level which marks the end of the first phase of rapid silting in the ditch (p. 74). This process is likely to have been completed within a few years of the digging of the ditch, if one may judge from recent observations of the rate of silting in modern excavations of comparable size in chalk. But once the rest-level had been reached, the secondary silting would accumulate above it very much more slowly. It is thus possible that the silt had accumulated only to the level of the earliest bluestone chips as late as fifty years after the digging of the ditch. If the latest date for the ditch is around 1700 B.C., it follows that the latest date for Stonehenge II is around 1650 B.C.

It would be unwise, however, to place very much reliance upon estimates of the rate of silting, since this depends very largely upon the prevailing climate, which was not then necessarily what it is today. None the less, a date for Stonehenge II somewhere in the seventeenth century B.C. accords fairly well with what is known of the history and activities of the Beaker people who appear to have built it (p. 157). These people were the first users of metal in Britain (copper and gold), and the distribution of their burials shows that after initial settlement on the east coasts and in Wessex, they expanded westwards along the natural routes to Ireland, at that time the principal source of metal in north-western Europe. One of these routes follows the south coast of Wales to Pembrokeshire, and it is probable that it was in this way that the bluestones of Prescelly became known to, and coveted by, the Beaker population of Salisbury Plain. But the transport of the bluestones from Pembrokeshire to Wiltshire is an undertaking of such magnitude that it is hardly likely to have been attempted before the Beaker community, and the trade route to Ireland, had already been firmly established for some time. Since the earliest date for the arrival of Beaker people in Britain is about 1750 B.C., it seems probable that Stonehenge II was not built until after 1700 B.C., at the earliest.

The finding of two fragments of Beaker pottery in the filling (strictly the refilling) of one of the Q Holes is of little significance, for this refilling took place after the dismantling of Stonehenge II, and is really contemporary with Stonehenge IIIa. The fragments may well have been lying in the surface soil for a century or more before they were accidentally incorporated in the rubble rammed back into the empty socket. All they tell us is that the refilling took place *not earlier* than the local arrival of Beaker people.

For the date of the sarsen structure, *Stonehenge IIIa*, there is no direct archaeological evidence in the form of associated pottery or other objects, and until recently the main argument for its date (apart from the astronomical theory discussed below) has been based upon the numerous round barrows which cluster thickly in the neighbourhood of the monument (fig. 8). Many of these barrows are of specialized form, and contain burials accompanied by rich and exotic weapons and ornaments, betokening widespread trade contacts with Central Europe and even with the Mediterranean. They obviously represent an aristocratic community of considerable power and wealth, and indeed the only one of which we know in Britain during the second millennium B.C. which could have commanded the resources of labour and craftsmanship necessary to encompass the transport and erection of the sarsen stones. This community, identified by Professor Piggott as the Wessex Culture of the Early Bronze Age, appears on the evidence of imported European objects in its graves to have flourished from 1550 to 1400 B.C. It is accordingly somewhere within this period, and presumably not too near its beginning, that the erection of the sarsen stones should be placed.

Striking confirmation of this date comes from the carvings found in 1953 (p. 44). All of these are within working distance from the ground, and were presumably executed *after* the erection of the stones. The best-preserved of the axe carvings are accurate full-size representations of a type of bronze axe-head, with broad crescentic cutting-edge and tapering butt, which is known to have been manufactured in Ireland, and distributed from there to Britain, between 1600 and 1400 B.C. The erection of the sarsens is thus likely to have taken place earlier than the later of these dates.

The dagger carving is even more informative. If the axe carvings represent a specific type of axe, of which numerous actual specimens survive, we are entitled to assume that the dagger carving also delineates a specific type of dagger, which was familiar to the person by whom, or under whose orders, the carving was executed. The weapon appears to have a straight-sided tapering blade with a sharp point, expanding into projecting 'horns' at its base, with a short hilt and a wide pommel with a flat top. No daggers of this form are known in the earlier Bronze Age either of Britain or indeed of Europe north of the Alps. On the other hand, fairly close parallels come from the famous Shaft Graves at Mycenae in southern Greece, the burials of the dynasty of warrior chieftains symbolized for us by the legendary figure of Agamemnon, which can be dated 1600–1500 B.C. Indeed, the best parallel of all for the form of the Stonehenge dagger is another carving, this time in relief, on one of the grave-stones set up over Shaft Grave V at Mycenae, showing a warrior armed with a dagger and driving a war-chariot. The only difference is in the pommel, which is spherical at Mycenae but flat-topped at Stonehenge.

One cannot insist, of course, that the Stonehenge carving *must be* a representation of a Mycenaean dagger, for such identifications are always in the last resort a matter of personal opinion. But the fact remains that no nearer parallels are known; and if it were the intention of the carver to represent a British type of dagger, he could have done so just as easily. In fact it would be easier, for the blade of such a dagger is broader and less angular in outline; and the technique employed to make the carving (p. 139) is one which lends itself to breadth and to curves rather than to the narrow and angular shape which has actually been portrayed. Moreover, among the grave-goods of the Wessex Culture there are several objects which provide clear evidence, to which no archaeologists have objected, for trade contacts between southern Britain and the Mycenaean and Minoan civilizations of the central Mediterranean; so that the idea of a Mycenaean dagger at Stonehenge is by no means as far-fetched as it at first appears to be.

If this is in fact what the Stonehenge carving represents, it follows that it must have been executed, at the latest, within the lifetime of someone who was familiar with this type of weapon in its home-land; and since the type goes out of fashion in Greece by 1500 B.C., the erection of the stones on which the carving occurs must have taken place by this date, or very shortly afterwards.

If the dagger were the only evidence for the date of the sarsens, it would be unwise to rely too much upon the suggested Mycenaean connection. But the fact that the evidence of the axe carvings and of the barrows both point to a date around 1500 B.C., at which time contacts with the Mycenaean world are independently attested, in itself goes some way to support this identification. It will be referred to again in connection with the possible origin of the remarkable architectural refinements exhibited by the sarsen stones.

The only other means that has been suggested for estimating the age of the sarsen structure is that propounded by the supporters of the astronomical theory of the purpose of Stonehenge, based on the apparent alignment of the axis upon the point of midsummer sunrise. So much time and ingenuity has been spent on this matter in the past that it deserves some attention here, if only to demonstrate the inadequacy of the arguments upon which it is based.

The significance of the midsummer sunrise is, of course, that it marks the furthest point northwards along the horizon at which the sun ever rises. In the spring, at the equinox, the sun rises due east. As the year advances, the point of sunrise moves northwards along the horizon, at first rapidly and later more slowly, until for several days around 20 June its position appears to be stationary. Thereafter it moves back again further and further towards the east, until it once more occurs due east at the autumnal equinox. In the winter half of the year the sunrise performs a similar advance and recession southwards, rising furthest to the south on the shortest day of the year, just before Christmas. Since the two occasions on which the sun rises furthest to the north and furthest to the south repeat themselves annually at the same times each year, they provide the simplest means whereby a fixed point in the annual calendar can be determined by observation of a heavenly body. And of the two the midsummer sunrise is to be preferred for such observations, since it is less likely to be obscured by cloud.

Although in any one man's lifetime the point of midsummer sunrise appears to be unchanged, it is in fact moving very slowly *eastwards*, and has been moving in this direction for many thousands of years. The movement is due to a very slight cyclical change in the inclination of the earth's equatorial plane to the plane of its orbit. It has a period of about 40,000 years, and is known as the Obliquity of the Ecliptic. The past values for the Obliquity have been calculated, and from these values it is possible to deduce the direction of midsummer sunrise at any given place at any past date.

The crucial observations on which the theory is based were made at Stonehenge by Sir Norman Lockyer in 1901. The arguments based on these observations are set out below, with comments upon their validity.

1. *The axis of Stonehenge was aligned accurately by its builders upon the point of midsummer sunrise at the date of its construction.*

This is an assumption which is entirely unverifiable. The alignment can have been accurate only within the limits of what can be done by eye, without instruments. In any case the *true* line of the axis cannot now be determined (p. 62).

2. *The Avenue is contemporary with the sarsen stones, and has exactly the same axis, which may be used as a substitute for the axis of the stones themselves.*

The first statement is now known to be false, and the second is probably false as well, and in any case is unverifiable.

3. *The azimuth (bearing) of the axis is 49° 34′ 18″ east of true north.*

This is an arbitrary axis chosen for reasons which are totally irrelevant to the question. Lockyer took two points on the estimated midline of the Avenue close to Stonehenge, and four more towards the far end of the first straight alignment of the Avenue. The azimuths of these lines were 49° 38′ 48″ and 49° 32′ 54″, with a mean of 49° 35′ 51″. None of these, however, was chosen as the axis. Instead, Lockyer observed that a line drawn through the centre of Stonehenge *approximately* on the mean axis passed close to or through an earthwork in Sidbury Hill, eight miles to the north-east, and another earthwork at Grovely, six miles to the south-west, neither of which, incidentally, is visible from Stonehenge itself. The azimuth which he finally selected for the axis (49° 34′ 18″) is that of an Ordnance Survey bench mark, erected in the nineteenth century A.D., near the former earthwork.

This extraordinary proceeding seems all the more remarkable in that the two earthworks are now known to be of the Early Iron Age, and to have been built not earlier than the fourth century B.C., when Stonehenge had already stood for more than a thousand years, and was probably already in part a ruin. The chosen line has just as much, but no more, significance than the fact that the same line, if prolonged, passes through Copenhagen.

4. *For the midsummer sunrise to have taken place on this axis the value of the Obliquity of the Ecliptic is 23° 54′ 30″.*

5. *This value of the Obliquity obtained about the year 1680 B.C.*

This calculation is based upon tables of the Obliquity published in 1873. More recent computations give for this value of the Obliquity a date of 1840 B.C.

6. *The date of the sarsen circle is therefore 1680 B.C. ±200 years to allow for experimental errors.*

For the reasons given above, this date should now be altered to 1840 B.C. ±200 years.

The objections put forward to the first three arguments above are sufficient in themselves to show the unsoundness of the theory. Three others of a more fundamental kind may be stated briefly. The first is that we have no means of telling what the original builders regarded as 'sunrise'. Was it the first gleam of light (as Lockyer assumed); or when the sun's disc was exactly cut in half by the horizon; or when the whole disc was just visible, with the horizon a tangent to its lower margin? The date computed using the first of these positions differs by nearly 4,000 years from that using the last.

Secondly, it should be observed that the assumed line of sight along the axis is not marked positively in any way, as are the sights of a rifle. The axis is determined by the mid-points of a number of empty spaces between pairs of upright stones (1 and 30, 15 and 16, 55 and 56), and the largest of these spaces (between stones 1 and 30) is 5 ft wide at eye height. An error of only one inch at this point makes a differ-ence of over two centuries in the calculated date, and for any given position of the head of the observer on the axis, the use of the left eye instead of the right, or vice versa, makes a difference of 500 years.

Thirdly, it must be remembered that Lockyer's observations were made with instruments of the highest precision, whereas the instruments used by the original builders were confined to their own naked eyes and, at the most, a number of straight sticks cut from the nearest hazel-thicket. The permissible limits of accuracy of the whole problem are necessarily fixed by the degree of precision of which the original builders were capable, and any conclusions based upon the use of narrower limits of accuracy are therefore wholly unreliable.

It should be added here that Mr R. S. Newall, who has de-voted a great deal of time and thought to this problem, is con-vinced that the layout of the sarsen structure at Stonehenge implies that the phenomenon observed in antiquity was not the midsummer sunrise, to the north-east, but the midwinter sunset, to the south-west. This suggestion is certainly worthy of serious consideration; but even if it is true, as a basis for calculating the date of the sarsens it is open to exactly the same objections that have been raised above.

In view of these objections it is indeed surprising that the date arrived at from astronomical observations should be so close to that given by purely archaeological evidence. None the less, neither method of approach can be taken to confirm the correctness of the other. The only conclusion to be drawn from astronomical considerations is that the structures of Stonehenge II and Stonehenge IIIa were aligned *roughly and approximately* on the midsummer sunrise. This is a fact; but it does not tell us either why or when it was done.

The date of the succeeding structures of *Stonehenge IIIb*, the setting of dressed bluestones and the Y and Z Holes, is again not known directly; only the Y and Z Holes were associated with objects of known date, and there is good reason to suppose that these found their way into the holes only long after they were originally dug.

The dressed bluestone structure may possibly have been planned as an integral part of the setting otherwise composed of sarsens, for the same techniques of dressing and jointing have been used in both. But even if it was not, the date of its erection is still likely to have fallen within the period of the Wessex Culture (that is, before 1400 B.C.), since the standard of craftsmanship is, if anything, even higher in the dressed bluestones than in the sarsens. The funerary record which, Stonehenge apart, gives us paradoxically our only evidence for the life of the contemporary population, suggests that in the two or three centuries after 1400 B.C. there was a marked decline in material wealth and technical virtuosity, and a reversion to an earlier and altogether more barbaric mode of existence.

The only evidence for the *duration* of phase IIIb is the amount of wear on the bearing surface of stone 36 (p. 53), where it rested on its upright. In view of the probable causes of this wear, the amount which has actually taken place represents more than a merely ephemeral life for the jointed structure of which this stone was the lintel. Nothing short of a very prolonged experiment would enable an accurate figure to be arrived at; but at a guess one can say that at the very least ten years, and possibly up to fifty years, must have elapsed for this degree of wear to develop.

Of the Y and Z Holes at least it is clear that they were *not* planned as an integral part of the great rebuilding represented by the sarsen stones. Had this been so, their circles would have been laid out accurately from the centre, when the ground was still unobstructed. The Y and Z Holes are obviously an afterthought; but how much later they are than the sarsens it is impossible to say. If they are really linked to the dressed bluestone structure, as has been assumed above (p. 81), then they also should fall within the fifteenth century B.C.

Until the excavation of holes Y16 and Z16 in 1953, any suggestion that the Y and Z Holes could possibly be of so early a date would have been greeted with ill-disguised disbelief, if not with derision; for it was already known from Colonel Hawley's excavations that the earthy filling of the holes contained numerous fragments of pottery, dating from the third century B.C. to the later part of the Roman occupation. It was accordingly assumed without question that the holes had been dug, at the earliest, in the pre-Roman Iron Age; and some archaeologists of less conventional spirit suggested with reserve that they might be ascribed to the Druids, the Celtic priesthood which is known to have flourished in Britain at this period.*

A recent analysis of the fine stoneless soil which forms the main part of the filling of the Y and Z Holes has now suggested, however, that the holes stood open for a very long period, to be measured in centuries, and that the filling itself is largely wind-blown material. It has also confirmed what ordinary observation has already suggested, that the soil is the ideal habitat for earthworms, whose activity, ceaseless but largely unseen, will steadily bury any small object dropped on the surface of such material. Consequently, though much of the Iron Age and Roman pottery occurs at quite low levels in the filling of the Y and Z Holes, one cannot, and indeed must not, assume that the holes were open at those levels when the pottery was originally dropped. On the contrary, it seems almost certain that at the time the earliest of the pottery was dropped the holes were already silted up. And since the process of silting was evidently a very slow one, there is nothing in the evidence which precludes the possibility that the holes were made as early as the fifteenth century B.C. Nothing could bring out more clearly the fallacy (accepted, I fear, by

---

* It may be remarked that Druids have so firm a hold upon the popular imagination, particularly in connection with Stonehenge, and have been the subject of so much ludicrous and unfounded speculation, that archaeologists in general have come to regard them as almost unmentionable in polite society.

not a few of my more distinguished colleagues) of supposing that archaeological sites are static, and that deposits and objects remain for all time in precisely the same state and position as that in which they were first formed or laid down.

Of the date of the final *phase IIIc,* in which the bluestones were re-erected in their present positions, there is little to be said. It has already been suggested (p. 85) that this re-arrangement followed some natural or human catastrophe which was itself the reason for abandoning the work of phase IIIb. If this is so, it is likely that the interval between the two phases was very short, and it is possible, therefore, that all the three phases of period III fall within a century, or at the most two centuries, after 1500 B.C.

The possibility of a deliberate destruction of the stones, either in the Roman period or in the Middle Ages, has already been mentioned (p. 85). It seems likely that the widespread scatter of stone chips all over the site can be connected with this destruction, since it is difficult to account for it as the result of dressing the stones on the spot.

There are two pieces of evidence which suggest that this scatter of chips (which is not necessarily confined, of course, to a single period of time) did not begin until a fairly late date. The first is the grave close to hole Y9 (p. 62), which is hardly likely to be earlier than the fourth century B.C. and more probably belongs to the time of the Roman occupation. The filling of this grave was earthy, and clearly contained a large proportion of soil derived from the adjacent surface. There were no stone chips at all in this filling, and the inference is that at the time the grave was dug the present scatter of chips did not exist.

The second piece of evidence comes from the filling of the Y and Z Holes. Apart from the deposits of bluestone chips right at the bottom, apparently made deliberately (p. 84), there were virtually no chips in the lower part of the filling. But in the middle and higher levels their numbers gradually increase. Now the vertical distribution of these chips is very closely and strikingly matched by the vertical distribution of fragments of Roman pottery in the same holes. And since both chips and potsherds are of the same order of size, and will therefore have been buried by earthworms at the same rate, it follows that they must have been dropped on the surface at the same time. It looks, therefore, as if there was some breaking-up of the stones during the period of the Roman occupation, but not earlier. This does not preclude further and deliberate destruction during the Middle Ages and later; and indeed it is known that individual acts of vandalism were common well into the nineteenth century (p. 191).

But the action of individual visitors in breaking off fragments of the stones at any period, either as keepsakes or for their supposed magical or medicinal properties, does not satisfactorily explain the *horizontal* distribution of chips all over the site, right out to and beyond the ditch. It must be emphasized that stone chips cannot travel horizontally by themselves; they have to be carried or thrown, and once allowed to lie on the surface for more than a few months they become buried by earthworms and can no longer move in any direction except downwards. The casual collection of fragments by visitors, who subsequently lose interest and drop them or throw them away, would certainly produce in time a scatter of chips all over the surroundings of the site; but one would expect the numbers of chips to fall off fairly rapidly as one leaves the immediate vicinity of the stones. In fact, while it is true that the highest concentrations of chips occur around the bases of the stones themselves, once one moves away from them the scatter is more or less uniform, and indeed there is at least as high a concentration in the ditch as there is in the vicinity of the Y and Z Holes. This is difficult to explain except in terms of the *deliberate* scattering of fragments broadcast, perhaps as a means of emphasizing the purposefulness of a partial destruction of the monument. The word 'partial' needs emphasis, for although the number of chips over the whole site can be estimated to run into tens of thousands, their average size is small, and in sum they represent no more than the volume of one average pillar of dolerite and of rhyolite respectively, and a rather smaller mass of sarsen. Except in the immediate vicinity of the stones the quantities of other rocks (volcanic ash and micaceous sandstone) are negligible.

Stonehenge from the air, seen from the west, before restoration

A The stones of Stonehenge from the air, seen from the south-east, before restoration

B The stones restored in 1958, seen from the west

The Heel Stone seen from the north-west

A A Z Hole after excavation

B Stone 10, with stones 34 and 35a in the foreground

Stone 16 seen from the north-west

A The curvature of the lintels over the entrance

B The tenons on stone 28

A The tenon on stone 56

B The entrance seen from within

The outer face of the second trilithon

The outer face of stone 60

A The rebate on the underside of the entrance lintel (stone 101)

B The projecting foot at the base of stone 55

A The carvings on stone 53

B The carvings on stone 4

A The carving on stone 57, before its restoration

B The lintel of the great trilithon (stone 156)

The outer face of stone 56

Shallow tooling on the north-eastern side of stone 52

A The upper part of the second trilithon

B The second trilithon, showing the inclination of the sides of the lintel

A A dressed bluestone from the horseshoe (stones 71 and 72)

B An undressed bluestone from the circle (stone 41)

A Outcrops of spotted dolerite on Prescelly Mountain

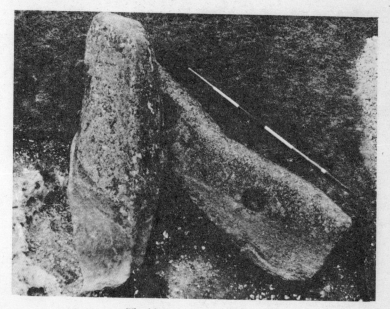

B The bluestone lintel 150 and 32

A The bluestone lintel 36, showing the seating for the upright

B A closer view of the seating, showing the marks of frictional wear

A Three stumps in the bluestone circle (stones 32, C, D, E,)

B The stump of the tongued bluestone 66

A The top of stone 69

B The remains of the tenon on stone 70

The grooved bluestone 68, with the second trilithon in the background

A The bluestone replica on a composite boat

B The bluestone replica on a sledge

A Broad tooling on stone 59

B Shallow tooling on the side of stone 16

The outer face of stone 28

The Stonehenge sequence may thus be set out in the form of a table, with very approximate dates:

1900–
1700 B.C.
Stonehenge I. Construction of the bank, ditch, and Aubrey Holes. Erection of the Heel Stone, stones D and E, and the timber structure A. Inception and use of the cremation cemetery.

1700–
1600 B.C.
Stonehenge II. Transport of the bluestones from Pembrokeshire. Erection of the double circle in the Q and R Holes. Filling up of the east end of the ditch at the causeway. Digging and filling of the Heel Stone ditch. Construction of the Avenue. Dismantling of stones D and E and timber structure A. Possible erection of stones B and C.

1500 B.C.
Stonehenge IIIa. Transport of the sarsen stones from near Marlborough. Dismantling of the double circle of bluestones. Erection of the sarsen trilithons, circle, Station Stones, and the Slaughter Stone and its companion. Carvings executed on the stones.

1500–
1400 B.C.
Stonehenge IIIb. Tooling and erection of stones of the dressed bluestone setting. Digging and abandonment of the Y and Z Holes.

1400 B.C.
Stonehenge IIIc. Dismantling of the dressed bluestone setting. Re-erection of these and the remaining bluestones in the present circle and horseshoe.

A.D. 50–
400
Possibly some deliberate destruction of the stones.

CHAPTER FOUR

The Techniques of Construction

THIS chapter is concerned with the technical aspects of the building of Stonehenge – the digging of the ditch, the building of the bank, the excavation of the various holes and sockets, the routes and methods used for the transport of stones, and the means whereby they were dressed to shape and erected.

For some of these operations, such as the dressing of the stones, there is surviving evidence in the form of the tool-marks on their surfaces, and even the tools themselves. But for others, like the transport of the stones or their erection, we have little direct evidence, and the methods used can be discussed only in terms of probabilities, on a common-sense basis. In cases such as these the archaeologist can never hope to arrive at the truth. The most he can do is first to determine what the problem was, then to assess the resources available for dealing with it, and finally to decide how he himself with those resources would have tackled the problem in question. But however much he may be convinced of the rightness of his own solution, he can never say with assurance 'This is how it was done'.

None the less, in what follows I have not hesitated to describe possible methods in detail, and to calculate the quantities of men and material that they would require, even though these calculations are mostly based upon assumptions for which no valid proof is ever likely to be discovered. For I believe that archaeologists *ought* to indulge in speculations of this kind, for it is only thus that they, and their readers, can begin to comprehend prehistoric monuments in terms of the human effort, ingenuity, and patience which brought them into being.

The Digging of the Ditch

The first operation in the building of the circular earthwork must have been to mark out its line. This was probably done by fastening one end of a piece of cord (of vegetable fibre or leather thong) to a peg in the centre, and swinging it round in a circle while keeping it straight and taut. The circumference described by the free end would be marked on the ground by hacking up pieces of turf, and these may well have been piled along a second circle, measured in the same way, to mark the centre-line or the inner edge of the bank to be built.

The turf and the topsoil taken off the site of the ditch were probably piled in a low bank on its *outer* edge, for the section through the remains of the *inner* bank shows chalk rubble resting directly on the original ground surface, without any intervening dump of soil.

The tools used for removing the turf were probably digging-sticks, with points hardened in a fire. For excavating the solid chalk the usual tool was the antler 'pick', of which about eighty were found by Colonel Hawley abandoned on the bottom of the ditch. These were made from the antlers of red deer, which under natural forest conditions grow to a much larger size than those now to be seen adorning the walls of successful stalkers. All the tines were cut off from the beam (that is, the main shaft of the antler) except the brow tine. The resulting tool has the shape of a figure seven, and is not unlike the small single-tined pick-axe still used by well-diggers and flint-miners in recent times for work in confined spaces. However, the antler pick does not seem to have been used as a true pick-axe, and indeed it is doubtful whether the material, tough as it is, would stand up to the continual shocks of prolonged use in this way, even in a rock so soft as chalk. Instead it seems to have been used as a handled wedge. The pointed brow tine was driven vertically into the chalk by hammering the back of the beam with a stone hammer, the marks of which are usually visible as a broad patch of abrasion. When the tine had been driven deep enough, the handle was pulled upwards, thus loosening the chalk and levering it away in fragments from the working face.

It will be seen that this method of working involves the initial sinking of a pit large enough to stand or crouch in, so that the loosening of the chalk can thereafter be carried out on a more or less vertical face. This seems to account for the very irregular character of the Stonehenge ditch, which is in fact a number of one-man pits strung together.

The crowns of the antlers (that is, the upper part of the beam and the two or three tines which branch from its end) were also found in the ditch, with their points abraded, showing that they had been used as rakes for collecting the loosened chalk into heaps.

For moving the rubble it is possible that wooden shovels were used, though no actual examples survive. But certainly small bone shovels were used, made from the shoulder-blades of oxen. These were probably held in the hand, like a modern coal-shovel, for they are too small and narrow for throwing up the loose material direct on to the bank.

The excavated material was probably carried up to be dumped on the bank in baskets, either supported on the head or suspended from the shoulders by leather straps, like the baskets still used today in western Scotland and Ireland to carry peat. Here again no actual remains of baskets survive, though there is indirect evidence for their use in Britain at this time. To enable the loaded carriers to climb out of the deeper parts of the ditch footholds may have been cut in the chalk sides (all traces of which will have been destroyed by subsequent weathering), or more probably notched wooden poles were used as ladders.

It is impossible to estimate the number of workers who were actually engaged on the construction of the earthwork. The half-circumference of the ditch excavated by Colonel Hawley is made up of about fifty pits, many of which have been run together to form a continuous but irregular excavation. The number of antler picks found abandoned on the floor of this area is about eighty. If one assumes that work was going on simultaneously round the whole circuit of the ditch, the number of diggers would thus be from 100 to 160, with an equal number at least of basket-carriers, probably women and children. But there is no reason to suppose that this was the case. It is more probable that only a few pits were dug at a time by a much smaller party, who gradually moved round the circle as each section was completed.

Even so, however, it must not be assumed that the building of Stonehenge I was the work entirely of only a small community of a few score persons at the most, for it includes the Heel Stone, a block which weighs at least thirty-five tons and would need a party of six or seven hundred men to haul it over the ground.

For the excavation of the various stone-holes the same tools and techniques appear to have been used as for the ditch, and indeed antler picks have been found on the bottom of several of them. For the narrower post-holes, however, digging-sticks alone are likely to have been employed, much as today the same result could be achieved, though more rapidly, with crowbars.

The Transport of the Bluestones

The source of the majority of the bluestones has been narrowed down, by petrological identifications, to an area of about one square mile at the eastern end of the Prescelly Mountains in north Pembrokeshire. There can be no question of the stones having been carried even part of the way towards southern England by ice during the Pleistocene period, and their appearance at Stonehenge can only be explained as the result of deliberate transport by man. The question to be answered is therefore quite clear: by what route, and by what means, were these eighty-odd stones, weighing up to four tons apiece, brought from Prescelly to Stonehenge, a distance as the crow flies of some 135 miles? Of the alternative answers of a land and a water route, it is safe to say that the second is overwhelmingly the more probable.

The enormous growth of rail and road transport in the last half-century has tended to obscure the fact that carriage by boat, either coastwise or on inland waterways, is by far the most economical means of moving bulky material from one place to another. The decline in such traffic (neglect of our inland waterways apart) is due chiefly to the fact that it is much slower than the alternatives of road and rail. In prehistoric times the undoubted advantages of water transport would have been even more apparent, for not only was time, rela-

tively speaking, of little importance, but in addition there
were no alternatives, as there are today. During the second
millennium B.C., at any rate, there were no wheeled vehicles
or even pack-animals. The only beast of burden was man
himself. Under these circumstances water transport was the
sole means of moving goods, and above all heavy goods,
with relative speed and economy. That this was widely realized
in prehistoric times is amply demonstrated by the relation of
the pattern of settlement to the river systems of the country,
and more particularly by the very large numbers of objects,
of all dates from the neolithic onwards, which have been
dredged in modern times from the rivers themselves.

It is thus inherently probable that the builders of Stonehenge II would seek to convey the bluestones from Pembrokeshire as far as possible by water, since this would mean a great
saving in labour. The number of men required to move a
stone of a given weight is discussed in detail below (p. 115),
but it may be said here by way of illustration that to haul a
stone weighing four tons on a sledge and rollers would need
about forty men for the actual pulling, and another twenty
to handle the rollers and steer the sledge by means of guide-
ropes. To carry the same stone by boat or raft would need a
crew of only twelve men at the most, and in sheltered waters
as few as half a dozen. The saving in man-power through the
use of water transport is thus of the order of 80 per cent.

Admittedly the journey by water is somewhat longer than
the shortest overland route, but the difference is only fifty
miles. Moreover the land route is one of exceptional difficulty,
for over the greater part of its length, from Prescelly to the
crossing of the Severn somewhere in the region of Gloucester,
it involves climbing and descending the slopes of the innumerable valleys of streams and rivers flowing southwards from the
mountains of southern Wales to the sea. Even if the route
kept as close to the coast as possible, a detour would be necessary whenever a river mouth was encountered in order to find
a crossing where the stream was narrow and the banks sufficiently firm. Indeed it is very doubtful whether a stone could
be hauled even as far as Gloucester without the use of boats
or rafts, and these would certainly be required for the crossing

of the Severn. If water transport had thus to be used occasionally in any case, it seems certain that, because of its manifest advantages, it would have been used as far as possible throughout.

What then is the most probable route for the carriage of the bluestones from Prescelly to Stonehenge, using boats or rafts wherever practicable? From the source of the stones

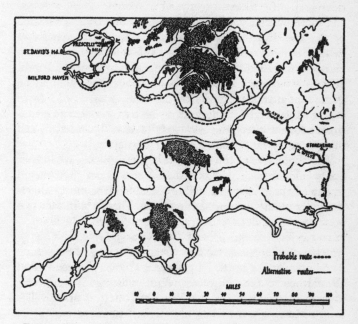

FIG. 4. The probable route for the transport of the bluestones

themselves, at the east end of the Prescelly Mountains (fig. 4), the shortest route to the sea is north-westwards down the valley of the River Nevern, some of whose tributary streams actually rise within sight of the outcrops from which the stones are derived. From these outcrops to the mouth of the river at Newport is about eight miles, and over this distance the stones would have been hauled on sledges, since the stream is too shallow to allow the use of boats until very near its mouth.

In fact, however, it is most improbable that this route to the sea was used, since it involves a very dangerous passage round the western peninsula of Pembrokeshire. From Newport Bay to the mouth of Milford Haven, a distance of some fifty miles, the coast is exceptionally forbidding, with steep cliffs and numerous submerged rocks off-shore; while off St David's Head and in the sounds between the mainland and the islands of Ramsey, Skomer, and Skokholm there are fierce tide-races of up to five knots, and dangerous whirlpools and eddies, to which any sensible navigator of today gives a wide berth. The distribution of prehistoric coastal settlement in Britain shows that then too the navigators of much frailer craft preferred at all costs to avoid such dangerous headlands, even to the point of making a portage overland. We may be quite sure that the carriers of the bluestones, borne down alike by the weight of their cargo and by their heavy responsibility for its safety, are not likely to have hazarded it, and their own lives, at the outset of their journey.

The alternative routes from Prescelly to the sea are longer, but would make it possible to load the stones in sheltered waters at a starting-point well to the east of the most dangerous parts of the Pembrokeshire coast. There are in fact two possible routes, both leading to Milford Haven. The first follows the line of the present Cardigan-Tenby road (A478), which passes less than two miles from the source of the stones. About two miles north of Narberth it joins the road from Carmarthen to Haverfordwest (A40), which runs westwards to cross the Eastern Cleddau River at Canaston Bridge. The bridge marks approximately the highest point to which the river is navigable by even shallow-draught boats, for above this it soon becomes a fast-flowing shallow mountain stream.

The second route follows the crest of the Prescelly Mountains westwards to the point where they are crossed by the road from Cardigan to Haverfordwest (B4329), and then joins this road to where it crosses the Western Cleddau River at the latter town, again at the highest navigable point. The two Cleddau Rivers flow southwards from these points for about six miles, and then unite to form the upper reaches of Milford Haven.

The existence of these two routes was pointed out by Professor W. F. Grimes, F.S.A. It is impossible to say which was the one chosen, though for what it is worth the concentration of prehistoric antiquities is somewhat greater along the first than on the second. But it seems certain that in either case the stones were shipped out from Milford Haven, since the only two varieties of foreign stone at Stonehenge which do *not* come from Prescelly have both been identified with outcrops on its shores. The micaceous sandstone of the Altar Stone occurs in the Cosheston Beds on the north bank, near Langwm, about two miles below the head of the estuary; while a second variety of micaceous sandstone, known at Stonehenge from chips only, can be matched very closely at Mill Bay, a narrow inlet on the south shore, four miles lower down. The occurrence of these rocks so close to each other, combined with the fact that the estuary and its tributary rivers do form the nearest *practicable* approach by water to the source of the stones, makes it overwhelmingly probable that Milford Haven was the starting-point of the sea journey to England.

From here the next and longest stage of the journey must have been coastwise along the shores of South Wales to the estuary of the Severn. There are admittedly a number of stretches of rocky cliffs along this coastline, particularly between the mouth of Milford Haven and Tenby. But there are also numerous gently shelving sandy beaches where boats or rafts could put in, and except for this initial stage there is hardly more than five miles of coast at a stretch in which there is no possibility of landing to wait for the passing of rough weather. Provided that it was possible to wait for fair conditions (and it must be remembered that this was the universal practice of all early navigators), there is no reason to suppose that this long coastwise journey would involve any special hazards, nor even any extraordinary efforts. For the spring tides along this coast average about three knots, and the prevailing wind is westerly. So long as there was no urgency, much of the journey could have been accomplished using the wind and tides, leaving to human effort only the task of keeping the vessels far enough off-shore to avoid submerged rocks and the more violent currents and eddies round the headlands.

From the estuary of the Severn there are two possible water routes to Stonehenge (fig. 4). The first, and by far the longer, follows the north coasts of Somerset, Devon, and Cornwall to St Ives Bay, then by land across the neck of the Penwith peninsula from Hayle to Marazion, to avoid the dangerous sea passage round Land's End, and thence up the south coast to the mouth of the Hampshire Avon at Christchurch, and so up the Avon itself to Amesbury.

The second route, which is not only some 400 miles shorter but also follows sheltered inland waters all the way, is up the Bristol Avon from its mouth to a point about seven miles above Bath, where the Frome joins it; then up the latter river to the town of Frome; thence overland to the head-waters of the River Wylye at Warminster, a distance of six miles; and finally down the Wylye to its confluence with the Avon at Salisbury, and so again to Amesbury and Stonehenge.

For every reason the second of these routes is to be preferred, and there is some evidence that this was the route actually used. On the chalk downs which form the north-western margin of Salisbury Plain, to the east of Westbury and Warminster, there are a number of Long Barrows, the characteristic burial-places of the Windmill Hill people (p. 149). One of these, Boles Barrow, lies in the parish of Heytesbury about three miles north of the River Wylye. It was partially excavated in 1801 by William Cunnington, who remarked that the central core of the mound was composed of piled boulders, chiefly of sarsen stone, among which was one of 'the Blue hard Stone also, ye same to some of the upright Stones in ye inner Circle at Stonehenge'. This stone, with others, was removed by Cunnington to his house at Heytesbury, and after many vicissitudes is now preserved in Salisbury Museum. Petrological examination has confirmed that it is of the same highly characteristic spotted dolerite from Prescelly that occurs at Stonehenge.

The occurrence of this boulder in a Long Barrow which could well have been built at or after the time of the transport of the bluestones to Stonehenge provides good reason for supposing that the River Wylye lay on the route. It cannot be *proved*, of course, that this boulder did not come from Stonehenge itself. But it is much less likely that the builders of the Long Barrow would have stolen it from there, in itself a dangerous act of desecration, and dragged it for fourteen miles (it weighs at least 600 lb.), than that they should have gathered it from the neighbourhood, where it may well have been discarded as useless by the original carriers after some accidental damage to a larger block.

If it is accepted that the bluestones were brought to Wiltshire by water, what type of craft was used? The alternatives are rafts, made of suitable solid logs lashed together, or true boats, either dug-outs hollowed out from the solid or composite boats formed of a skin hull stretched on an articulated wooden frame. For the sea journey the raft has some marked advantages over the boat, in that it is unsinkable and cannot be swamped in rough weather. On the other hand a raft to support a given weight is very much larger and heavier than a boat, or composite vessel of several boats lashed together, to carry the same burden, and is therefore more difficult to propel by paddling, and far less manoeuvrable in an emergency. Moreover, while it is possible that rafts were used at sea, it is very doubtful if they would be practicable for the inland part of the journey.

The minimum size of raft required is determined by the weight of the heaviest stone together with that of the appropriate crew. In their present dressed state the largest of the Stonehenge foreign stones is the Altar Stone, with a weight of $6\frac{1}{4}$ tons. One may assume that in its original state, before dressing, it weighed in the region of 7 tons, and would need a crew of a dozen men averaging 11 stone apiece. The total burden to be supported by the raft is thus about 17,500 lb.

The lightest timber likely to be available in quantity is pine, which when dry weighs about 35 lb. per cubic foot. A cubic foot of water weighs about 60 lb., so that floating pinewood will support a maximum load of about 25 lb. per cubic foot. The required raft must therefore contain not less than 700 cubic feet to carry the calculated load with its upper surface just awash. A log raft must necessarily consist of at least two layers of logs, one laid at right-angles to the other, and to keep its dimensions to a minimum it must be square in plan.

It follows, therefore, that a raft to carry the Altar Stone and its crew, if built of logs with an average diameter of one foot, would measure 21 ft square, with a draught of 2 ft, if built in two layers; 17 ft square, with a draught of 3 ft, if built in three layers. In practice these dimensions would have to be rather greater, both to give some free-board (that is, to raise the surface of the raft above water-level) and to allow for the gradual waterlogging of the wood after prolonged immersion.

It can be said quite confidently that even today it would be impossible to navigate rafts of this size along the suggested course of the Avons and the Wylye; for if the draught is kept small enough to avoid grounding in shallow places the width becomes too great, while if the width is reduced to a practicable figure the draught immediately becomes impossibly large. If such navigation is ruled out today, it would certainly be impossible in prehistoric times, when the depth of the rivers was more variable and in general shallower, owing to the existence in many places of multiple channels, many of which have today been artificially suppressed or controlled.

For the inland part of the journey, therefore, boats must have been used. What kind of boats were they? Fortunately we have plenty of evidence, in the form of actual remains dredged from the beds of rivers, for the use of dug-out canoes in Britain from neolithic times onwards, and indeed before. It is not impossible that skin boats were used as well, though no actual remains survive. The Eskimo *umiak*, the Irish curragh and on a smaller scale the Welsh coracle are all modern representatives of the type. It need not be considered further here, however, as it is structurally unsuitable for carrying the loads envisaged.

The dug-out canoes were made by splitting a large tree trunk longitudinally and hollowing out the interior, probably with the help of fire in the initial stages, until a one-piece hull was obtained with walls some 2–3 in. thick. The size and shape of such boats is determined by the available raw material, which is usually oak. Exceptional examples have been recorded with a total length of 55 ft, but for present purposes it will be wise to assume a maximum length of 35 ft, a beam of 4 ft, and a depth of 2 ft. The shape of these vessels resembles that of an unusually deep punt, with a more or less flat bottom and vertical sides.

Theoretically a single canoe of this size will carry a weight of about 8,700 lb. with a displacement of half its depth. Two such boats lashed side by side could therefore support the Altar Stone and a crew of at least ten men, with a freeboard of 1 ft. In fact, however, three or more boats would make a more satisfactory composite vessel. With two boats only the load on each gunwale would be of the order of 1¾ tons, and this load would be concentrated in the central half of the vessel, measured longitudinally, so that there would be a tendency both for the sides of the individual canoes to spread or buckle and for the vessel as a whole to break its back in the middle. Three canoes, each of the same beam and draught, but only 24 ft in length, would carry the same weight far more safely distributed. The stone would rest, of course, on bearers extending the full width of the vessel, so that the load was evenly divided between the six gunwales. These same bearers would also serve to lock the three canoes together, and if they were notched to fit over the gunwales would at the same time act as stretchers preventing the sides from spreading under the applied load.

The practicability of this arrangement was proved in an experiment devised by the writer and his colleagues in collaboration with Mr Paul Johnstone of the B.B.C. Television Service, which formed part of a television programme on Stonehenge broadcast in July 1954. Three 'canoes', built of elm boarding and measuring 12 ft by 2 ft 3 in. by 1 ft 6 in., were fixed together by four transverse bearers and floated on the river Avon near Salisbury. A repilca of a bluestone in reinforced concrete, measuring 7 ft 6 in. by 2 ft by 1 ft 6 in., was lowered on to the vessel by a mobile crane. The total load, including a crew of four boys from Bryanston School, was about 3,600 lb. and gave a draught of 9 in. The crew punted the loaded vessel up and down a stretch of the Avon with the greatest ease, and it was clear that it could have been propelled, at least in slow-flowing water, by a single man. Indeed, the operation had much in common with the pleasant pastime of punting agreeable companions (built happily upon less uncompromisingly monolithic lines) upon the quiet waters of the Cherwell or the Cam (Plate 22a).

This practical trial leaves very little doubt that some such arrangement of dug-out canoes was used for the inland part of the voyage from Prescelly. The possibility of using the same craft *at sea* is another matter, and has not so far been put to the test. There is every reason to suppose that such canoes were used at sea in prehistoric times, though not usually with so heavy a load. But in any case, as we have seen, rafts could have been used for this part of the journey, and would have some advantages over boats.

The route suggested above includes at least twenty-four miles of land transport: sixteen miles from Prescelly to Canaston Bridge, six miles between Frome and Warminster, and two miles up the Avenue from the Avon to Stonehenge. Over these distances the stones must have been dragged on sledges.

The almost universal use of wheeled vehicles today makes us forget that sledges are not merely for use in snow, but are also by far the best way of carrying heavy or bulky goods over dry ground, where wheeled vehicles or pack-animals are not available. Indeed there are still farms in Wales and Ireland today where the horse-drawn sledge is the main and sometimes the only vehicle. One can safely assume the existence of such dry-ground sledges in prehistoric Britain (though drawn by men, not animals), though owing to the perishable nature of their timbers no certain example has survived. What may be the remains of such a sledge, however, were found by the writer, in a condition so decayed as to render identification uncertain, in a grave near Dorchester-on-Thames, where it had apparently been used to transport the body of the dead man from a distance. Significantly, perhaps, he belonged to the Beaker culture, to which the earliest bluestone structure should probably be assigned.

The practicability of sledging the bluestones was also tested successfully in the television programme referred to above. A sledge was made to the writer's specification of roughly squared 6-in. timbers, with an overall length of 9 ft and a width of 4 ft, and the replica of the bluestone was lashed in place upon it (Plate 22b). The loaded sledge was then dragged

over the down immediately south of Stonehenge by a party
of thirty-two schoolboys, arranged in ranks of four along a
single hauling-rope, each rank holding at chest level a wooden
bar to whose centre the rope was fastened. It was found that
this party could just haul the sledge, weighing some 3,500 lb.
in all, up a slope of about 4° (1 in 15), though it is doubtful
whether they could have continued this effort for long. The
sledge slid easily over the long rank grass, and left no sign of
its passage apart from some slight crushing.

The use of wooden rollers under the runners of the sledge
allowed the hauling-party to be reduced from thirty-two to
fourteen, that is, by 56 per cent, and it is certain that if the
rollers had been more carefully selected for roundness a further reduction to a dozen or even less could have been made.
The saving in man-power is not quite as great as it looks,
however, because a separate party is needed to shift the rollers
as they emerge from behind the sledge, and lay them again
some distance in front of it, so that there is always a sufficient
number in place to form a track. Moreover as soon as rollers
are used the problem of steering the sledge arises, as especially
when climbing a slope obliquely it has a natural tendency to
slip sideways off the rollers. To counteract this, guide-ropes
were fixed to the four corners of the sledge and each was
manned by two people. These ancillary tasks occupied at least
a dozen people, so that the total number required to move
the stone *with rollers* would be twenty-four, against thirty-two
without rollers.

The experiment was carried out with senior schoolboys
from Canford School, who were naturally unaccustomed to
this particular activity; and the figures given are critical figures,
that is, the *minimum* number necessary to move the stone. It
seems safe to assume, however, that if the same numbers of
trained and experienced men were employed, the stone could be
moved continuously for several miles a day without undue
exertion. The total required is thus in the region of sixteen
men per ton weight, or about 110 men for the Altar Stone,
the heaviest of the foreign stones.

There is no means of telling, of course, how many of the
bluestones were transported at one time, nor how long a

journey took. But for the sea and river voyage, at least, it is probable that there were convoys of perhaps up to a dozen vessels, whose crews would provide a body of men sufficiently large to ensure that help could rapidly be given to any individual vessel that found itself in difficulties.

The Transport of the Sarsens

It is now generally agreed by archaeologists and geologists that the origin of the Stonehenge sarsens must lie on the Marlborough Downs, in the area where sarsen blocks still litter the surface in many places today. In the past it has been suggested that the stones came from some other and smaller deposit of sarsen on Salisbury Plain, much closer to Stonehenge, which has since been entirely worked out. There is no evidence to support this. It is inconceivable that this hypothetical deposit should have consisted entirely of blocks of just the right size and number for the building of Stonehenge, for even in the thick concentrations of boulders near Avebury examples comparable in size with even the smaller uprights at Stonehenge are very rare. Had this deposit existed, it must have contained many smaller boulders suitable for modern building, and some of these at least would now be incorporated in the houses and barns of the neighbouring villages. In fact, it is only around Avebury that sarsen is used for building at all. In the villages of the Pewsey Vale, east of Devizes, in the upper valley of the Avon and on the Plain itself, sarsen in buildings is almost unknown. This in itself is sufficient to disprove the notion that the Stonehenge sarsens came from anywhere nearer than the Marlborough Downs.

The method of transport to Stonehenge must certainly have been by sledge-hauling overland all the way, for there is no possible water route. The difficulties of this operation must have been enormous, for though the total distance, about twenty-four miles, is almost exactly the same as for the haulage of the bluestones (p. 114) the weights involved are about seven times as great, both for the heaviest stones and for the aggregate of them all. Moreover, the shortest route involves a river crossing and the negotiation of a steep escarpment of the chalk.

There is no certain evidence, of course, for the route actually followed, but an inspection of the One Inch O.S. Map, supplemented by field-work on the ground itself, suggests one which is certainly possible, and even probable, since it is the only route which avoids excessively steep falling and rising slopes without deviating far from a direct line. Its practicability is evidenced by the fact that it is still followed by existing roads, which until the recent advent of the petrol engine always tended to take the line of least effort compatible with directness (fig. 5).

The effective starting-point was probably at Avebury. It is not to be supposed, of course, that the stones themselves originated there, for doubtless all the larger slabs in the vicinity had already been used for the building of the great circles at Avebury itself. But Avebury stands at the lowest point on the River Kennet at which exceptionally heavy sarsens could be dragged across a ford; lower down elaborate bridge-works of timber would be necessary for their passage. This then was probably the starting-point, to which selected stones were dragged from many different areas of the downs to the east and north; for we have seen (p. 38) that the builders of Stonehenge were hard put to it to find sufficient stones of the right size, and it is out of the question that all of them lay ready to hand in a single valley of the downs.

It is tempting, too, to think that Avebury may have served as the starting-point for other than purely practical reasons. Here, after all, was the greatest and doubtless the most renowned and revered sanctuary then existing. What could be more fitting than that the stones of the new monument, which was to eclipse it 'as St Pauls doth a parish church', should ceremonially be dragged through its already ancient circles, so that their bearers could receive from the presiding arch-priest that spiritual benison and encouragement of which their forthcoming physical exertions were soon to leave them so sorely in need?

From the fording of the Kennet just west of Avebury the

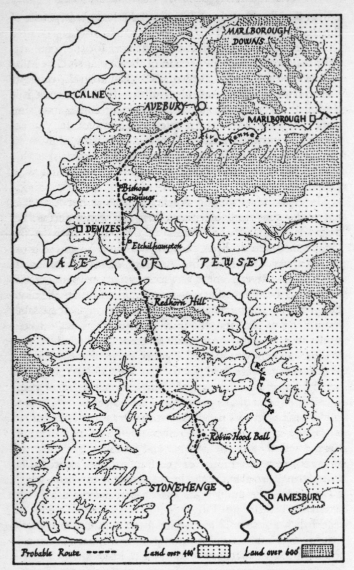

FIG. 5. The probable route for the transport of the sarsens

route follows the line of the modern road through Beckhampton towards Devizes (A361), a notably straight and level stretch which is an open invitation to the modern motorist (frequently and disastrously accepted) to overtax his engine. About a mile south-west of Shepherds Shore, where the road crosses the Wansdyke, a minor road leads southwards to Bishops Cannings and thence to Coate and Etchilhampton, falling and rising gently but avoiding the marshier bottom of the Vale of Pewsey. It is only by this route that one can avoid a difficult crossing of the northern escarpment of chalk that marks the edge of the Vale, which elsewhere is exceedingly steep. It need hardly be said that the difficulties of manoeuvring a fifty-ton stone *down* a slope of, say, 1 in 4 are not less than those of hauling it *up*; in either case, such slopes were to be avoided.

The route thus described as far as Etchilhampton leads to the narrowest crossing of the Vale of Pewsey itself, now marked by a portion of the modern road A342, which itself perpetuates a much earlier trackway known as the Lydeway. After running for two miles across the bottom of the Vale, significantly enough on the only line athwart the Vale which involves no crossing of a stream, the Lydeway reaches higher and firmer ground at Foxley Corner. From there the route follows approximately the line of the old Devizes–Salisbury road, now virtually closed to the public by the establishment of artillery ranges along its course. This road runs within two miles to the west of Stonehenge, and for the greater part of its course keeps to the natural ridgeway with the minimum of rise and fall. The only difficult point is where it climbs the steep southern escarpment of the Pewsey Vale at Redhorn Hill. Here the road makes a dog-leg kink to ease the climb, and doubtless the builders of Stonehenge did the same. Indeed, they had no alternative, for the escarpment is equally steep for nearly four miles to east and west, and to make a detour to find a gentler slope would be to sacrifice the advantages of the subsequent easier going on the ridgeway.

For the actual methods used in hauling the stones we must fall back once more upon conjecture aided by common sense. Clearly rollers must have been used to reduce friction, and the stones must have been cradled in massive timbers, or bound on to enormous sledges, in either case to provide uniform runners to rest on the rollers and a means of attaching the hauling-ropes, which could not be fixed to the stone itself. The operation must therefore have necessitated the cutting and dressing of very considerable quantities of timber, almost certainly oak.

The ropes were probably of twisted or plaited hide thongs, such as were in use in cart-horse harness at least until the early nineteenth century; for it is doubtful if any native vegetable fibre existed capable of being fabricated into ropes of the required diameter and breaking strain. This in turn must have involved the preparation of enormous lengths of narrow thong, from hides either collected over a long period beforehand, or very likely from beasts specially slaughtered for the purpose. Huge amounts of animal fat must also have been prepared for keeping the leather ropes supple and waterproof.

We have seen that the comparatively light bluestones required a hauling-party of some sixteen men per ton weight. To arrive at the minimum numbers for hauling the sarsens (that is, sufficient to haul the heaviest stone) it is not sufficient, however, merely to scale up this figure by the appropriate factor. The far greater weight of the sarsens, for instance, would require both a closer setting of the rollers, in order to distribute the weight and prevent their being driven into the ground, and a larger diameter of roller as well, to avoid breaking them when passing over irregularities of the surface. Since the weight of a hardwood roller measuring 12 ft by 9 in. is in the region of 300 lb., at least two men would be required to lift and move it; and the rate of progress of the stone would be limited by the speed at which the re-laying of the rollers could be carried out. The proportion of the total party engaged in shifting the rollers would thus have to be doubled at least, and the overall total of men for a given weight increased accordingly.

For purposes of estimating the *minimum* labour force required we may therefore take a figure of twenty-two men per ton weight and an average rate of progress of half a mile per day. The heaviest stones, which weigh about fifty tons, would therefore need some 1,100 men to move them, one at a time, over the twenty-four miles to Stonehenge, and would take about seven weeks for the journey. But even this is not enough, for it allows only for hauling up gentle slopes. To negotiate the steep escarpment at Redhorn Hill would certainly require a substantial addition, bringing the total up to perhaps 1,500 men. Moreover, some time must be allowed for the return journey from Stonehenge, presumably with the cradles or sledges, now empty, and the rollers; and even more for very necessary rest and recuperation. It would not be too much, therefore, to allow nine weeks for the round trip.

On this basis it can be calculated that the smallest requirements for the transport of the eighty-one sarsens to Stonehenge would be 1,500 men working for five and a half years, and working, moreover, without more than a few days' rest between trips. In fact, of course, it would have been impossible to maintain continuous working in this way for so long. Not only would there be interruptions owing to bad weather, but at certain seasons of each year the workers would perforce have to return home to attend to their crops and herds. It is thus safe enough to assume that the transport of the stones, all told, took upwards of ten years, unless the number of men employed was far larger than there is any reason to suppose.

Even in these days of dense populations and large-scale works of civil engineering, the employment of so many men upon a single project for so long would be worthy of remark. In prehistoric Britain, a land by modern standards extremely sparsely populated, the withdrawal of so many farmers and shepherds from their normal occupations for parts of the year, and their concentration in a single area upon a task of unwonted physical difficulty, must have been an entirely revolutionary proceeding, whose repercussions on the daily life of the countryside must have extended for many score miles beyond Stonehenge and Avebury. One has only to think of the problems of feeding and sheltering this number of people today to realize how profound must have been the upheaval thus occasioned in a society of so much simpler structure and communications, living so much nearer the borderline of subsistence. The implications of this extraordinary feat of organization for the nature of this society are considered in Chapter VI.

One final problem connected with the movement of the stones remains to be considered, namely how they were brought into the site of Stonehenge itself. Obviously they were not dragged *over* the surrounding earthwork, for even though the bank was denuded and the ditch silted up almost to their present levels (p. 74), they would still have presented a serious obstacle. But if the stones were brought in by the obvious route, through the entrance, they must at some point have been dragged across the northern bank and ditch of the Avenue, which provides the only means of approach to the entrance. There is no sign of such passage, and one must assume that either the ditch and bank of the Avenue were protected from damage by timber-work, or an alternative route was used through a breach in the main earthwork, possibly the South Causeway (p. 21), though it would hardly seem wide enough. This remains one of the minor unsolved mysteries of Stonehenge.

The Tooling of the Sarsens

Once the stones had been brought to Stonehenge, the next task of the builders was to dress them to shape, a process about which a good deal more is known. It is probable, indeed, that some preliminary shaping had already been carried out *before* they were moved at all, for clearly most of them have been much reduced in size from their parent blocks, and this reduction must have been made at the start, in order to avoid the hauling of unnecessary weight.

Many of the Stonehenge stones are tabular sarsens, that is, they are derived from slab-like blocks with two broad parallel faces, formed originally by the solidification of a bed of sand of uniform thickness. The great stones of Avebury exhibit a number of examples of such tabular slabs in their natural state, and it is clear that many of the sarsen deposits of the district were of this kind.

The Avebury stones also demonstrate an important characteristic of tabular sarsen, namely that it normally occurs in the form of polygonal slabs, the commonest shape being a quadrilateral of approximately lozenge form. Pillar-like shapes of rectangular section, like the uprights of Stonehenge, appear to be very rare. Consequently although the builders started with raw material on which two parallel surfaces had already been formed by nature, much preliminary work would still be necessary in order to reduce the width of the natural slabs to form pillar-like shapes of the required dimensions.

It is not known for certain how this was done. It is known, however, that sarsen stone will split most easily in a plane at right-angles to its tabular surfaces, and it is probable that this preliminary shaping was effected by splitting off comparatively large masses, rather than by the very laborious process of slow attrition used in the final dressing of the surfaces (p. 124). The detaching of these masses was probably carried out by two methods. Where a natural crack existed on or close to the required line, this could be opened up and deepened by careful pecking with stone tools, so as to allow a line of close-set wooden wedges to be driven in. The soaking of these wedges in water would cause them to swell and open the crack still further, finally splitting the stone in two. This primitive but effective method is of great antiquity, though there are no physical traces of its use on the stones of Stonehenge; but one would expect all such traces to be obliterated by later dressing.

Where no natural crack existed it would be necessary to make one. The stone would first be heated by lighting fires on its surface along the required line, and then suddenly cooled by pouring on cold water in a narrow stream, thus setting up an internal strain. Then, at a given signal, men stationed beside the line would simultaneously dash down upon the surface a number of heavy stone mauls, about the size of a football, whose impact would either detach the required mass outright, or else would start a crack which could be enlarged and opened up by wedges as before. This method is known to have been used in native Indian stone quarries during the present century, and very similar means were employed, so we are told by Stukeley, for breaking up the stones of Avebury in the eighteenth century 'to get a little dirty profit'.

Once delivered on the site at Stonehenge the stones had to receive their final dressing, reducing them to the correct shape and section, with the surfaces tooled to approximate planes. One would naturally expect this work to be done *before* their erection, both for ease of movement around the stones, and because with the means employed it is far easier to tool a horizontal surface than a vertical one. That this was done in fact is shown by the occurrence of tooled surfaces below ground level, and by the finding of numerous *used* stone hammers deposited as packing-blocks in the stone-holes.

Fortunately for the archaeologist much of the tooling was left in a half-finished state which allows one to reconstruct the methods used with some confidence. The chief technique was the very laborious one of pounding the surface of the stone repeatedly with heavy stone mauls. These are natural boulders of sarsen stone, ranging from the size of a football to that of a cricket ball, which formerly occurred commonly on the surface of the downs, and are still occasionally turned up by the plough. The heaviest weigh about 60 lb.

In view of the relatively advanced level of technology exhibited by many other aspects of the design and construction of Stonehenge, it may seem surprising that so apparently primitive a method should have been used for dressing the stones. In fact, however, no other method is possible in the absence of modern mason's tools of steel, and the pounding process is dictated entirely by the intractable nature of sarsen. It is not generally realized that sarsen is the most difficult of all British rocks to work, and requires from two and a half to three times the effort necessary to produce a comparable result on granite, itself considered to be one of the least tractable of building stones. Sarsen is so hard that it turns the edge of all but the most modern alloy-steel tools, and in modern times it is dressed entirely by splitting. We have already seen that this method was probably used in the initial shaping before the stones were moved. But it was clearly impossible to *finish* by this method surfaces of more than 150 square feet in area. The method of dressing by pounding was thus the only one which could be employed to produce a presentable surface finish.

Surviving examples of tooling on the stones suggest that the dressing was carried out in several stages of increasing delicacy. Initially, the rough and irregular surface appears to have been reduced by working parallel grooves about 9 in. wide and 2–3 in. deep, generally running longitudinally, using the larger mauls of 20–30 lb. in weight. Examples of tooling left in this state can be seen on the upper (outer) face of stone 59 (Plate 23a) and on the lower part of the outer face of stone 54 (Plate 8).

The next stage seems to have been the removal of the ridges left between the broad grooves, by bashing at them sideways with the heaviest mauls weighing up to 60 lb. This is the only operation in which actual *chips* of sarsen were detached; the normal pounding produces only fine sand and dust. This accounts for the relative scarcity of sarsen chips on the site, though it is certain that much if not all of the dressing was carried out on the spot. Statistical sampling of a number of areas suggests that the chips represent a total volume of no more than a dozen cubic feet, a tiny fraction of the total volume of stone removed in the course of dressing. On the other hand analysis of soil from the site has shown that it contains an abnormal proportion of siliceous sand, clearly the product of dressing the stones.

The coarse dressing was followed in many cases by finer work, consisting of smaller and shallower grooves, not exceeding 9 in. in length, 2 in. in width and ¼ in. in depth, which often cover the whole of a surface. Excellent examples of such tooling, arranged longitudinally, occur on stones 16 and 52 (Plates 5, 14, 23b), and transverse tooling of the same kind can be seen on the outer face of stone 52 at the base, and high up on the east side of stone 53 (Plate 15a).

A third variety of tooling has been used in places to remove particularly prominent protuberances. One of the best examples of this can be seen high on the west side of the outer face of stone 28 (Plate 24), where three short deep grooves are thrown into sharp relief by the glancing rays of the setting sun.

The penultimate stage of dressing consisted in removing all traces of grooves and ridges by pounding the whole surface uniformly with a stone maul, leaving the stone with a characteristic pocked texture, like the surface of orange-peel much magnified. Few traces of this kind of dressing now survive above ground, owing to the smoothing effect of subsequent weathering, but below the surface it is preserved intact in many places. An excellent example can be seen in the Devizes Museum, on a large flake of sarsen found detached from the base of stone 56 at the time of its re-erection in 1901.

The final operation of dressing was to grind the surfaces of the stone smooth, presumably with heavy sarsen grinders, perhaps hauled back and forth by ropes, and some suitable abrasive mixed with water. Experiment has shown that the local greensand has no cutting action upon sarsen, but possibly crushed flint would have been effective.

This polishing seems to have been carried out only sporadically, and now survives only on the inner faces of certain stones, such as the lower part of stone 10 (Plate 4b), and in small patches on surfaces left in the second or third stage of dressing. A good many polished surfaces, however, have probably been reduced in area or obliterated altogether by subsequent weathering.

A careful survey of the various degrees of tooling and polishing to which the stones have been subjected shows that the main concern of the builders was to produce a presentable finish on those surfaces which would be seen from the *interior* of the site. The best finish thus occurs on the inner faces of the uprights. Their sides have often been left in the second (shallow groove) stage of dressing, while their outer faces are frequently very rough, with large irregularities only perfunctorily reduced by deliberate coarse tooling. The chief exceptions to this rule are the sides and outer faces of the uprights of the great central trilithon (55, 56), which have been finished as carefully as the inner face. This suggests that one of the principal ritual stations in the monument may have been *behind* this trilithon, from which these surfaces would be visible. It is notable, too, that the finish of the lintels is in general much higher than that of the uprights.

Some evidence exists for the way in which the work of dressing the stones was parcelled out among the various masons. In a number of places there are sudden changes of level in the dressed surfaces, marking the boundary between the areas allotted to different workers. A good example can be seen high on the south-west side of stone 54 (Plate 15b), where a rectangular patch measuring about 3 ft high and 2 ft wide is sunk noticeably below the adjacent surface of the stone.

Few visitors to Stonehenge have any true idea of the immense labour and patience involved in the tooling of the stones. Experiments made for Mr E. H. Stone, the author of *The Stones of Stonehenge*, by a professional mason in 1923 showed that the process of pounding a sarsen with a stone maul removed about six cubic inches an hour, entirely in the form of sand and dust. If we assume that on the average a thickness of two inches has been dressed away from all the surfaces of the uprights and lintels (and this may well be a gross under-estimate), the total volume of stone removed would be of the order of *three million* cubic inches. It would take a force of fifty masons, working ten hours a day and seven days a week (one may safely assume the absence of Union rules and other restrictive practices), a period of some two years and nine months to finish the dressing of the stones alone; and this takes no account of the subsequent polishing, or the equally laborious task of forming the mortice-and-tenon and tongue-and-groove joints on the uprights and lintels.

These joints have been formed by the same techniques of pounding and grinding. The tenons have been shaped by the gradual removal of the whole of the top of the stone from around them, in itself an extremely long and laborious task. On each upright of the five trilithons, for instance, the volume removed amounts to not less than 3,000 cubic inches, which would occupy two masons, at the rate suggested above, for nearly four weeks. The mortices were doubtless started by the method of pounding, and continued, as the depression deepened, by grinding. Similar methods seem to have been employed for forming the tongues and grooves on the ends of the lintels of the outer circle. All this work has been most carefully finished with a smooth, though not a polished, surface and clearly far more labour was expended, area for area, upon the surfaces to be jointed than upon the exposed faces and sides of the stones. One must not forget, however, that the degree of finish on surfaces that were originally in contact is likely in any case to be better preserved since such surfaces were for long protected from the weather.

For reasons explained below (p. 134) it is clear that unlike the rest of the dressing, the production of the joints and bearing-surfaces must have taken place *after* the erection of the uprights.

The amount of devoted and patient labour involved in the dressing of the stones is the more surprising when it is realized that Stonehenge is unique among the megalithic monuments of Europe in having its stones dressed over their whole surface. The only other occurrences of deliberate dressing are confined to areas of a few square feet only in the great chambered tombs of New Grange in Ireland and Maes Howe in Orkney. This remarkable stage in the construction of Stonehenge must therefore have been undertaken without any traditional background of experience in this particular craft, and this alone may well account for the curiously uneven finish of many of the surfaces. It points also, as do other features of the monument, to the probability of direct influence from the contemporary urban civilizations of the central Mediterranean, in which the practice of building in dressed stone was already well established. It should be observed, however, that the basic technique of dressing a stone by abrasion must already have been well known in Britain, though on a small scale only, since this is the normal way in which the surface of the domestic quern for grinding grain was prepared.

One last problem connected with the dressing of the stones deserves a brief mention. It has often been assumed in the past that much of the tooling was carried out with hammer stones of *flint*, and some support was lent to this notion by the discovery by Colonel Hawley of quantities of shattered fragments of flint, forming a layer several inches thick, beneath the turf in the areas which he excavated within the sarsen circle. It was further supposed that the apparent distribution of these alleged remains of flint hammers *within the circle only* proved that the lintels of the circle had been erected by means of an earthen ramp piled up *on the outside*, the presence of which would prevent the accumulation there of discarded fragments of broken hammers, which would be cleared away with the ramp when the latter was moved.

This argument is an excellent example of the many beliefs about Stonehenge which appear plausible enough until their foundations are examined critically and, in particular, by practical experiment. Such experiment shows that in fact it is impossible to produce any effective abrasion of sarsen by pounding with a flint nodule; the only effect is to abrade, and ultimately, as the blows and the exasperation of the experimenter alike become more violent, to shatter the hammer. Moreover, a careful examination of the layer of flint fragments and of Colonel Hawley's records shows first, that the layer itself extends well outside the entrance on the north-east side, and in fact forms a pathway of flint gravel from the entrance of the earthwork to the stones; and secondly that the fragments of flint themselves show no signs whatever of being the broken pieces of hammer-stones. The date and purpose of this layer of flint gravel is admittedly obscure, but it clearly has nothing whatever to do with the dressing of the stones. The chief argument for the use of an earthen ramp for erecting the lintels thus falls to the ground (p. 134).

The Erection of the Uprights

The problem of how the upright sarsen stones at Stonehenge were erected was worked out in great detail by Mr E. H. Stone in 1923, and published in his *Stones of Stonehenge* (1924). As an experienced engineer, then retired, he was well equipped to tackle this problem, and his conclusions were all carefully tested by experiments with models which he made at a scale of 1:12. Since then no one has had any reason to call any of his main contentions seriously in question. Much of this section, therefore, is based upon the work, with some additions or variations occasioned by the subsequent finding of fresh evidence.

One must assume that by the time the sarsens had arrived on the site and were being dressed, the double circle of blue-stones of Stonehenge II had been uprooted, the stones removed from the site, and the empty sockets filled up with chalk rubble, tightly rammed. The next problems to be solved were the finding of the centre upon which the new building was to be laid out, and the determination of the axis of symmetry aligned on the point of midsummer sunrise.

The centre could be found either by trial and error, by swinging a measuring-line from an assumed centre and shifting the latter until the circumference coincided with the crest of the bank or with the circle of Aubrey Holes, which must still have been visible as shallow depressions; or by a geometrical construction, using datum-points on the bank or the Aubrey circle as before. Which method was used we do not know; but it is significant that the four Stations do appear to be related geometrically to the centre and axis of the sarsen circle, which implies some knowledge of applied geometry, including the setting-out and bisection of a right-angle. It is generally assumed that the four Stations are connected with this subsequent process of finding the centre of the earlier monument of period I, though admittedly no one, myself included, has so far supplied any convincing description of the exact construction used by the surveyors.

Once the centre was fixed (it differs, incidentally, from that of period I by over two feet) the determination of the axis was a simple matter of observing successive sunrises around midsummer and marking their directions, as seen from the centre, either by hazel wands stuck in the ground, or possibly, if greater accuracy was required, by plumb-lines suspended from an overhead frame of wood. There is some reason to suppose that the use of the plumb-line was known to the builders (pp. 133, 139).

When the centre and the axis had been fixed, the circumference of the circle on which the inner faces of the uprights of the sarsen circle were to lie must have been marked out, presumably by wooden pegs driven in flush with the surface of the ground. This operation had necessarily to be carried out at this stage, even though, for obvious reasons, the central trilithons had to be erected first. For once the latter were in position, no true circle could be struck from the centre.

The diameter of this circle is 97·3 ft, and corresponds very

closely to 100 Roman feet, a unit of much greater antiquity
than the classical period. Whether this is to be regarded as
anything more than a chance coincidence is a matter of personal choice. It may be observed, however, that if it were
desired to set the sarsens in a circle so that the average gap
between them ($3\frac{1}{2}$ ft) was just half their average width (7 ft),
their inner faces would have to lie on a circle of just this
diameter. It is hardly possible to argue, conversely, that the
width of the uprights has been deliberately adjusted to give
this relationship on a circle of that predetermined diameter,
since in fact their widths vary considerably.

It has already been observed (p. 38) that in order to avoid
the accumulation of errors of spacing due to this variation in
width, the *centres* of the inner faces are set at equal intervals
of $10\frac{1}{2}$ ft round the circle. It is these points which were presumably marked by pegs.

It is clear that by reason of their greater length and weight
the uprights of the trilithons were erected first, and the sarsen
circle afterwards, the trilithon lintels being moved into the
circle, though not necessarily raised into position, before the
latter was complete. In both settings of uprights the process
of erection appears to have been the same, except that the
trilithons were pulled up from within outwards, whereas the
stones of the circle were raised from the outside towards the
centre.

The first task was to dig the stone-holes, whose depths
must have been carefully adjusted to the variable lengths of
the stones, so that when upright their tops were at the correct
level. These holes have an approximately rectangular plan,
matching that of the stones but some 9 in. to a foot wider all
round. Three sides are steep, but the fourth, towards the
centre of the site in the case of the trilithons and away from
it in the circle, is in the form of a ramp sloping from the base
of the hole proper to the surface, at an angle of about 45°.
Against the back of the hole (that is, opposite the ramp) a
number of wooden stakes, 4–6 in. in diameter, were set in a
row, their purpose being to protect the chalk side from being
crushed by the toe of the stone as it was raised, thus bringing
down on to the bottom a mass of loose rubble which would

make an unsuitable foundation and upset the levels. This device of anti-friction stakes (the decayed remains of the stakes
themselves survive in a number of instances) had already been
used in the erection of the Heel Stone in period I at Stonehenge, and in the great stone circles at Avebury.

The stone to be erected was then aligned radially upon
the stone-hole, supported horizontally on rollers of large
diameter, so as to raise it as far as possible above the surface.
It was then dragged forward, still on a radial line, so that the
front end, that is, the base, began to overhang the ramp. By

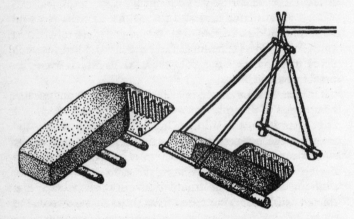

FIG. 6. Two stages in the erection of the uprights

previous trial and error the rollers would have been positioned so that as the centre of gravity of the stone passed over
the leading roller (which would be checked at this point by
stakes driven into the ground) it overbalanced, tipping the
base squarely into the hole, the lower part of the outer face
resting on the ramp. This manoeuvre, illustrated in fig. 6, thus
raised the stone half-way to the upright position by the force
of gravity alone, and substantially diminished the effort required to bring it from the horizontal to the vertical position.

The final stage of the operation could doubtless have been
achieved merely by attaching ropes to the top of the stone
and hauling it upright by brute force. The direction of the

pull would necessarily be at an acute angle to the length of
the stone, however, and for that reason inefficient. Mr E. H.
Stone has pointed out that the use of a large pair of timber
shear-legs located behind the stone-hole (fig. 6) would greatly
diminish the effort required. A cross-bar at the base of the
legs prevents them from spreading or closing, and another
nearer the apex forms an anchorage for ropes attached to the
top of the stone and is positioned so that the initial pull is at
right-angles to its length, the most efficient direction; the
ropes used by the hauling-party are attached at the apex, the
difference in height between it and the upper cross-bar pro-
viding some multiplication of leverage. Experiments with
scale models showed that with this device the pull required
to raise a stone of the outer circle, weighing 26 tons, would
be 4½ tons, representing a force of 180 men each exerting a
pull of 56 lb.

Once approximately upright the stone would require final
adjustment to bring it truly vertical, a process which it is
difficult to believe could be carried out without the use of a
plumb-line. Doubtless with this purpose in view, the bases of
all the uprights have been left roughly pointed, so that a
movement of a degree or two in any direction could fairly
easily be obtained. Once the position of the stone was considered satisfactory, the space between its base and the sides
of the hole was packed tightly with stones and boulders, many
of them being discarded mauls, used in the dressing of the
surfaces previously. The presence among these packing-
stones of fragments of rock from Chilmark, eleven miles away
to the south-west, has never been satisfactorily explained,
though it suggests a local scarcity of suitable material, perhaps because so many local sarsen boulders had already been
used up as mauls.

Once the ramps had been filled with tightly rammed chalk
rubble, it seems probable that the uprights were then left
alone, perhaps for a year or more, before any further work
was done. It would certainly be desirable to leave an interval
during which any instability could manifest itself and be corrected; and more particularly it would be necessary to let the
uprights settle in the relatively soft chalk foundation in which

they stood, for until all settlement had ceased the work of fashioning seatings for the lintels at a uniform level could not be begun.

The Raising of the Lintels

It is probable that the work of preparing the tenons and dished seatings for the lintels (p. 39) was done first, the mortices being sunk in the undersides of the lintels to match them afterwards, the necessary dimensions being transferred by measurement from one to the other. This seems the most satisfactory way of minimizing errors of fit, and of avoiding the necessity of frequent trial fittings, which would obviously occasion much difficulty. Even so, however, errors did occur, as is shown by the fact that at one end of lintel 102 there are two adjacent mortices, with centres differing by about 9 in.

The problem of how the lintels were raised into position is one which most frequently troubles the visitor to the site, and has taxed the imagination of archaeologists for many years. The solution most commonly propounded (among others by Mr E. H. Stone) is that of an earthen ramp built against the pair of uprights on which the lintel was to be placed, up which it was hauled, or perhaps rolled in a timber cradle, much as barrels of beer are today parbuckled up a pair of planks into a brewer's lorry. The origin of this notion, as applied to Stonehenge, seems to lie in the belief (almost certainly correct) that this method was used in dynastic Egypt for the erection of colossal stone statues, and indeed of the Pyramids themselves.

So far as Stonehenge is concerned, there are two main objections to this otherwise plausible theory. The first is the effort and time involved in digging away and rebuilding the ramp for each fresh lintel to be raised. The second is the absence of any evidence for the origin of such a ramp (which must have had a volume of not less than 10,000 cubic feet for the sarsen circle lintels alone, to say nothing of the much higher trilithons) in the form of a quarry, even refilled, in the vicinity of the site. It can safely be said that neither the material of the bank nor the silting of the ditch has been re-used in this way.

The alternative of a timber ramp, or scaffolding with one sloping side, is more feasible, and a working model of such a structure was demonstrated by the writer in the television programme on Stonehenge mentioned above (pp. 113, 114), and is now in the Salisbury Museum. To a lesser extent, however, the same objections apply to this solution as to that of an earth ramp, namely the labour of repeatedly assembling and dismantling the framework for each fresh operation of raising a lintel; for such a structure would necessarily have its component beams fixed together either by tree-nails (wooden pegs) or by lashings. Moreover, the erection of such a timber structure would involve the sinking of a considerable number of post-holes to support its vertical members, and its repeated construction around the circle would produce a recognizable and recurrent pattern of post-holes. No such pattern was revealed by Colonel Hawley's extensive excavations, and such post-holes as he did find were too few and too irregular in their spacing to represent a timber structure of the kind envisaged.

There remains, however, a third method of raising the lintels, originally mentioned as a possibility, though an improbable one, by Colonel R. H. Cunnington in his *Stonehenge and Its Date* (1935), and since convincingly urged upon the writer and his colleagues in correspondence by Mr G. A. Gauld, B.SC., M.I.C.E., an engineer with practical experience of raising heavy weights by primitive means. This method involves the building of a timber 'crib', that is, a structure of alternate layers of parallel timbers laid horizontally, the direction of the timbers in one layer being at right-angles to that in the layers above and below it. As Mr Gauld points out, this means is still commonly used today for raising or lowering massive pieces of machinery on to their foundations where cranes and other mechanical lifting devices are not available.

The procedure suggested is as follows (fig. 7). The lintel is first positioned on the ground a few feet from its uprights and parallel to the position which it is ultimately to occupy. By means of a long wooden lever one end of the stone is then raised a few inches, and a short packing-piece of squared timber is inserted beneath it, close to the end. The other end

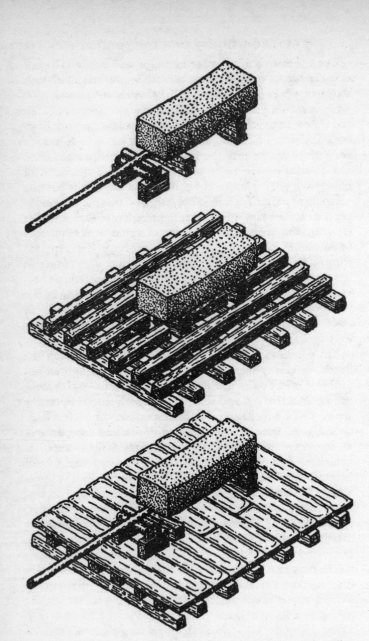

FIG. 7. Three stages in the raising of a lintel by means of a crib

is then lifted and packed up in the same way, and the process
repeated alternately at each end until the stone is raised on
two piles of packing a foot or two above the ground. At this
stage the packing tends to become unstable, and the construction of the crib is accordingly started. A row of long
timbers is laid down, parallel to each other and to the existing
packing-pieces, at intervals of a foot or two both under the
raised stone and beyond its ends. On these a second layer of
timbers is laid at right-angles, that is, parallel to and outside
the longer sides of the lintel. A third layer is then laid parallel
to the first, and so on until the top of the crib is close beneath
the lower surface of the stone. The top of the crib is then
decked over with planks to form a working platform, and the
stone is again lifted by levering so that its weight is transferred from the original piles of packing to new packing-
pieces resting alongside the old on the decked surface. The
old packing is then lifted out, the decking completed, and the
whole process started again from the beginning. The initial
stages are illustrated in fig. 7.

It would be necessary, of course, for the crib to be large
enough to accommodate not only the lintel but also the party
operating the lever and positioning the packing and timbers.
The force required to raise one end of a lintel of the outer
circle, which is $10\frac{1}{2}$ ft long and weighs $6\frac{3}{4}$ tons, is just over 3
tons, if it is supported on packing one foot within its other
end. This lifting could be achieved by a gang of seven men,
each exerting a pressure of 100 lb., towards the end of a lever
measuring about 13 ft in length, with a fulcrum one foot from
the lifting end. The minimum size of the crib would thus be
about 18 ft square, assuming that the lever was used at right-
angles to the length of the lintel and that the latter lay close to
the inner side of the crib (i.e. on the side nearest the uprights).
In practice it is probable that the dimensions of the crib would
be somewhat larger, in order to surround the pair of uprights
on which the lintel was to be placed, and so ultimately to provide a working-platform at the level of their tops. It may well
be, in fact, that such an enlarged crib was used for the whole
of the operations of forming the tenons and seatings on the
uprights, the lintel being first raised alongside to the required

height in a semi-finished state, that is, with its surfaces dressed but without mortices and tongue-and-groove joints. These would then be tooled to fit the tenons already formed and the joint on the adjacent lintel already in place. The lateral movement of the lintel for trial fittings and for its final setting in place would be effected with levers as before, swinging each end of the stone sideways a few inches at a time.

A crib of the required size would need about a mile run of timber 6 in. square, in lengths of about 20 ft. This is admittedly a formidable requirement. But it must be remembered that such a structure can be built and dismantled speedily, and requires few replacements, since none of its timbers are fastened together, but merely rest on each other. Thus in spite of the labour of cutting and squaring so much wood, the total time and effort involved in raising the lintels by this means would certainly be far less than if the builders used a fixed ramp or scaffold of timber, pegged or lashed together. Moreover, the use of the crib is consonant with the archaeological evidence, in that it does not require the digging of a recurrent pattern of post-holes.

The method outlined above seems to the writer and his colleagues to be the most satisfactory solution so far propounded, and it is for this reason that it has been explained and illustrated in detail. But it is not, of course, the last word on the subject, for which it is unlikely, in any case, that conclusive evidence for one method rather than another will ever be found.

One problem posed by the raising of the lintels still requires discussion, namely how their levelling was achieved. We have already seen that the builders achieved a surprisingly close approximation to a true horizontal plane in the setting of the lintels (p. 40), and it seems inconceivable that this was done by eye alone. If instruments were used, as they must surely have been, what were they?

There appear to be two possible answers to this question. The first is some form of water-level, akin to the modern builder's spirit-level and used in the same way. This might well have taken the form of a narrow trough of wood, or more probably of sheet bronze, with vertical sides very carefully worked to exactly the same height above the base all round. If this tray were filled with water to just below the edge, and rested on the edge of a suitable rigid wooden bar of uniform depth, levels could be transferred from one point to another with considerable accuracy, particularly if the modern practice was followed of reversing the actual instrument end for end for each reading, and taking a mean.

The second type of instrument that could have been used is a large wooden square, shaped like the letter L on its side, like an enlarged version of the modern joiner's square, with a plumb-line suspended from the apex. Provided that the angle of the two sides was a true right-angle, a matter which can very easily be checked, the long side would necessarily be horizontal when the plumb-line hung in coincidence with the edge of the short side. Such an instrument could equally well have been used to transfer levels from one point to another, and its use at Stonehenge is perhaps rather more probable than that of the water-level. In either case, however, the degree of accuracy with which the lintels have been levelled, both in the circle and on the trilithons, makes it morally certain that some device of this kind was known to and employed by the builders.

The Production of the Carvings

All the prehistoric carvings at Stonehenge seem to have been executed by methods akin to those used in dressing the surfaces on which they appear, that is, by 'pecking' and abrasion. The hammer-stones used would of course have been much smaller than the usual sarsen mauls, and indeed were probably natural quartzite pebbles about the size and shape of a rather narrow-ended egg. The use of flint chisels has been shown by experiment to be ineffective; the only result is to splinter and bruise the edge of the tool. The use of bronze chisels admittedly cannot be ruled out entirely, if only because it is possible, as the numerous modern inscriptions show, to produce incisions on sarsen with a metal tool, though only with the utmost labour and at the cost of ruining the tool itself. But it is clear from the study of other carvings of the same prehistoric period, which have been preserved in their pristine state on the interior walls of chambered tombs in Ireland and elsewhere, that edged tools of any material were hardly ever employed, the usual technique being that of hammering with a suitable stone held in the hand, or striking a narrow stone punch with a wooden mallet. In either case the result is to crush and abrade the surface, not to cut it. There is no reason to suppose that the techniques used for the Stonehenge carvings were not the same, even where, as on the two uppermost axes on stone 4 (Plate 11b), there are the remains of a narrow groove with a sharp bottom outlining the edge of the figured weapon; the appearance of this groove suggests that it has been produced by scratching or linear abrasion, and not by actual cutting with an edged tool.

As has already been pointed out (p. 92), these techniques lend themselves more readily to the production of curved rather than angular designs, a point of considerable importance in assessing the archaeological significance of the angular outline of the Stonehenge dagger.

The Dressing of the Bluestones

Careful examination of the dressed bluestones in the horse-shoe (p. 54) and of the two lintels in the circle (p. 51) shows them to have been dressed to shape in exactly the same way as the sarsens. Traces of shallow transverse grooving can be seen on the outer face of stone 70 and on the upper surface of the prostrate stone 67, while an exceptionally clear example was revealed by the excavations of 1954 on the outer end of the fallen lintel 150. These, however, are the only surviving traces of this intermediate stage of dressing. Elsewhere the surfaces have been worked smooth, probably by very fine overall pecking with light hammers. Actual grinding seems to have been restricted to the production of the mortice holes on the two lintels, which are noticeably smoother even than those surfaces, such as the inner end of the lower surface of the lintel 36 (Plate 18a), which have always been protected from weathering.

In general, the standard of tooling on the dressed bluestones far surpasses even the most careful work on the sarsens; and the finish of certain individual stones, and particularly stone 36, must be accounted among the finest achievements of the mason's craft in prehistoric Europe. It is one of the most curious features of Stonehenge that the art of dressing stones with such skill, and to shapes so aesthetically satisfying, should here have reached so high a pitch, and yet was not imitated, even in the crudest fashion, on any other British monument of later date.

CHAPTER FIVE

The Builders of Stonehenge

IN the preceding chapters we have examined the structure of Stonehenge, the evidence for the succession of phases in the monument and their date, and the techniques used by the builders. Here we are concerned with the builders themselves. Who were they? What do we know of them? What kind of lives did they live? And above all how far do their achievements at Stonehenge itself illumine the picture of social structure, political organization, and economic relations in pre-historic Britain, and indeed in western Europe, during the second millennium B.C.?

The very existence of monuments like Stonehenge, the product of communal effort on a large scale, implies the existence of contemporary social unities whose individual members share not only a common tradition of material culture but also, presumably, a common body of religious belief and a common allegiance to a pattern of social structure which provides the necessary condition for effective concerted action. It is thus undisputed, except perhaps by the most stringently academic of archaeologists, that the prehistorian is justified in thinking of the prehistoric past in terms of the development and interaction of social groups, whose nature is approximately identified by the terms 'folk', 'people', 'tribe', and 'community'. None the less, the communities whose life and relations the prehistorian attempts to reconstruct must be regarded, in a sense, as fundamentally other, and even less real, than those later communities which are the actors upon the stage of history.

The historian, by definition, uses *documents* as his raw material, for it is the presence or absence of *written* evidence that distinguish History and Prehistory one from the other, in the chronological sense of these terms. The invention or adoption of writing, however, is a phenomenon which makes its appearance only in communities which have reached a level of economic organization and social complexity which requires some system of permanent (that is, non-oral) record for the maintenance of its social and economic structure. That is to say, by and large writing and the making of records is a function of civilization in the strict sense of the word, a way of life based upon living in cities, with all the complexities of economic dependence, social hierarchy, and political power which are its necessary concomitants. It is *ipso facto* with communities of this relatively advanced kind that the historian deals, and History itself is the interpretation of their inter-related growth, impact, and decay.

These historical communities are real communities, in the sense that they form social, political, and religious unities of a kind which are familiar, or at least readily comprehensible, to us today. And in addition their reality as historical entities is guaranteed by their own surviving documents, which betray, explicitly in some cases and tacitly in many, their own consciousness of internal coherence and of differentiation from neighbouring and contemporary communities.

It is this factor of the *survival* of evidence of self-awareness, of consciousness of nationhood, if you wish, that constitutes the fundamental difference between the study of history and that of prehistory. There is no reason to suppose, of course, that in prehistory communities did not exist of fundamentally the same kind, socially and economically speaking, as those known to us in history, even though they had not reached that level of development of which the appearance of writing is an index. Nor, equally, should one doubt that such communities were conscious of themselves *as communities*. The difference lies in their conceptual status. For whereas the reality of historical peoples, nations, religious orders, and commercial organizations is guaranteed by their own surviving records, the 'communities' of prehistory are inferential constructs, created in the minds of those who study their surviving remains. Those remains are of an entirely material and non-verbal kind. Though they constitute valid evidence for the reconstruction at least of the basic technological and economic aspects of prehistoric life, they tell us nothing directly of social structure, of the exercise of political power, or of religious belief. Nor do they give any indication of what their makers and users thought and felt about themselves and about the essentially non-material factors which united them or divided them from their fellow men. All this is a matter of inference in prehistory, and inference, moreover, from evidence which by its very nature is largely silent upon those aspects of communal life and human relationships which can only be expressed explicitly in verbal form.

I do not for a moment deny, of course, that the study of history itself is essentially inferential and interpretative. Nevertheless, the existence of contemporary records of historical communities does seem, to me at least, to confer upon such communities a conceptual status that is necessarily lacking in the case of their prehistoric counterparts.

It is for this reason that the archaeologist generally fights rather shy of using terms, applied to prehistory, such as 'folk', 'people', 'tribe', and the like. Instead he uses the term 'culture'. This, in its strict sense, may be defined as an assemblage of material remains, both objects and structures, together with such practices and customs (e.g. burial rites) as can validly be inferred from such remains, which are recurrently found in association with each other. Such an assemblage can be distinguished from another, whose components again are found in association with each other, but not with those of the first. Within each such assemblage variants will be apparent, chiefly differentiated on a geographical basis. The classification of archaeological material into families of cultures, individual cultures, and sub-cultures thus resembles the taxonomic classification of living creatures into phyla, genera, and species. In both cases though the categories may in theory be exclusive in practice they overlap, with the occurrence of intermediate forms which are placed in one or the other group purely as a matter of convenience. In both cases too the adoption of such a system of categories is an essential condition for the extraction of useful information, even though it is clearly understood that the conceptual framework is the product of the investigator, and not necessarily inherent in the material itself.

The word culture is used by archaeologists also in a secondary though equally valid sense as a substitute, though by no means a synonym, for 'community'. Just as in geology, for instance, the Principle of Uniformity is recognized, whereby the occurrence of similar fossils in dissimilar deposits is taken to imply not only the existence of a distinct class of creature with a uniform biological inheritance, but also the broad contemporaneity of the deposits concerned: so too in archaeology the occurrence in separate places of similar pottery, accompanied by similar stone tools in similar houses or tombs, is taken to imply the existence, broadly at the same time, of members of a 'community', that is, a group of people linked together by the possession of a common cultural inheritance. Such 'communities', however, are far more shadowy and conceptually far less real than the known and named communities of history, for in the last resort they are no more than workable categories invented by archaeologists, in order to permit the transformation of mere inanimate sticks and stones into the history of living men.

The use by archaeologists of terms such as 'Windmill Hill culture', 'Beaker culture', 'Wessex culture' must not be regarded, therefore, merely as one more instance of the tendency of specialists to obscure their meaning by the invention and use of unnecessary jargon. In this sense the word 'culture' has a precise meaning, and is itself a recognition by archaeologists that the nature of their material is such that it cannot permit the full range of inference open to the historian.

To me at least, the chief value of the study of such monuments as Stonehenge is that they do, in a sense, provide evidence for that self-conscious awareness of social unity which, in the absence of contemporary documents, is otherwise lacking from the purely material remains of the prehistoric past. In other words, their positive indications of the existence of communal effort and communal organization go a long way to validate the equation which the archaeologist must make, if he is to interpret prehistory in human terms at all, between his 'cultures' – mere categories of inanimate objects – and real communities of living men and women. For if there is any value in archaeology at all, it is as a study of *people*, of whom we ourselves are the descendants and heirs, not of the dry and dusty objects ranged on the shelves of a museum.

The period of prehistory to which the successive buildings of Stonehenge belong, namely the early and middle part of the second millennium B.C., is one of exceptional interest but also of great complexity, for it witnesses the arrival in Britain of a number of immigrant foreign cultures, with their impact both on each other and on the indigenous inhabitants, resulting in the formation of distinctively British cultures in which many variant strands of tradition are closely woven. To understand Stonehenge in terms of the people who built it one must know something of the contemporary history of southern Britain as a whole, and not merely of those individual cultures which appear to have been directly responsible for the several phases of construction. In what follows, therefore, I have attempted a brief sketch of the main British cultures of the earlier part of the second millennium B.C. A more detailed picture is given in such standard works as Stuart Piggott's *Neolithic Cultures of the British Isles* (1954), the same author's *British Prehistory* (1950), and *Prehistoric Britain* by Christopher and Jacquetta Hawkes (1958).

The Indigenous Inhabitants

Up to a few centuries before the first building at Stonehenge, the native population consisted of scattered groups of savages, living entirely by hunting, fishing, and the gathering of wild fruits and berries, practising no form of agriculture and having no domesticated animals other than the dog. Their way of life, typical of this Mesolithic* stage of economy, differed little in its essentials from that followed by their forebears for hundreds of centuries, save that the improvement of the climate after the retreat of the Pleistocene ice-sheets provided a warmer and more benign environment, and a greater range and quantity of natural foodstuffs. Their settlements, mere temporary camping-places of rough platforms of light tree-

*So called because it is intermediate between the Palaeolithic (the Old Stone Age of the Pleistocene period) and the Neolithic (the New Stone Age, marked by the introduction of agriculture and stock-raising).

trunks, or shallow pits in the ground, protected perhaps by a screen of branches as a wind-break, were located either on the banks of rivers, or on the shores of lakes (then more numerous than today), or in upland regions clear of the dense forest covering the valleys and the Midland Plain, where a lighter growth of scrub permitted the unimpeded hunting of game. Their equipment consisted entirely of tools and weapons appropriate to such an existence: axes for the cutting of timber chipped from flint, knives and scrapers of the same material for the cutting and dressing of skins, and arrowheads for hunting. Enormous use was made of bone and antler, worked skilfully into a wide range of hunting weapons, particularly for the spearing of fish.

By and large, if allowance is made for differences in physical environment and in available raw materials, the life of these native Mesolithic inhabitants of Britain must have resembled in many respects the nomadic and precarious existence of the present-day aborigines of Australia. Like them, they lived from hand to mouth, unable to accumulate any store of surplus food against the capricious uncertainties of nature, which through drought, forest fire, or epidemic disease might at a stroke rob them of their accustomed livelihood. They built no houses, made no religious or funerary monuments, and indeed left no mark at all upon the British countryside.

These people, of course, made no direct contribution to the building of Stonehenge, even though a few scattered bands of them may still have been roaming the country, untouched culturally by their more advanced neighbours, at the time the first monument there was under construction. Nevertheless they are important as the direct ancestors of those Secondary Neolithic cultures (p. 153) to which that same first monument must be ascribed. And indeed even later, at the time of the building of Stonehenge III, when the introduction of agriculture and metal-working had already raised the standard of living a measurable distance towards the heights of civilization, the old traditional Mesolithic skills in the gathering and preparation of natural raw materials, animal and vegetable, must have played a considerable part in the vast organization necessary for the transport and erection of the sarsen stones.

The Windmill Hill Culture

About 2300 B.C. there arrived from the continent on the southern shores of Britain, in scattered groups from Sussex to Devon, the first neolithic colonists, known to archaeologists as the Windmill Hill culture. For some time their advent was doubtless unnoticed, or at least ignored, by the indigenous population; yet they were the bearers, literally, of the seeds of a revolution, in the form of fertile grain and horned beasts. For it was the practice of agriculture and stock-raising, that is, the deliberate *production* as opposed to the mere gathering of food, that allowed the population of Britain for the first time to gain mastery of its environment, and so to rise from brute savagery to the higher levels of barbarism. It is only then that men, no longer constrained by the harsh exigencies of mere existence, could find opportunity and energy for those expressions of faith through works of which, among many minor monuments, Stonehenge is the most notable.

The Windmill Hill culture is the British representative of a whole family of cultures, collectively known as Western Neolithic, whose expansion can be traced from somewhere in the eastern Mediterranean to Iberia, France, Switzerland, and ultimately to the Channel coasts. In Britain their settlements are widespread on the chalk downs of Wessex and Sussex, in the upper valley of the Thames and in East Anglia, with northward extensions reaching finally to the shores of the Moray Firth. These settlements seem for the most part to have been only temporary (though isolated instances of permanent houses are known in south-western Britain), doubtless because the grazing of cattle and the practice of primitive hoe-agriculture alike impose a semi-nomadic life upon their exponents. None the less, there is evidence for the localization in separate districts of groups of these farmer-shepherds, in the form of large embanked enclosures, often with several concentric rings of earthwork. These are known, misleadingly, as 'causewayed camps', from the discontinuous character of their quarry-ditches. The best known is the type-site of the culture on Windmill Hill, near Avebury, and the nearest to Stonehenge is Robin Hood Ball, about three miles away to the north (fig. 5).

These enclosures appear to be cattle-corrals, used chiefly in the autumn for the impounding of beasts for marking (doubtless by nicking the ear with a flint knife), gelding, and for the slaughter of the young animals for whom there was no winter

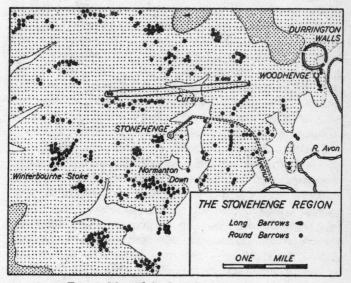

FIG. 8. Map of the Stonehenge region

feed. During these periods the ditches were occupied for temporary shelter, and it is the remains of such camping that were mistaken in the past for evidence of permanent settlement.

The size of these enclosures and the volume of their earthworks suggest that they were built and used communally, and hence imply the existence of some social unit larger than the individual family. The same conclusion must be drawn from the characteristic burial places of the culture, the Long Barrows which form striking landmarks on the Wessex downs. These are elongated mounds of chalk rubble, often 10 ft or more in height, piled up from a deep quarry-ditch on either side over the collective burial of from half a dozen to a score of bodies, many of them deposited already in a skeletal condition. Most of these barrows are over 100 ft in length, and a number are over 300 ft. Such monuments to the dead are clearly beyond the capacity of a single family to construct, and must again be regarded as evidence for some kind of 'tribal' or 'clan' organization.

There are about 100 Long Barrows in Wiltshire alone, and of these ten are sited within two miles of Stonehenge (fig. 8), a sufficient concentration to suggest that already during the *floruit* of the Windmill Hill culture, and possibly even before the first construction at Stonehenge itself, the region was regarded as one of especial sanctity. This is reinforced, moreover, by the occurrence close to the north of Stonehenge of one of the most remarkable but least known of Wiltshire antiquities, namely the Cursus, discovered and so named by William Stukeley in the early eighteenth century.

This is an immense elongated enclosure with parallel sides 300 ft apart, each marked by a low bank and ditch, which runs roughly east and west for a distance of a mile and three-quarters, and is closed by a rounded continuation of the same bank and ditch at either end (fig. 8). Just beyond the east end is a Long Barrow, now almost obliterated by a trackway, upon which the Cursus was obviously aligned deliberately. Among the score or so of cursus monuments known elsewhere in Britain there are several with even more direct connections with Long Barrows and other ritual structures of Windmill Hill origin. These leave little doubt that the Cursus must be counted among the achievements of the culture.* The occurrence of this example of exceptional length (it is exceeded by only one other, in Cranborne Chase) so close to Stonehenge itself implies a preceding tradition of sanctity attached to the region. A find of a fragment of micaceous sandstone on the outer lip of the ditch of the Cursus suggests, however, that it was not built much before the erection of Stonehenge II.

The purpose of the Cursus and of its analogues elsewhere is

---

*The 'Lesser Cursus' to the north-west of the west end of the main structure was discovered and named by Sir Richard Colt Hoare early in the nineteenth century, but is not in fact a true cursus at all, though it may well be of neolithic date.

unknown, though it is obviously religious or ceremonial in character rather than secular, and is presumably connected in some way with the cult of the dead interred in the Long Barrow at its end; and whatever ceremonies took place within it must surely have been of a processional kind.

In this connection it is significant that Stonehenge too has its processional way, the Avenue, a structure unparalleled elsewhere but in many respects similar to the Cursus. Both monuments seem to have been built at about the same time, and it would not be too rash to suggest some kinship of intention and function between them, though modified in the case of the Avenue by considerations of expediency in the dragging of the bluestones from the Avon to Stonehenge (p. 67). This is not to suggest, of course, that the Avenue was built by people of the Windmill Hill culture, for this seems to have been the achievement of the Beaker culture responsible for Stonehenge II (p. 159). There is indeed no evidence for the direct participation of the Windmill Hill culture in either of the earlier constructions at Stonehenge itself, though it is perhaps significant that fragments of their characteristic pottery have been found in each of the three sanctuaries, in Oxfordshire and West Lothian, which form the closest analogues of Stonehenge I (p. 156).

The Megalith Builders

Some three or four centuries after the first arrival of the Windmill Hill culture another group of small bands of neolithic colonists landed in various places on the western coasts of Britain. Whereas the earlier immigrants brought with them the means of purely economic advancement, these new arrivals were the bearers of what was evidently a most potent and attractive religious doctrine, which found its practical expression in the erection of vast and elaborate chambered tombs. It is indeed only through the tombs that their builders are known, and the secular aspects of their life are unrepresented, save by such selected objects of daily domestic use as it was thought proper to deposit in the tomb as a viaticum for the dead.

The various British groups of these tombs represent the most northerly extent of a movement originating in the Mediterranean area, probably at its western end, and spreading into south-western France, and up the Biscay coast to the Breton peninsula, a movement in which the persuasive force of the doctrines thus diffused seems to have been far greater than the numerical strength of their bearers. Of the British groups of tombs only one need concern us here, since it alone is significant for the building of Stonehenge.

The tombs of this group, known to archaeologists as the Severn-Cotswold type, are distributed principally on the limestone uplands of Gloucestershire, with important extensions into South Wales and north Wiltshire. In their earliest form, represented at Notgrove in the former county, they consisted of an elongated pear-shaped mound of rock rubble, covering beneath its broader end a series of connected burial chambers, built of large slabs of stone set on edge, with similar horizontal slabs resting on them to form the roof. In plan the tomb has an axial gallery or passage, with a terminal chamber at its inner end and two pairs of chambers opening off its sides, in the manner of transepts in a church; for this reason the type is known technically as a transepted gallery-grave. The gallery is entered from a cusp-shaped forecourt, open to the sky, set in the broad end of the mound, the actual doorway being normally closed by dry-stone walling, except when a burial was actually in progress. As in the Windmill Hill culture, burial was collective, though here the bodies were interred successively, whereas all the burials beneath a Long Barrow must have been deposited at the same time, even though many of the individuals had already long been dead.

In the later and more devolved forms of these tombs the chambers are simpler, opening from the sides of the mound, and though the forecourt is retained the doorway at its centre is a dummy, of symbolic significance only. The best example is Belas Knap, just south of Winchcombe in Gloucestershire. This change of plan seems to have taken place fairly rapidly, and any tomb which retains the original transepted plan can accordingly be assigned to an early place in the series.

The southwards extension of these tombs comprises Wayland's Smithy on the crest of the Berkshire Downs and an important group in the immediate vicinity of Avebury, mostly represented today only by vestigial remains. The most complete and by far the largest is the West Kennet chambered Long Barrow on the crest of a down just south of Silbury Hill, which was excavated by Professor Stuart Piggott and the writer in June and July 1955. This excavation showed that the tomb was a perfect example of the transepted plan, and that it must represent an early offshoot from the primary area of colonization in the Cotswolds. The chambers are built on a monumental scale, with a roof-height in the gallery and terminal chamber of 8 ft internally; while after the final burial the original semicircular forecourt was blocked by a massive façade of upright stones which extended right across the front of the mound. Many of these stones, and indeed many of those in the tomb itself, are very large, and the heaviest weighs nearly twenty tons.

The present significance of this remarkable tomb, the largest in England and Wales and to be counted among the finest achievements of megalithic architecture in Europe, is that it must represent the first introduction into Wiltshire of the techniques of moving and erecting massive stones. It thus forms the starting-point of the local tradition of megalithic construction which was later to find expression in the great stone circles and avenue at Avebury, and achieved its final and finest flowering in the sarsen structure of Stonehenge itself. It is in this sense, as the founders of a tradition of craftsmanship rather than as direct participants, that the builders of the Severn-Cotswold chambered tombs contributed to the building of Stonehenge.

The Secondary Neolithic Cultures

One would expect that the useful arts of husbandry, and other technological innovations such as the making of pottery, which were introduced by the primary neolithic colonists, would in time be adopted by the indigenous inhabitants, to their own manifest advantage. This is indeed what seems to have happened. Contact between the two led to the exchange of cultural traits, the Windmill Hill people receiving certain Mesolithic influences, evidenced particularly by certain types of antler tool and by decoration on their pottery reminiscent of basket-work; while in the case of the native population the results of contact amounted in effect to the creation of a new and distinctively insular group of cultures, in which the new arts of husbandry and potting were absorbed into, and at the same time modified, the continuing traditions of Mesolithic life. These new cultures, happily named by Professor Piggott 'Secondary Neolithic', are secondary to the primary colonizations in time, and secondary also in the sense that they depend for their genesis upon the impact of those colonizations upon the indigenous savage population. They thus represent the first development of distinctively insular and British traditions; though it should be made clear that the concept of Secondary Neolithic cultures is not confined to Britain, for in many parts of Europe the same processes of impact and fusion produced comparable phenomena, each distinctive of its own region.

Because in Britain the process of fusion took place more or less simultaneously in widely separated areas, the resulting Secondary Neolithic cultures exhibit a considerable range of variation, evidenced in particular by pottery, some types of which show clear signs of derivation from basketry prototypes. But behind this diversity there is a fundamental unity of culture represented by a uniform assemblage of bone and stone tools, many of which betray an obviously Mesolithic ancestry and show that the older traditions of hunting, fishing, and gathering must have continued in vigorous form, in spite of the introduction of primitive agriculture and the domestication of beasts. Indeed the absence of any permanent settlements (apart from the well-known groups of houses, built and furnished in stone, at Skara Brae and Rinyo in the Orkneys, which cannot be regarded as typical) and the distribution of temporary camping-sites chiefly on the banks of rivers and on coastal sand-dunes show that much of the nomadic life of the earlier Mesolithic must have persisted unchanged.

We can envisage these Secondary Neolithic peoples, there-

fore, living much as tinkers and gypsies still do in many parts
of Europe today, moving about at will with small herds of
somewhat ill-favoured cattle, hunting in the forests, fishing
in the streams and on the shore, and engaging in sporadic
dealing in such natural products as antlers, hides, vegetable
ropes and cordage, dried fish, nuts, and herbs. They thus
seem to have played in an unorganized way a considerable
part in the economic life of neolithic Britain. The most
notable and best-documented of their activities is perhaps the
exploitation of flint mines and of natural outcrops of igneous
rocks for the manufacture of axes, whose distribution shows
that they were traded regularly over distances of several hundred miles.

In spite of this unsettled and roving existence, however,
there must have existed within the Secondary Neolithic cultures some kind of 'tribal' organization, however loosely knit.
The evidence for this lies in a number of widely distributed
embanked circular enclosures, which must be regarded, for
want of better names, as sanctuaries or temples.

These 'henge monuments' (the name is coined from that of
Stonehenge itself) are of widely different sizes and structure,
but almost all of them show the common feature of a circular
enclosing bank with its ditch on the *inside*, an arrangement
which distinguishes them sharply from almost all contemporary and later earthworks of domestic or defensive purpose.
The circular earthwork is normally broken either by a single
entrance, or by two entrances on opposite sides. Finds from
excavated sites suggest that the latter kind of henge monument belongs to the slightly later Beaker cultures (p. 157),
but that the former were built by the Secondary Neolithic
population, who seem actually to have invented this new type
of religious monument. For not only are some of the single-
entrance henges demonstrably *earlier* than the local arrival of
Beaker people; it is also clear that no examples of either type
exist outside Britain, so that the idea cannot have been introduced by alien immigrants from abroad. It is to this single-
entrance type that Stonehenge I belongs.

The internal structure of these earlier henge monuments is

very variable.* At Woodhenge, two miles north-east of Stonehenge (fig. 8), excavation revealed six concentric ovals of post-holes, which can only be interpreted convincingly as the ground-plan of a roofed wooden building. At Arminghall, just outside Norwich, the central feature was a horseshoe of large wooden posts, probably free-standing. The Stripple Stones on Bodmin Moor and Mayburgh near Penrith both enclosed settings of upright stones. In a number of other sites there is now no trace of any internal structure at all. For our present purpose, however, the most important of these monuments is a small group distinguished by the presence of an internal ring of pits, and by the reversal of the more normal position of bank and ditch, the latter being here on the *outside*, both of them features which occur in Stonehenge I. Two of these sites have been excavated at Dorchester-on-Thames, Oxon. (sites I and XI), while a semicircular setting of similar pits, without any earthwork enclosure, formed the first structure in a series of ritual monuments at Cairnpapple in West Lothian. At all these sites, as in Stonehenge I, cremated burials were associated with the pits, accompanied by characteristic forms of Secondary Neolithic bone pin. Similar cremated burials also occurred in small embanked cemeteries, without internal structures, at Dorchester-on-Thames (sites IV, V, VI), many of them being deposited in the partly silted ditch exactly as in Stonehenge I (p. 28).

It is thus clear that it was one of the component groups within the Secondary Neolithic cultures that was responsible for the building of Stonehenge I, a structure which even if not unique in its plan is none the less marked out by its great size and by the accuracy of its design as perhaps the leading sanctuary of its time in Britain.

The Beaker Cultures

By the end of the first quarter of the second millennium B.C. the distribution of settlements in Britain reveals a complex

*For fuller details, see R. J. C. Atkinson, C. M. Piggott, and N. K. Sandars, *Excavations at Dorchester, Oxon.* (Ashmolean Museum, 1951), vol. I, chap. VIII.

pattern of discrete but interlocking cultures: the Windmill Hill people mainly in the south and east, the builders of megalithic tombs chiefly in the north and west, and the Secondary Neolithic cultures almost everywhere. At this point the pattern is still further complicated by the arrival on the eastern shores of Britain of a number of distinct groups of immigrants which constitute the Beaker cultures, so called from the pottery drinking-cups which are the most characteristic item of their material equipment.

The archaeology of these cultures is still by no means properly understood, but it is clear that in the south at least we have to deal with two main groups of population, distinguished by the forms of their pottery as the Bell-Beaker and Necked-Beaker cultures. The former are representatives of a whole group of related cultures widely distributed in southwestern and central Europe; the proximal origin of the British immigrants lies in the Rhineland. The Necked-Beaker culture, on the other hand, is an indigenous development in Britain, apparently the result of the impact upon a Bell-Beaker population already established here of bands of warrior invaders arriving on our north-eastern coasts from some point, not yet identified, on the opposite side of the North Sea. These invaders seem to be offshoots from yet another great group of Continental cultures, extending across the great plain of northern Europe from the steppes of Russia to the Rhine, and characterized as the Corded-Ware-Battle-axe cultures from their common use of impressed cord ornament on pottery and of perforated stone battle-axes as weapons. It is these peoples, among whom an element of martial display and warlike panoply suggests the institution of chieftainship, that are commonly supposed to have introduced to the West the Indo-European speech which lies at the foundation of most European languages today.

The arrival of the Beaker cultures in Britain introduced a number of radical innovations, the chief of which is the practice of individual inhumation burial under a round barrow, a sharp break with the tradition of collective burial hitherto followed almost universally in these islands. The two main component cultures are distinguished by a marked difference in the size and height of these barrows, those covering Necked-Beaker burials being usually much the larger.

In addition the Bell-Beaker peoples at least brought with them the knowledge of the use, if not the fabrication, of metal objects, and the demand for these new products seems rapidly to have spread to the Necked-Beaker culture also, not merely because of the technical superiority of metal over flint, but also for the prestige which the possession of such rare novelties must have conferred upon their owners. At this time one of the chief European centres of metal-working, in copper and soon afterwards in bronze, was already being established in Ireland. The distribution of Beaker remains in Britain suggests that trade-routes to the West were rapidly prospected and opened up. One of these routes to Ireland lay along the south coast of Wales, and is of particular significance in connection with the transport of the bluestones from Pembrokeshire to Stonehenge.

Of the daily life of the Beaker cultures we know virtually nothing, for almost their sole remains are their graves. The absence of settlement-sites suggests that they were nomadic pastoralists, growing crops only sporadically and incidentally; while the wide variation in the richness of their grave-goods coupled with the occurrence, particularly in Necked-Beaker graves, of objects of warrior's panoply such as battle-axes, implies that we are dealing here with a society in which differences of wealth and status are far more strongly marked than in the earlier neolithic communities of Britain. Indeed already we have here the signs of the emergence of a warrior-aristocracy, intimately involved in the trade in metal products, which was to play so notable a part in the succeeding Wessex culture (p. 160).

Apart from graves, however, the Beaker cultures appear also to have built two kinds of related religious monuments, namely free-standing stone circles and henge monuments of the second class, the latter often with stone circles inside the enclosing earthwork. Stone circles are notoriously among the least understood of British antiquities. Relatively few have been excavated, and of these most have yielded no evidence of their date and culture. In Wiltshire, however, there is one group, at Avebury itself, which can with some confidence be ascribed to the Beaker peoples. The earliest construction there seems to have been the two central circles of Avebury, together with the avenue of two lines of upright stones which runs towards them, though originally it did not reach them or even point directly at them. The southern end of the avenue led to a smaller double circle of stones on Overton Hill, which itself apparently superseded an earlier wooden building erected by Secondary Neolithic people. If one can judge by burials placed at the foot of some of the stones, and by potsherds in some of the stone-holes, these structures were built by Bell-Beaker people. The double circle at the Sanctuary on Overton Hill is of particular significance in connection with the double bluestone circle of Stonehenge II.

The subsequent structures at Avebury, the great earthwork enclosing the two earlier circles with a ring of 100 huge stones just within the ditch, and the extension of the avenue to the southern entrance of the earthwork itself, are probably the work of a Necked-Beaker community which settled in the district somewhat later. Though the evidence on this point at Avebury itself is not as explicit as 'one might wish, other henge monuments of the same class can be assigned to the Necked-Beaker culture with confidence.

It appears, therefore, that at least in north Wiltshire the practice of megalithic architecture and the skills which it required had been assimilated by the Beaker cultures from sources which must have included the neighbouring West Kennet Long Barrow and its lesser analogues. By comparison with their achievements there, the erection of the double circle of Stonehenge II is an insignificant feat; though the *transport* of the bluestones is indeed a heroic undertaking, fit to rank with the building of Avebury itself. The possible reasons for it are discussed below (p. 175).

It must be admitted that the evidence for assigning Stonehenge II to the Beaker cultures is chiefly circumstantial, rather than direct. The conclusion rests first upon the occurrence of Beaker sherds in the Stonehenge ditch at a level corresponding to the first arrival of the bluestones (p. 74), and in one of the Q Holes (p. 91); secondly, upon the fact that the nearest analogue for the double stone circle, itself an uncommon type of structure, may with some confidence be regarded as the work of Beaker people; thirdly, upon a similar parallelism of function between the Stonehenge and Avebury avenues, though admittedly they differ in actual construction; and fourthly, upon the occurrence of fragments of the Stonehenge foreign stones in two monuments of Beaker type. One of these is a miniature henge monument with two entrances encircling a Beaker grave, in Fargo Plantation, a mile north-west of Stonehenge; the other is Avebury itself, where a fragment of micaceous sandstone, almost certainly to be identified with the material of the Altar Stone at Stonehenge, was found during the nineteenth century close to the 'Cove' at the centre of the Northern Circle. Moreover, it had always been something of a puzzle that the Beaker people, so active at Avebury, should have left no mark at Stonehenge. The discovery of Stonehenge II thus fulfils an expectation which already existed even before the evidence came to light in 1954. In the absence so far of any facts to support an alternative hypothesis, it may therefore be accepted that this second phase of construction at Stonehenge was the work of the Beaker cultures.

The Wessex Culture

Reference has already been made (p. 144) to the similarities between the classification of archaeological material and the taxonomic arrangement of the various forms of living creatures. This biological analogy can usefully be extended to the study of the growth, change, and decay of archaeological cultures, for these too, like the men and women which they represent, are dynamic rather than static in their nature.

In the evolution of living creatures, the high road of biological development is peopled with life-forms whose survival has been assured by lack of specialization and by a genetical vigour expressed in prolific variation. The side roads, ending ultimately in cul-de-sacs, are filled with forms which have become adapted, through a greater degree of specialization of function, to one particular mode of existence. Being thus more sensitive to changes of environment, such forms are the more liable to extinction.

The history of the neolithic cultures of Britain suggests an analogous process of natural selection. The Primary Neolithic cultures arrived in these islands already fully formed, with a pattern of economic life based upon husbandry which implies some degree of physical immobility and of adaptation to a particular environment of climate and vegetation. On the other hand, the Secondary Neolithic and Beaker cultures (that of the Necked-Beakers in particular) are largely native growths within these islands, whose relative lack of economic specialization permitted them more freely to adapt themselves to contemporary changes of physical environment, and more readily to exploit to their own advantage such technological innovations as the introduction of metallurgy. Moreover, the greater physical mobility of these communities made for more frequent opportunities for contact between them, and thus for the development of that 'hybrid vigour' which in the biological field so frequently results from the cross-fertilization of different strains.

It would be unwise to push this biological analogy too far. None the less it may serve to illumine, even if it does not accurately describe, the course of British prehistory towards the close of the first half of the second millennium B.C. For already before 1500 B.C. the Primary Neolithic cultures were in decline, and indeed, so far as southern England is concerned, almost extinct; whereas the Secondary Neolithic and Beaker cultures still flourished vigorously, no longer, it is true, in their original forms, but as a single new culture partaking of both, but also transcending both in enterprise and in its level of material wealth. One may hazard the guess that the main causes of this decline and growth were, on the one hand, a gradual drying-up of the climate, doubtless intensified by the deforestation brought about by neolithic pastoralism; and on the other the growth of Irish metallurgy, which was radically to transform the part played by Britain in the economic structure of prehistoric Europe and create opportunities of quite exceptional advancement for the peoples of southern England, lying on the trade-routes from Ireland to the Continent.

The growth of this new culture, known as the Wessex culture of the Early Bronze Age, is marked in the archaeological record by the appearance of numerous burials of exceptional richness and elaboration; for here too, as in the earlier Beaker cultures, evidence of the living comes almost entirely from the tombs of the dead. The barrows themselves are of specialized form, which illustrates very well the hybrid and yet unitary character of the new culture. For though the body is still placed singly beneath a round mound, the mound itself is commonly surrounded by a ditch with an external bank. We thus have here the apparent fusion of two traditions: the round barrow appropriate to the Beaker cultures; and the circular embanked enclosure of the Secondary Neolithic henge monuments. These two elements are combined in various forms to make a group of types, known collectively as 'circle-barrows'. They range from bell-barrows, in which the mound is of considerable height and occupies almost the whole of the enclosed area, leaving only a narrow strip between its edge and the ditch, to disc-barrows, in which the burial lies beneath an insignificant tump in the centre of an otherwise flat circle like a small henge monument, though without entrances. Between these two extremes there are a number of intermediate types.

It is significant too that bell-barrows, whose large mounds must surely represent the earlier traditions of the Necked-Beaker culture, commonly contain the burials of men accompanied by objects of martial panoply such as battle-axes; whereas the disc-barrows, to judge from the associated objects, are the graves of women. Moreover, whereas men were sometimes buried by the Beaker rites, as crouched inhumations in a proper grave, the women were invariably cremated and their bones placed merely in a shallow pit, an old Secondary Neolithic rite which gradually became universal during the *floruit* of the Wessex culture.

The burials thus give us a picture of a culture in which earlier traditions have fused into a distinctive form, and in which the warrior-chieftain element, already discernible in embryonic form in the Necked-Beaker culture, now achieves a dominant place, though ultimately to be absorbed, in the decline of the culture, by the less spectacular but more persistent heritage of the Secondary Neolithic.

The occurrence in the graves, particularly of men, of rich assemblages of bronze tools and weapons and of gold ornaments implies that we are dealing here with a 'heroic' society in which the ordinary population is dominated and controlled by a caste of warrior-chieftains, essentially the same type of society, that is to say, as those of the Homeric epics, of the Norse sagas, and of the early literature of Wales and Ireland. But it is clear that in spite of the element of martial display represented by skilfully wrought battle-axes and mace-heads of stone, and by bronze daggers with hilts richly ornamented in gold, the fundamental feature of the Wessex culture is commercial success. Whatever their pretensions to warlike valour, the dead buried in the Wessex circle-barrows were essentially hard-headed and successful business men, who had made the best of their position as middle-men in the metal trade between Ireland and the Continent.

The evidence for this commercial activity is chiefly in the form of metal tools and weapons. Not only, for instance, are bronze axes and halberds known from European finds, whose distinctive form and decoration mark their Irish origin; but also in the graves of the Wessex culture itself there appear objects which are either direct imports, or close native copies of such imports, from the principal continental centre of metallurgy in South Germany and Bohemia. It is thus clear that the Wessex culture played an integral part in a commercial system which now, for the first time in European prehistory, achieved a truly international character. The complexity of this system is nowhere better illustrated than in a couple of Wessex graves which yielded complex necklaces of amber beads. These had clearly been obtained, not directly from the sources of amber in Scandinavia, but from *entrepôts* far to the south in Central Europe, on the long overland route by which amber was traded to the Mediterranean from the north.

Indeed the Mediterranean itself was not outside the orbit of trade from Wessex, for in each area there occur gold objects which must have originated in the other. Here, however, it is likely that it was the south that played the active and the north the passive role in the exchange. For at this time there flourished in the central Mediterranean the great maritime empire of Minoan Crete, and its offshoot and competitor on the Greek mainland, centred upon Mycenae, the city of Agamemnon. It has long been recognized that the stories of Odysseus and of the Argo enshrine in legendary and heroic form the more prosaic commercial exploits of merchant-venturers from these two great centres, within the limits of the tideless Inland Sea. From Britain there is most suggestive evidence that exceptionally perhaps, but none the less success-fully, they dared to voyage beyond the Pillars of Hercules into the inhospitable waters of Ocean, no longer wine-dark, but grey beneath anything but a halcyon sky.

Among the most exotic of the objects found in Wessex graves, chiefly those of women, are small ribbed beads of blue faience, often fragmentary with their brilliant colour dulled by fire and by the stains of time, which clearly had sometimes been handed down as treasured heirlooms before their final burial. Careful examination leaves little doubt that these beads are of Egyptian manufacture, and their sporadic occurrence both in Crete and on the Atlantic coasts of Iberia and France suggests forcibly that they reached Britain by sea. It is diffi-cult not to see in them the exact counterparts of those gaudy glass beads, strung on lengths of copper wire, which were carried as trade goods by the Western explorers of Africa in the nineteenth century A.D. Is it then too fanciful to regard this handful of trinkets, insignificant in themselves, as the tangible relics of some unsung Odyssey? And may not the Golden Fleece have been fetched from the Island of the Hyperboreans, no less than from Colchis?

Whatever may have been the precise part played by the Wessex culture in this widespread network of European trade, it is clear that here, and here alone, in Britain have we a community able to command the immense resources of labour and craftsmanship necessary for the building of Stonehenge III. This conclusion is confirmed by the very notable concentration of burials of the Wessex culture close to Stonehenge, where they cluster in great barrow-cemeteries on the crests of the neighbouring downs (fig. 8). When one stands within the stones looking out over their ruins southwards to the barrows on the skyline of Normanton Down, one can be sure that in them the builders of Stonehenge themselves now rest from their labours.

And yet were these Wessex chieftains *alone* responsible for the design and construction of this last and greatest monument at Stonehenge? For all their evident power and wealth, and for all their widespread commercial contacts, these men were essentially barbarians. As such, can they have encompassed unaided a monument which uniquely transcends all other comparable prehistoric buildings in Britain, and indeed in all Europe north of the Alps, and exhibits so many refinements of conception and technique? I for one do not believe it. It seems to me that to account for these exotic and unparalleled features one *must* assume the existence of influence from the only contemporary European cultures in which *architecture*, as distinct from mere construction, was already a living tradition; that is, from the Mycenaean and Minoan civilizations of the central Mediterranean. Admittedly not all the refinements of Stonehenge can be paralleled in detail in Mycenaean or Minoan architecture, though it is noteworthy that the structure of the Postern Gate at Mycenae is very similar to the trilithons at Stonehenge, even to the use of the mortice-and-tenon joints to hold the lintel in place. But even without this specific parallel, the architecture of the central Mediterranean provides the only outside source for the sophisticated approach to architecture exhibited at Stonehenge. We have seen that through trade the necessary contacts with the Mediterranean had been established. The Stonehenge dagger too may be seen, if one wishes, to point more directly at Mycenae itself. We know from Homer that architects, like the poets of whom he himself was one, were homeless men, wandering from city to city. Is it then any more incredible that the architect of Stonehenge should himself have been a Mycenaean, than that the monument should have been designed and erected, with all its unique and sophisticated detail, by mere barbarians?

Let us suppose for a moment that this is more than mere conjecture. Under what circumstances, then, could a man versed in the traditions and skills of Mediterranean architecture find himself working among barbarians in the far cold North? Only, surely, as the skilled servant of some far-voyaging Mycenaean prince, *fortis ante Agamemnona*; or at the behest of a barbarian British king, whose voice and gifts spoke loudly enough to be heard even in the cities of the Mediterranean. Have we then any evidence in Britain for the concentration of power in the hands of a single overlord, native or foreign?

Here too, I believe, Stonehenge itself provides the answer. For one must remember that Stonehenge is not only unique in the refinement of its details; it is unique also as the *only* monument, great or small, which can be assigned to the Wessex culture, apart, of course, from the barrows. The great sanctuaries such as Avebury all belong to an earlier age, and by the time Stonehenge was built there can have been no living and active tradition of communal building of this kind. The building of Stonehenge is thus unlikely to have been the expression of the common will, but rather the fulfilment of a purpose imposed from above. Now in the rich and martially furnished Wessex graves we can admittedly see evidence for chieftainship, and the grouping of the graves in cemeteries may imply whole dynasties of chiefs. Yet the pattern of society which they represent is surely that of so many other heroic societies, in which clan wars with clan, and rival dynasties carry on a perpetual struggle for power. Under such conditions, can the construction of Stonehenge, involving the displacement of so many hundreds of men from their homes for so long, have been attempted, still less achieved? Surely not; for such great works can only be encompassed by a society at peace within itself. And in such a society of conflicting factions, how is peace imposed except from above?

I believe, therefore, that Stonehenge itself is evidence for the concentration of political power, for a time at least, in the hands of a single man, who alone could create and maintain the conditions necessary for this great undertaking. Who he was, whether native-born or foreign, we shall never know; he remains a figure as shadowy and insubstantial as King Brutus of the medieval British History. Yet who but he should sleep, like Arthur or Barbarossa, in the quiet darkness of a sarsen vault beneath the mountainous pile of Silbury Hill? And is not Stonehenge itself his memorial?

CHAPTER SIX

The Meaning of Stonehenge

IN the preceding chapters I have tried in turn to answer the principal questions which every inquirer will ask about Stonehenge. *What* is it? *When* was it built? *How* was it done? *Who* did it? This chapter is concerned with the final question: *Why?* Why was anything built at Stonehenge at all? Why, once built, was it rebuilt no less than four times? Why were the various structures built in these particular ways? What does it all *mean*? To all these questions beginning 'Why?' there is one short, simple and perfectly correct answer: We do not know, and we shall probably never know.

The percipient reader will have observed that the answers given in the earlier chapters contain an increasing proportion of hypothesis to fact. This is merely an illustration of an inherent characteristic of archaeology, namely that it can answer only certain kinds of questions. As my friend Professor Christopher Hawkes has put it, there are four main kinds of archaeological evidence: technological evidence, economic evidence, evidence for social and political structure, and evidence for those non-material aspects of life subsumed under the term 'religion'. These four types of evidence are here arranged in decreasing order of reliability. On technological questions, of how objects were made or structures built, the evidence is good. These things are largely matters of fact, in the ordinary sense of that phrase. Again, we can learn a good deal about economic facts, of how communities obtained their livelihood, to what extent they engaged in trade and with whom, and even something of the lines on which such trade was organized; though even here there are many conclusions which remain strictly hypothetical. When it comes to questions of social organization and political power, the archaeologist is on very shaky ground, as the reader of the last chapter will have realized; and even though he may feel justified in stating certain tentative conclusions, he cannot pretend that they are much better than reasonable guesses. When finally he comes to matters of faith and religion, he is usually inclined to take refuge altogether in silence, on the ground that archaeology can deal only with the results of human actions, not with human motives.

This attitude is natural enough. One has only to think how difficult would be the task of future archaeologists if they had to reconstruct the ritual, dogma, and doctrine of the Christian Churches from the ruins of the church buildings alone, *without the aid of any written record or inscription*.

We thus have the paradoxical situation that archaeology, the only method of investigating man's past in the absence of written records, becomes increasingly less effective as a means of inquiry the more nearly it approaches those aspects of human life which are the more specifically *human*. It is a perfect case of the higher, the fewer.

This paradox is known only too well by archaeologists themselves, but is not generally appreciated or understood outside professional archaeological circles. The ordinary visitor to Stonehenge, for instance, is at least as much interested to know what the place was for, as to learn how and when and by whom it was built; and rightly so. So that when he is told that we just do not know, his reaction is one of disappointment not untinged with disbelief.

I do not myself believe that the archaeologist who offers his wares to the public has any right to take refuge in a smug nescience, by an appeal to the strict canons of archaeological evidence, when faced with perfectly legitimate questions of this kind. Nevertheless the plain fact of the matter is that on such points there can be no certainty, or even any very high degree of probability, as long as written evidence is lacking. If, then, the archaeologist is willing to leave the dry land of fact and set out upon the uncharted sea of conjecture, in an attempt to find answers for questions of this sort, he must first make it quite clear what he is doing. In what follows, therefore, it must be understood that I am indulging in speculation upon subjects about which there is no possibility of greater certainty.

The one thing about Stonehenge upon which everyone is

agreed is that it is primarily a 'temple', a structure in which it was possible for man to establish contact and communication with extra-mundane forces or beings. This much we may take for granted. Yet we must beware of imposing upon prehistoric life the division into sacred and profane activities which is a commonplace in much of the modern world. In 'primitive' communities this antithesis is meaningless. Every act, every object, every building is invested with significance beyond its superficial content and appearance, and everywhere the unseen is coterminous and coexistent with the seen. Whatever it was for, we can be quite sure that Stonehenge was not a place to be attended on Sundays, soberly dressed, and left echoing and empty for the rest of the week. Indeed it may well have been used for many activities which today have no overt connection with religious belief or practice, such as political councils and the dispensing of justice; or even for more frankly secular purposes like the holding of markets.

These, however, are activities which are unlikely to have left any tangible traces. If we are to learn anything from the physical remains of the monument itself, it is concerning the religious practices and beliefs of which it was the scene and the expression.

Stonehenge I

The main structural features of the earliest monument are the ditch and bank, the ring of Aubrey Holes, the Heel Stone and the wooden structure, perhaps a triple gateway, which stood close to it.

The symbolic as well as the physical function of the earthwork is surely that of a barrier, a boundary between the sacred and the secular, or the initiated and the profane. This implies that whatever rituals or ceremonies took place inside the earthwork, they demanded for their performance a particular location, in which alone communication could be established with the unseen powers. It implies also that the function of the earthwork was not merely to *exclude* but also to *enclose*. It is thus not only possible, but even probable, that there existed in the centre of the site some timber building, a *sanctum sanctorum* in which resided the numinous principle of the place, either as a disembodied presence or represented by some tangible object of worship and veneration. Admittedly there is no archaeological evidence for such a structure. But the area in which it is most likely to have stood, the very centre of the site, has not so far been explored. I for one shall not be surprised if future excavations here do reveal the traces of a former shrine.

Of the rituals and ceremonies performed within the monument we have no evidence, except for the Aubrey Holes. It is now clear that these have no structural function; that is, they were never intended as the emplacements for any kind of upright of wood or stone. They are simply pits; and the same is true of the similar but smaller rings of holes in the analogous monuments mentioned above (p. 156).

Now we know that in classical times the digging of a pit in the ground was an essential part of a ritual designed to open the way to the chthonic deities, the Gods of the Nether World. In Greece such pits had a special name, *bothros*; and the most celebrated account of this ritual in classical literature occurs in the Sixth Book of the Aeneid, where the descent of Aeneas into Hades to consult the spirit of his father Anchises was thus effected. It is well known that the roots of classical religion lie deep in the prehistoric past (indeed the very names of many of the Greek pantheon go back to Mycenaean times in the late second millennium B.C.). It is thus not at all impossible that a ritual of this kind, involving the opening of a symbolic door to the nether world and the pouring into it of propitiatory and prophylactic libations, often the blood of slaughtered beasts, may have existed even as early as 2000 B.C. and even in so remote a place as Britain. Indeed, for what it is worth, more than one of the pits in site XI at Dorchester-on-Thames, one of the lesser analogues of Stonehenge I, showed signs of having been filled with a pool of liquid; though admittedly this *may* have been nothing more exciting or significant than rain-water.

Here then is a possible explanation for the Aubrey Holes. If it is the right one (and remember that it may just as well be wrong), it implies that this particular Secondary Neolithic community conceived of a *nether* world of spirits, and that in turning to their gods they looked not skywards but into the deep and dark recesses of the earth.

The occurrence in so many of the Aubrey Holes of cremated burials must not be taken as evidence that their purpose was primarily sepulchral, for in many cases the burned bones were deposited only *after* the holes had been dug and refilled. Their presence shows no more than that the holes were sacred, and a fit resting place of the dead. They may also be a sign of the belief that the spirits of the dead were not entirely released from attachment to their physical bodies by the purifying action of the funeral pyre, and that thus placed they could still act as mediators between the light and living world above and the shadowy other world below.

There is one question, raised by the presence of these burials associated with a ritual structure, which must be considered, namely the possibility that they represent human sacrifices. This is a notion to which archaeologists are seldom, perhaps too seldom, willing to accord serious respect and objective consideration, principally because in the public mind it forms so prominent an element in that uncritically romantic approach to the past which is the antithesis of scholarly research. Moreover Stonehenge itself is the very last context in which it would be felt proper to consider this suggestion, precisely because human sacrifice is so firmly established among the popular Druidical fantasies in which today the monument is enwrapped.

There is, of course, no warrant at all for supposing that the Druids had anything to do with Stonehenge. None the less it is a fact recorded historically that Druidism did involve this abhorrent practice. Though the historical records of Druidism go back only a few centuries B.C., it is probable that the roots of this barbarian Celtic religion lie no less deep in the past than those of contemporary classical religions. There is thus no reason to suppose that human sacrifice did *not* occur, occasionally at least, among the Secondary Neolithic communities of Britain. Indeed, there is evidence that it did occur; for the infant with its cleft skull buried at the centre of the neighbouring sanctuary of Woodhenge can hardly be interpreted in any other way. Thus, although personally I incline to the view that the burials in the Aubrey Holes represent natural deaths, the possibility that they were sacrifices performed as part of some propitiatory ritual cannot by any means be ruled out.

Of the remaining structures, the Heel Stone and the wooden 'gateway' near it, there is little to be said. Single standing stones are a common form of prehistoric antiquity, but their significance is entirely unknown. The 'gateway', however, if that is what it was, implies by its position some distance from the entrance of the earthwork that, even in this earliest stage, the monument had to be approached on an axial line, an obligation more concretely expressed by the Avenue in the succeeding phase. It is doubtful, however, whether the direction of the approach had any particular significance, for the plans of other henge monuments of the same class exhibit no uniformity in the orientation of their entrances.

Stonehenge II

The new monument consisted of a double circle of Pembrokeshire bluestones at the centre of the earlier earthwork, and of the Avenue linking the entrance with the River Avon. It is difficult even to guess how far this new structure represents any radical change of belief and practice. We have already seen that in the earliest phase it may be supposed that the direction of communication with the other world was downwards. Among the Beaker peoples, on the other hand, there are reasons, equally slight, for believing that to establish such contact the worshipper looked skywards. For in the henge monuments of the second class, associated with the Necked-Beaker culture in particular, there is a consistent tendency towards uniformity in the orientation of the entrances. Though the significance of the preferred direction (north-north-west to south-south-east) is unknown, the existence of this uniformity must surely be related to observations of the rising and setting of heavenly bodies; for in the absence of maps or the compass, this is the only means of obtaining consistent lines of direction. Among the Bell-Beaker people too the occurrence of circular gold discs ornamented with a central cross, plausibly interpreted as sun-symbols, may point in the same skyward direction.

In Stonehenge II there is indeed specific evidence that the sun played some part, and perhaps the central one, in the beliefs of the builders. For the orientation of the entrance of the circle, itself unequivocally marked by additional stones, towards the midsummer sunrise can hardly be accidental, and seems to show that in this respect at least the new monument represents a new orientation of religious belief.

Of the actual significance of the stone circle itself we know nothing. Were the stones merely a ritual fence, like the earthwork of the earlier phase, but symbolically rather than physically effective? Or were they, like the monoliths still erected today by the hill tribes of Assam, the resting places of the spirits of departed ancestors? Did they perhaps form the fixed framework of some mobile and sinuous pattern of communal dance, like the circles of wooden posts reported by early settlers to have been so used by the Indians of Virginia? Here surely we have one possible answer to the kind of ritual performed in these circles. For there is physical evidence, in the form of buried surfaces compacted by the rhythmic pounding of feet, for the part played by dances in the burial-ritual of certain round barrows; and it is perhaps significant that in surviving folk-lore there attaches to so many stone circles the legend that they are really dancers, frozen into petrified immobility for thus impiously disporting themselves upon the Sabbath.

At Avebury it has long been observed that in the avenue and in the great circle the shapes of the stones are predominantly of two kinds, a tall pillar and a broad lozenge. It has been suggested that these two forms are symbolic of male and female, and that their deliberate selection and alternative arrangement point to the existence of some kind of fertility cult. The suggestion is appropriate enough for a community of pastoralists, whose livelihood and prosperity depended upon the ability of their flocks and herds regularly to increase and multiply.

It seems possible that the same shapes of stones may have had some symbolic significance also in Stonehenge II. Certainly among the undressed bluestones in the circle there are both tall pillars and broader flatter stones, both of entirely natural form but possibly selected deliberately. Moreover it is perhaps significant that the two bluestones now flanking the entrance (31 and 49) each represent one of these two contrasted shapes. It must be admitted, however, that to judge from the few sockets of the double circle (Q and R Holes) so far excavated, the two shapes did not alternate regularly, and there appears to have been a preponderance of the pillar form.

Of all the aspects of Stonehenge II by far the most remarkable is the fact of the transport of its stones from Pembrokeshire. What can have been the motives which prompted this extraordinary undertaking, for which there is no parallel in European prehistory, apart from the transport of the Stonehenge sarsens themselves? To an earlier generation of antiquaries the bluestones represented a monument which had already stood in Wales, and had been dismantled, transported, and re-erected at Stonehenge in its entirety. In support of this thesis they claimed that there was a great concentration of stone circles and other megalithic constructions in the immediate vicinity of Prescelly, which marked the area as one of the chief religious centres of Britain. The translation of the stones was explained, if it was explained at all, as the result of a shift to Wessex of the seat of ecclesiastical power, an event for which, incidentally, the bluestones themselves were the only evidence.

Quite apart, however, from the manifest absurdity of this circular argument, more rigorous field-work by a later generation of archaeologists, and in particular by Professor W. F. Grimes, F.S.A., has shown this great concentration of megalithic monuments to be a myth. Certainly some sites have survived scrutiny; but they are too few to justify the view that here was once a great religious centre.

None the less, I am myself convinced that to the Beaker people who opened up the trade-route to Ireland along the south coast of Wales the mountain of Prescelly had a very

special significance – that it was, in fact, a sacred mountain.*
A glance at the map shows that Prescelly Top, 1,760 ft above
sea-level, is the highest point anywhere in the south-western
peninsula of Wales, and dominates the landscape for miles
around. On a clear day it can even be seen on the far horizon
from the hills above Aberystwyth, fifty miles away to the
north. To the traveller humping his pack along the ridgeways
of south Pembrokeshire on the last stages of the land-route to
the West, its cloud-wrapped summit must have seemed no
less the home of gods than did Mount Ida to a voyager in the
Cretan plain; and to the trader returning across the sea from
Ireland, shielding his eyes from the spray as he peered across
the bows of his laden boat, the same summit would be the
first welcome sign of land ahead.

I believe, therefore, that the awe-inspiring character of
Prescelly Mountain is alone sufficient to account for the special
significance of the rocks which crop out along its crest. But
there is another way in which a special demand for these rocks
may have been created in Wessex. Among the stone battle-
axes used by Necked-Beaker warriors there are a few made of
preselite, that is, the spotted dolerite of Prescelly. Admittedly
they are very few; but one must remember that for every object now in a museum many more must originally have been
in circulation. It must be realized, too, that weapons, and axes
in particular, had a significance in prehistoric times beyond
that of mere efficacy or utility. Like Excalibur, they possessed
symbolic and magical qualities, qualities that might well be
transmitted to the material of which they were made. May it
not be, then, that the particular virtues of this Prescelly rock
became celebrated in Wessex through the medium of these
weapons of prestige, and that when the time came to build at
Stonehenge a monument of especial significance and sanctity,
it was this rock, from the cloud-capped crest of the sacred
mountain far to the west, that was chosen in preference to all
others?

*I am encouraged in this view, formed as the result of two spells of
field-work in Pembrokeshire, by finding that it is shared by Sir Cyril Fox,
the foremost living authority on Welsh prehistory.

Stonehenge III

There is no need to labour the point that the sarsen structure of Stonehenge III is unique. As such, it is all the more hopeless to try to interpret it in terms of belief and ritual. It need not be supposed, however, that the suppression of the bluestone circle of period II and its replacement by the sarsens *necessarily* implies a fundamental change of faith, any more than the rebuilding of a medieval church on a larger scale involved more than a reconstruction to the greater glory of God. The new structure preserved the circular pattern of the old, and perpetuated the former alignment on the midsummer sunrise. This in itself shows that there must have been some continuity from the earlier to the later phase.

The distinctively novel features are in the *elevation* of the new monument, with the unique use of stone lintels. These, as their joints confirm, must be copies in stone of wooden prototypes. In other words, the sarsen structure must surely be related in some way to the *framework* of a circular wooden building. Now remains of wooden buildings of any kind are scarce enough in second-millennium Britain; and of sites apparently dedicated to a religious purpose only two are known, both in Wiltshire and both of the Secondary Neolithic cultures – Woodhenge and the Sanctuary on Overton Hill near Avebury. Is it not possible, therefore, that the sarsen structure at Stonehenge echoes that fusion of earlier traditions which we have already seen exemplified in the circle-barrows of the Wessex culture? Does it not combine both the stone circle of the Beaker cultures and the framed wooden shrine of the Secondary Neolithic, now no longer roofed but open to the sky? And if for a moment one can accept again the notion of a unifying kingship, by whose fiat the building of the sarsens was achieved, cannot one see in the fusion of two separate traditions of religious architecture a deliberate act of policy?

Let us suppose temporarily that this is the true picture, instead of a mere flight of fancy. How then should the later changes of plan in phases IIIb and IIIc be interpreted? In the first, we have the larger bluestones dressed to shape, like the sarsens, and erected *within* the sarsens in a setting which included two trilithons; while *outside* the sarsen circle preparations were made for setting the remaining bluestones once more in a double circle (in the Y and Z Holes), echoing the pattern of the older Beaker circle. But this latter project was never completed. Instead, the dressed stones were dismantled and all the bluestones, dressed and undressed alike, were re-erected in a new plan which copies the setting of the sarsens. May we not see here the interplay and conflict of two traditions, resolved finally by the adoption once more of a neutral plan? And may this not be the very first recorded example of the typically British art of compromise?

It is easy, and indeed fascinating, to erect an inverted pyramid of hypothesis of this kind upon an entirely insufficient foundation of fact, and I make no pretence that these speculations are anything but the purest fancy. Nevertheless I rehearse them quite unrepentantly, for it seems to me that this is the *kind* of information that archaeology should seek to collect, if only the evidence is available. Even fifty years ago, most modern archaeological doctrine would have been unthinkable, and archaeologists would have protested that the nature of the evidence was such that it could not permit such interpretations as are now drawn from it. The change is not due to the development of scientific techniques of research, but simply to the growth of ideas about what archaeology is *for*. The wildest fancies of today may thus well become the commonplace orthodoxies of tomorrow.

The Carvings

The Stonehenge carvings are among the most surprising and intriguing aspects of the monument, and certainly not the easiest to interpret. The axes and dagger may, of course, be nothing more than symbolic offerings, substitute simulacra of the weapons themselves, which could not be fixed to the stones. On the other hand there is evidence from more than one part of Europe for the existence of definite axe-cults during the second millennium B.C. In Minoan Crete the symbol of the bronze double-axe, the *labrys*, occurs everywhere, and even gave its name to the royal palace at Knossos, the House of the Axes or Labyrinth. In the megalithic tombs of Brittany, too, and in chalk-cut burial chambers in the valley of the Marne there are carved representations of stone axes on the walls. Even in Britain carvings of bronze axe-heads, similar to the Stonehenge examples but cruder in execution, occur in two burial-cists in Argyll and on a stone slab in a Wessex culture round barrow in Dorset. It may be, therefore, that the Stonehenge carvings are not mere substitutes for real weapons, but rather the symbols of a cult, just as the cross is such a symbol today.

The symbol on stone 57 (p. 44) is of particular interest. In so far as its weathered and abraded state allows interpretation, it seems to be a version of a symbol which occurs on many standing stones, and occasionally in chambered tombs, in Brittany. Its appearance at Stonehenge provides one more link between Wessex and the Breton peninsula in the middle of the second millennium B.C. For it is clear that there too a warrior-aristocracy was engaged in the European metal trade, and the occurrence in their graves of daggers with hilts richly decorated in gold, in characteristically British style, suggests that the Breton culture may itself be an offshoot from Wessex.

The religious implications of this symbol are even more important. For it seems probable that this, and other variants, are degenerate versions of a representation of a mother-goddess, whose cult is intimately associated with the Western family of neolithic cultures as a whole, but has no place in the skyward-looking eastern cultures of which the builders of Stonehenge III were the heirs in Britain. We have here one more piece of evidence for the fusion of diverse religious traditions in the final and greatest period of building at Stonehenge.

The Druids

There remains the question of the Druids and Stonehenge. In popular belief the two are inseparable, and I have no illusions that anything I may say, however forcibly, will do much to break the connection.

Nevertheless, let it be said once more that there is *no* evidence for connecting the Druids with Stonehenge in any way whatsoever. This is not to say, of course, that the Druids never existed. Far from it; for they are described by Julius Caesar and other classical writers, from whom we know that they were a Celtic priesthood flourishing in Gaul and particularly in Britain. The earliest mention of them dates from about 200 B.C. But it is reasonable to suppose that Druidism had already by then been in existence for some time, for it is only an established and influential religion that is likely to have come to the notice of classical writers, who were not after all particularly interested in the manners and customs of barbarians. On the other hand, the society in which Druidism flourished, the La Tène cultures of western Europe, only came into being after 500 B.C., and in Britain not until two centuries later. By this time Stonehenge had been built for more than a thousand years, and may already have been a ruin. Even if the monument was still venerated, there is no reason for the Druids to have taken any interest in it, since their places of worship and observance were 'groves', that is, clearings in the forest. There is no mention in classical accounts of any kind of artificially constructed temple.

Admittedly, if it could be shown (which it cannot) that Stonehenge had definitely been destroyed by the Romans, this in itself would be good evidence for a genuine Druidical association with the monument. For the almost universal policy of Rome towards the religions of conquered peoples was to foster and modify them towards ultimate absorption in the Roman pantheon. Almost alone among such religions, Druidism was stamped out with unrelenting ferocity, probably because it included the practice of human sacrifice, abhorrent to the Roman mind. (The more cynical observer will reflect that the extermination of the Druids, potentially the core of a troublesome resistance-movement, must materially have eased the path of conquest.) Had there been any Druidical connection with Stonehenge, the monument might well have been destroyed as part of this deliberate campaign. Unfortunately, however, the evidence for a Roman destruction is at least equivocal.

The association of the Druids with Stonehenge, now so firmly established in popular imagination, is really of quite recent growth, and its origins lie no further back than the seventeenth century, when John Aubrey first suggested that Stonehenge and other stone circles might be Druidical temples, a suggestion which in the existing state of archaeological knowledge was perfectly reasonable. This notion was taken up and expanded enthusiastically in the eighteenth century by William Stukeley, and popularized in the many guide-books and other works, often based upon his book, which appeared during the following hundred years. Its continuing popularity is doubtless due to its romantic appeal, and not least, I believe, to the fascination exercised on the public mind by the idea of human sacrifice, to which the columns of the popular Sunday press bear eloquent witness.

What then is the real significance of Stonehenge, not as a mere structure, or as evidence for archaeological chronology, or as a technological achievement, but as a document of British history? For me, at least, it represents in epitome the growth and flowering of our earliest British communities, of whom we today are still in part the descendants and heirs. It stands as a symbol, as St Paul's Cathedral may stand for a later age, of the first incorporation of Britain, however transitory, within the orbit of the Mediterranean world, the cradle of European civilization. And, in spite of its relative crudities, it so far transcends all other European monuments of its age that it can justly be counted among the highest achievements of the human spirit in the prehistoric past.

CHAPTER SEVEN

Stonehenge and the History of Antiquarian Thought

THE recent work at Stonehenge, whose results are described and interpreted in detail for the first time in this book, is merely the latest manifestation of a persistent spirit of inquiry whose origins can be traced back to the seventeenth century and even beyond. It is perhaps fitting, therefore, to conclude this account of the most recent views on the history and significance of the monument by some consideration of their antecedents, the more particularly since the history of speculation and research on the problems of Stonehenge serves well to illustrate, in miniature, the history of antiquarian thought in Britain, and the development of the attitudes and methods of the modern archaeologist from their earliest beginnings.

The inquirer into the history of Stonehenge cannot be said to lack material. On the contrary, he is faced by a bulk of literature which is positively embarrassing, for no prehistoric monument in Britain, or for that matter in Europe, has been the subject of more speculation and controversy. In 1901 there was published* a bibliography of no fewer that 947 items relating to the great monuments of Stonehenge and Avebury, of which the great majority refer to Stonehenge alone. Though no complete bibliography of works published since that date has been attempted, it is safe to say that they run into many hundreds of items.†

Much in this huge mass of literature is ephemeral, much

* *Wiltshire Archaeological Magazine*, XXXII (1901), 1–169. The reader is referred to this work for bibliographical details of the books published up to this date which are mentioned in this chapter.

†I cannot pretend to have read more than a tithe of this voluminous literature. In writing this chapter I have relied largely and gratefully upon a comprehensive recension of the literature of Stonehenge compiled in manuscript by the late Harold Peake, F.S.A., and now in the possession of Professor Stuart Piggott. It was evidently intended to appear in the form of a novel, in which were to be recounted the researches of an 'ingeniose

again purely repetitive; and a high proportion is the product of that lunatic fringe of archaeology to which Stonehenge has always acted, and still acts, as an irresistible magnet. But, though the process is exceedingly laborious, a handful at least of fertile grain can be winnowed from this vast deal of chaff, and it is this residue of description, inference, and conjecture that forms the necessary background for the most recent research. It falls naturally into three periods. The first ends with the inception of specifically antiquarian studies around A.D. 1600. The second comprises the seventeenth, eighteenth, and nineteenth centuries, in which such studies grew apace, though still unsupported by research in the field. The third period begins with the earliest deliberate excavations at Stonehenge in 1901.

The Period of Legend

In view of the relative paucity of classical accounts of Britain, it is hardly surprising that no certain mention is made of Stonehenge by any ancient author, even though it must surely have been regarded as one of the wonders of the world, had it been known to them. A passage from a lost *History of the Hyperboreans*, ascribed to Hecateus of Abdera (*c.* 300 B.C.) and quoted by Diodorus Siculus in his *History* (book V), has sometimes been taken to refer to Stonehenge, though without sufficient justification. 'Hecateus and some others', says Diodorus, 'tell us that over against the land of the Celts there is in the Ocean an island not smaller than Sicily, situated under the constellation of the Bear, which is inhabited by the Hyperboreans ... The inhabitants honour Apollo more than any other deity. A sacred enclosure is dedicated to him in the island, as well as a magnificent circular temple adorned with many rich offerings ...' The recent discovery of the carvings of weapons at Stonehenge, which may be votive representations, makes it tempting to see in them a confirmation of the 'magnificent circular temple' of Apollo. But the temptation

---

young man', Sidney Gadge, at the behest of a wealthy patron. Had it ever been published, it would have been a most notable addition to the long catalogue of bizarre works upon Stonehenge.

must be resisted; for it is not even certain, though admittedly probable, that the island of the Hyperboreans was in fact Britain.

The first specific mention of Stonehenge by name in English literature occurs in the *Historia Anglorum* of Henry of Huntingdon, written about A.D. 1130. In describing the four wonders of Britain, he says 'The second is at Stonehenge, where stones of an amazing size are set up in the manner of doorways, so that one door seems to be set upon another. Nor can anyone guess by what means so many stones were raised so high, or why they were built there.'

A few years later, about 1136, another chronicler, Geoffrey of Monmouth, gave a less factual but intrinsically far more interesting description of Stonehenge, which was to serve as the model for all future accounts for centuries to come. The story he tells is briefly as follows. Aurelius Ambrosius, King of the Britons, wishing to commemorate the nobles treacherously slain by Hengist the Saxon and buried in the convent at Ambresbury (the modern Amesbury), summoned Merlin the prophet, a man of the greatest genius in the prediction of future events and in the making of mechanical contrivances, to consult him on the proper monument to be erected to the memory of the dead. Merlin replied, 'If you wish to honour the grave of these men with an everlasting monument, send for the Giant's Dance which is in Killaraus (perhaps Kildare), a mountain in Ireland. For there is a stone structure, which no one today could raise without a profound knowledge of the mechanical arts. They are stones of a vast size and wonderful quality, and if they can be brought here they will stand for ever.'

Accordingly an expeditionary force was sent to Ireland which, having defeated the Irish in battle, proceeded to the mountain of Killaraus. There, however, all their efforts failed to dislodge the stones of the monument, until Merlin, having prepared his own engines, dismantled them with incredible facility, and having carried them by sea to Britain, re-erected them in the same form at Stonehenge, thereby giving a manifest proof of the superiority of art over brute force.

This pleasing tale shows clearly enough the awe and wonder inspired by the engineering achievement of Stonehenge in the Middle Ages. But it also contains a most surprising suggestion of the persistence right up to the twelfth century A.D. of a genuine folk-memory of the actual building of Stonehenge (that is, Stonehenge II) some twenty-five centuries earlier.

For a long time the story of the transport of the stones of Stonehenge from Ireland was regarded as a mere flight of fancy. But the growing belief that the bluestones came from some locality a long way off, finally identified as Pembrokeshire in 1923, and the high probability that they were carried from there most of the way by water, puts an entirely different complexion on the story. The correspondence between the legend and the fact is so striking that it cannot be dismissed as mere coincidence; for to do so imposes at least as great a strain upon credulity as to suppose that behind this correspondence there lies a genuine memory of recorded events. Professor Stuart Piggott, who has discussed in detail the sources used by Geoffrey of Monmouth,* concludes that we cannot rule out the possibility that he had access to a written or oral tradition, now lost but then still current in Wales, which embodied the story of the carrying of the bluestones from Prescelly to Stonehenge. Among the many extraordinary hypotheses concerning Stonehenge this is by no means the least credible. For the story of the carriage of so many stones over so great a distance would be one worthy of note and remembrance even in the Middle Ages, and still more so among the illiterate societies of prehistoric times, in which the oral transmission of tales of legendary and heroic feats was a commonplace.

However this may be, in his own day and for many years thereafter Geoffrey's account was accepted and repeated by other chroniclers, with that unquestioning credence of the written word so characteristic of the medieval mind, and so foreign to our own more rational, or more cynical, habits of thought. Not until the fifteenth century was there any breath of disbelief, when the anonymous author of the *Chronicle of England* commented pithily upon Geoffrey's account with the

Antiquity, XV (1941), 269-86, 305-19.

words 'Credat Judaeus Apella, non ego'. From then until the beginning of the seventeenth century the Merlin legend, though still quoted, was increasingly regarded as a fairy-story.

During this period from 1130 to 1600, which constitutes the first, and one might say the purely passive, phase in the history of Stonehenge research, only three additions were made to the original account of Geoffrey of Monmouth. The first of these was the suggestion, later to gain wider currency, that the material of the sarsens was an artificial cement.* The second was a variant of Geoffrey's story, in which Merlin fetched the stones not from Ireland but from a point on Salisbury Plain, 'which was both near the site fixed upon, and was also remarkable for the enormous size of its blocks', evidently the first tentative recognition of the true origin of the sarsen stones.† The third was the notion, again to be revived later, that Stonehenge was the work of the Romans.‡

The Period of Record and Speculation

The year 1620 saw the opening of a new and more active period of interest in Stonehenge, which lasted until the first organized excavation only a little more than half a century ago. In or about that year King James I was staying at Wilton House as the guest of the Earl of Pembroke, and being taken by his host to view the neighbouring wonder of Stonehenge was moved to instruct the architect Inigo Jones, 'the Vitruvius of his age', to make a plan of the monument and to furnish some account of its nature and origins. Unfortunately neither Jones's original plan nor his observations were published during his lifetime. It was only in 1655, three years after his death, that his son-in-law John Webb issued a volume entitled *The Most Remarkable Antiquity of Great Britain, vulgarly called Stone-Heng, Restored*, which he stated to have been prepared from 'some few indigested notes' left by Inigo Jones. It is difficult to be sure of the measure of Jones's own con-

* John Rastall, *The Pastyme of People, or The Chronicle of the Realm of England* (1530).

† John Leland, *Commentari de Scriptoribus Britannicis*, ed. Anthony Hall (1707).

‡ Folkersheimer, *Letter to Simler*, Zürich Letters, 2nd series (1845).

tribution to this work, but it would be charitable to suppose that he was not himself responsible for the plan, a piece of highly imaginative reconstruction which it is difficult to reconcile with any objective observation of the site. Though it may be noted that in his own book on Stonehenge Webb expressly states that his father-in-law was the first actually 'to take the measure of any stones of Stonehenge'. If so, the result speaks more for the fertility of his imagination than for his accuracy. The main conclusion, though whether formed by Jones or by Webb we do not know, was that the stones came from the 'quarries at and about Aibury', and that the monument as a whole was a temple of the Tuscan order of architecture erected by the Romans to the god Coelus.

A few years later this view was hotly disputed by Dr Walter Charleton, who published in 1663 a rejoinder entitled *Chorea Gigantum or Stone-Heng Restored to the Danes*, in which he asserted the view, supported by arguments of indifferent cogency, that Stonehenge was 'erected by the Danes ... to be a Court Royal, or place for the inauguration and election of their Kings'. Two years later Webb returned to the attack with his *Vindication of Stone-Heng Restored*.

None of these volumes does anything to advance our knowledge of the monument, and even in their own day seem only to have served to sharpen the edge of acrimony. Nor does either of the later ones contain any fresh plan, both authors being content to rely upon the 'restoration' already published under the name of Inigo Jones. But though today all three make remarkably tedious reading, they do at least illustrate the greatly enhanced interest that by then attached to the site. This interest, at any rate within the academic world, is amusingly displayed in a play, circulated in manuscript and performed in the hall of St John's College, Oxford, entitled *Stonehenge: A Pastoral*, the work of John Speed the son of the historian and cartographer.

At this same time that remarkable man John Aubrey, the discoverer twenty years before of the great circle of Avebury, was turning his attention to Stonehenge, and casting upon it a notably more objective regard than any of his contemporaries. His plan, though only a sketch, is important as the first record of the 'cavities' on the inner edge of the bank, rediscovered only during Colonel Hawley's excavations, which are now known in his honour as the Aubrey Holes. His other great contribution was the suggestion, now made for the first time, that Stonehenge and other stone circles were temples of the Druids. His manuscript, the *Monumenta Britannica*, in which these monuments are described, has never been published in full.* It was evidently known, however, either directly or more probably through a transcript, to the eighteenth-century antiquary William Stukeley, who did so much to popularize the Druids as an essential ingredient of British antiquarian thought. Nevertheless it is ultimately Aubrey who must bear the responsibility for the Druidical associations of Stonehenge which still have so firm, and indeed ineradicable, a hold upon the popular imagination.

During the next three-quarters of a century the literature of Stonehenge continues the controversy concerning its date, purpose, and builders, though it includes only one work wholly devoted to the monument, *A Dissertation on Stonehenge* (1730) by S. Wallis. Virtually the only new contribution made during this period was the suggestion that the uprights and lintels had been erected with the help of inclined planes or ramps of earth, subsequently removed.

In 1740 William Stukeley, the leading antiquarian of his century, published his folio volume *Stonehenge, A Temple Restored to the British Druids*, which was to become the leading source-book for more than a hundred years. The fieldwork which it records had been completed many years before, in 1721–4. Stukeley's description is a great advance on anything which had gone before. His plan, though inaccurate by modern standards and still a 'restoration' rather than a delineation of the monument as it actually was, is the result of many careful measurements, from which he deduced that the unit of measurement used by the builders was a 'Druid cubit', a length of 20.8 in. He was the first observer to record the

---

*The section of the *Templa Druidum*, the first part of the *Monumenta Britannica*, which deals with Stonehenge, was published with two facsimile plans by William Long in *Wiltshire Archaeological Magazine*, XVI (1876). I hope one day to produce a critical edition of the whole manuscript myself.

existence of the Avenue, whose course he traced for a distance of nearly a mile from Stonehenge. Much of the further part of this course was later obliterated by cultivation, and was only rediscovered by the dramatic medium of air-photography some two centuries later. He was also the discoverer of the Stonehenge Cursus, and drew attention to the significance of the barrows clustering round Stonehenge, some of which he excavated. His observations, particularly of the methods of construction employed, compare very favourably with the work of many of his successors a century or more later.

Perhaps the most surprising and unusual aspect of Stukeley's researches at Stonehenge is his attempt to ascertain the date of the monument from the known rate of change in the variation of the magnetic compass, a device which he assumed to have been known to the Druidical builders. His assumptions, and the date which he deduced (about 460 B.C.), are of course entirely false. But his attempt is none the less of the greatest interest, as the first known example of the application of science to the solution of an archaeological problem, and forms a most striking parallel to the attempt made two centuries later by Sir Norman Lockyer to date Stonehenge from the variation in the azimuth of midsummer sunrise.

During the latter half of the eighteenth century Stonehenge became increasingly popular as a resort of the curious, largely owing to the publication of Stukeley's book. This tendency is illustrated by the appearance of a spate of guide-books, many of them published in Salisbury and based, sometimes *verbatim*, upon Stukeley's account; and by the almost invariable inclusion of a description of Stonehenge and its surroundings in the numerous *Tours* and topographical surveys published during this period. Interest was still further stimulated by the sudden and dramatic fall of the fourth trilithon on 3 January 1797. In most of these accounts the Druidical associations so fervently canvassed by Stukeley were accepted without question. But one writer at least, James Douglas, the author of the *Nenia Britannica* (1793), asserted roundly that Stonehenge 'was erected long before the time of the Druids, but it may have continued in use as a place of convocation even to Anglo-Saxon times'.

The next landmark in the progress of Stonehenge researches was the publication in 1812 of the first volume of Sir Richard Colt Hoare's *Ancient Wiltshire*. This contains one of the first tolerably accurate plans of the monument in its contemporary state and not as a 'restoration'. It also includes a survey of the Avenue, of which the major part already recorded by Stukeley was evidently still visible, and of the Lesser Cursus, now identified for the first time. Though Colt Hoare did no digging at Stonehenge itself, he was indefatigable in excavating the surrounding barrows, and it is largely upon the results of his depredations that our present knowledge of the archaeology of the Stonehenge region is based. In the course of this work he confirmed an observation already made by Stukeley, that fragments of the stones occurred in some of the surrounding barrows, thus demonstrating that the monument must have already been erected when some of the barrows were built.

During the succeeding years of the nineteenth century the flow of new guide-books, and of articles in popular journals, continued unabated. Many of them contain absurd and wholly fanciful statements, as for instance that the ruination of Stonehenge was due to the Deluge, the greater dilapidation of the south-western side showing the direction from which the monument was overwhelmed. But there were also many serious contributions. In particular, the growth of geological knowledge focused attention upon the petrology of the stones. A number of articles appeared on the nature and origin of the sarsen stones, and the identity of the Stonehenge sarsens with those of the Marlborough Downs came to be generally admitted. At the same time the foreign nature of the bluestones was recognized, and the conjecture advanced that the bluestone structure was of a different date from the sarsens.[*]

Practical interest in the stones was not confined, however, to the learned world, for the general public, now visiting Stonehenge in ever-increasing numbers, was evidently loath to leave the site without detaching a fragment or two as a souvenir. Of course, this sort of destruction was nothing new. Already in the middle of the previous century one of the

[*] *Gentleman's Magazine*, new series II (1865), 307–18.

earlier anonymous guide-books laments 'the unaccountable Folly of Mankind in breaking pieces off with great Hammers', a practice ascribed to the belief that the stones were factitious and were possessed of unusual powers of healing. A century later this belief can hardly still have served as an excuse for vandalism, but the desire for souvenirs was evidently at least as compelling, and it was the common practice of visitors to furnish themselves in Amesbury with a hammer, hired out for the express purpose of detaching fragments of the stones as keepsakes.

The cumulative effect of this petty destruction, coupled with the growing realization among the educated public of the corporate responsibility of the nation for the safety of its antiquities, led to an outcry in the local and national press, beginning about 1870 and continuing in increasing volume to the end of the century. A number of well-meaning attempts were made by archaeological societies and by individuals to persuade the owner of Stonehenge to safeguard the monument by fencing it in, but all of them were abortive, chiefly for lack of agreement on the measures to be adopted and because of the opposition of a section of the public, principally the local residents, to the idea of hindering access to the site, which even though still in private possession was now regarded as a national monument. The only positive result of this agitation was the scaffolding of certain of the stones which were leaning dangerously, a wise proceeding which stimulated a further public demand for the restoration of the site. At the same time there was a growing feeling that it was improper for our leading monument of antiquity to remain in private hands, and a number of approaches were made to the owner to sell Stonehenge to the nation. In 1899 Sir Edmund Antrobus, who had just succeeded to the estate, did in fact offer to sell Stonehenge and 1,300 acres of the surrounding land for £125,000, an offer which was not accepted and, perhaps not surprisingly, raised a storm of indignant protest.

Matters were finally brought to a head by the sudden and unexpected fall, on the last evening of the nineteenth century, of one of the uprights of the sarsen circle and the lintel which it had hitherto supported (stones 22 and 122). This raised the agitation for preservation and restoration to a new pitch, and after much negotiation the owner accepted a number of re-commendations for action put forward by a committee of experts convened to advise him. As a result the site was fenced in during May 1901, an action which though sensible and long overdue aroused a storm of protest which it is difficult to understand today; it was even proposed by the objectors to test the legality of this proceeding by a law-suit.

Early in September of the same year work was started on the raising of the leaning upright of the great trilithon (stone 56), which had already slipped before the middle of the sixteenth century, and was gradually slipping further, being supported by the bluestone pillar (stone 68) in front of it. This work, conducted by Professor William Gowland and brought to a successful conclusion in October, marks the beginning of the third phase of research at Stonehenge, in which speculation gave way to active exploration of the site itself.

The latter half of the nineteenth century saw the production of an immense volume of literature on Stonehenge, for the most part consisting of sterile and repetitive controversy concerning its date and the identity of its builders. The candidates for this honour range from the 'little folk' – the supposed builders of megalithic tombs – through the Celts, Phoenicians, Belgae, and Romans to the Anglo-Saxons and even the inhabitants of Atlantis. But some of the antiquaries of the day, at least, realized that little was to be gained merely from the mulling over of the statements and theories of previous writers, and that the fog of conjecture could be dispersed only by practical research on the site itself. Several proposals were made for excavations, in conjunction with the re-erection of the trilithon which had fallen in 1797, but perhaps happily none of them came to fruition.

Meanwhile in 1880 Flinders Petrie, whose early contributions to British prehistory have been entirely overshadowed by his career as an Egyptologist, then still all before him, laid the foundation of all future research at Stonehenge by the publication of his monograph *Stonehenge: Plans, Descriptions and Theories*. This contains the most accurate plan of Stonehenge ever likely to be made (unfortunately reproduced at a scale which compels the use of a powerful magnifier if measurements are to be scaled off with the full precision of which the plan is capable), and a concise statement of the evidence, as it then existed, for the date of the site and the sequence of its construction. Petrie also introduced his own system of numbering the stones, which has since been universally adopted.

The Period of Modern Research

Petrie's admirably factual approach may well have influenced Professor Gowland in his presentation of the results of his excavations carried out in 1901.* His report is extremely clear and succinct, and shows commendable caution in drawing conclusions from what was admittedly scanty and uncertain evidence, in marked contrast to the untrammelled speculations of many contemporary writers on Stonehenge. It also forms a landmark, incidentally, in the history of archaeological method, in that it contains the earliest drawn sections from a British site actually to be measured *in situ* from individual cuttings. Sections published by previous workers, including General Pitt-Rivers who is rightly regarded as the father of modern excavation, had always been either purely diagrammatic, or average sections conflating into one a number of separate exposures.

The digging supervised by Professor Gowland was confined to the base and the immediate vicinity of stone 56, and extended only as far as was necessitated by the engineering operation of returning the stone to the vertical. His work threw considerable light on the methods used by the builders for dressing and erecting the stone, but yielded only negative evidence of date. Gowland very cautiously concluded that the stones were probably erected in the late neolithic period, when metal was only just coming into use, to which he assigned a date of around 1800 B.C. However, perhaps because of the lack of any new and striking evidence of the date of the monument, this admirably conducted and presented piece of research created little stir, and was indeed almost entirely ignored by many subsequent writers on Stonehenge.

*Archaeologia, LVIII (1902), 38 ff.

A few months before these excavations began another attempt had been made to date the monument by entirely different means. The orientation of the stones and the Avenue upon the midsummer sunrise has long been recognized, and during the latter part of the nineteenth century a number of suggestions had been made for dating Stonehenge by astronomical means, not all of which were based upon a sufficiently profound knowledge of the technicalities involved. No such charge could be made against Sir Norman Lockyer, who earlier in 1901 made the very precise observations of the direction of the axis which have already been mentioned (p. 94). As we have seen, Lockyer's conclusions will not stand up to a critical examination; not, of course through any error of observation or computation, but because the basic assumptions which he made are archaeologically unsound. None the less his attempt is important as an early example of the application to archaeology of techniques drawn from scientific disciplines, which is one of the characteristic features of modern archaeological research.

During the first two decades of the present century publication and research on Stonehenge showed a marked decline, and apart from some forthright exchanges between Lockyer and his critics, a volume by Mr Edgar Barclay* and a guidebook by Mr Frank Stevens† little of importance was produced. Meanwhile Stonehenge itself was put up for sale by public auction in Salisbury on the death of the proprietor in 1915, and was knocked down for £6,600 to Mr (later Sir Cecil) Chubb, who most generously presented it to the nation in 1918. The formal transfer of the title-deeds to the First Commissioner of Works took place at Stonehenge itself, with speeches from representatives of the Government, the British Museum, the leading national and local archaeological societies, and, appropriately enough, the latter-day Druids.

It may be noted in passing that towards the end of the First World War an aerodrome was constructed immediately southwest of Stonehenge. It is said that the authorities concerned

*Edgar Barclay, *The Ruined Temple, Stonehenge* (1911), a revision and amplification of the same author's *Stonehenge and Its Earthworks* (1895).

†Frank Stevens, *Stonehenge Today and Yesterday* (1916).

demanded, in all seriousness, that the monument should be demolished, as its stones constituted a dangerous hazard to low-flying aircraft.

As soon as the end of the war permitted, arrangements were put in hand for the restoration and stabilization of a number of stones in the outer circle (1, 6, 7, and 30) which were leaning dangerously and had for many years been shored up with unsightly props of steel and timber. The barbed-wire fence was enlarged to its present position, and the trackway which until then had crossed the site close to the stones was diverted to the west. At the same time the Society of Antiquaries was granted facilities for excavation, and Lt-Col. William Hawley was appointed to supervise the work.

The restoration of the leaning stones and the accompanying excavations were started in September 1919, and not unnaturally received considerable publicity. By the end of 1920 the engineering operations were successfully completed, the stones having been slowly returned to the vertical by means of screw-jacks and their bases set firmly in beds of concrete. The archaeological investigation continued, however, until the autumn of 1926.

During this period of seven years rather more than one half of the total area of Stonehenge (to the east and south of the axis) was completely stripped to bedrock, including the filling of the ditch and the wide flat area between the bank and the stones, together with the whole width of the Avenue up to the Heel Stone. For the most part this huge undertaking was accomplished by Colonel Hawley with the help of only one workman, with occasional assistance from small parties of undergraduates from Oxford and Cambridge. For some parts of the work, notably the excavation of the Aubrey and Y and Z Holes and the drawing of sections and perspective sketches, he had the invaluable collaboration of Mr R. S. Newall, F.S.A., whose personal recollections have provided an indispensable link between these and the more recent excavations, and to whom my colleagues and I are indebted for information on many points which never found its way into Colonel Hawley's published reports.

These prolonged researches naturally threw a great deal of

light upon the history of the monument, succinctly summarized by Mr Newall in 1929.* The most striking discoveries were the ring of Aubrey Holes inside the bank, and the Y and Z Holes outside the stones in the centre; while the renewed interest in the petrology of the stones occasioned by these excavations led to the conclusive identification of the source of the bluestones in 1923.

Nevertheless, though it must readily be admitted that Colonel Hawley's excavations did much to advance our knowledge of Stonehenge, it must equally be confessed that seen in retrospect they form one of the more melancholy chapters in the long history of the monument. No one will deny that Colonel Hawley was a most devoted and conscientious excavator. But unfortunately he was obsessed with the danger, or at least the undesirability, of forming any kind of working hypothesis or of framing any specific questions to be answered by excavation.† As a consequence, he continued the mechanical and largely uncritical stripping of the site far beyond the point at which his work ceased to yield significant information. This process, coupled with a regrettable inadequacy in his methods of recording his finds and observations and, one suspects, an insufficient appreciation of the destructive character of excavation *per se*, has left for subsequent excavators a most lamentable legacy of doubt and frustration. For it is now clear that there are a number of problems connected with the history of Stonehenge which it will never be possible to solve by excavation in the future, because the evidence has already been totally destroyed without record of its nature or significance.

It is, of course, only too easy to criticize the shortcomings of one's predecessors, and it is with some misgivings that I make these strictures upon an investigation to which, whatever its failings, all subsequent researchers at Stonehenge must be indebted. But the inadequacy of this earlier work,

---

* *Antiquity*, III (1929), 75–88.
† The late Dr O. G. S. Crawford recently revealed that Colonel Hawley also had a fixed aversion from pottery. Since in general excavators tend only to find what they are looking for, it is probable that a good deal of evidence of this kind may unwittingly have been overlooked.

even measured by the standards of its own day, has long been recognized, and is not the least of the causes contributory to our present state of knowledge, or ignorance, about Stonehenge. The lapse of time may now be considered sufficient to justify the publication of a view which has long been expressed by archaeologists, with even greater vehemence, in private.

The principal results of Colonel Hawley's work are incorporated in the earlier chapters of this book, and need no further elaboration here. Naturally the excavations aroused considerable interest, and led to the revival of a number of earlier theories and controversies. In particular the astronomical theory of dating propounded by Lockyer was enthusiastically supported by Mr E. H. Stone in a number of articles, and finally in his book *The Stones of Stonehenge* published in 1924. In this he gives an admirably full and factual account of the physical details of the monument and the lithology of its stones, and makes a number of ingenious suggestions concerning the methods adopted by the builders to dress and erect them.

The end of the excavations in 1926 saw a gradual diminution in the volume of publication, and during the next twenty years the only work of note wholly devoted to the subject was Colonel R. H. Cunnington's *Stonehenge and Its Date*, which appeared in 1935. This is an admirably concise, practical, and remarkably prescient treatment of the problems of Stonehenge, in which the author anticipated a number of the discoveries made during the recent excavations, particularly in connection with the settings of the bluestones.

With the revival of archaeological research after the end of the war in 1945, attention was once more turned to Stonehenge. It was by then generally agreed that our knowledge of the structure and history of the monument was unsatisfactory, and that further progress could be made only by renewed excavations. Three British archaeologists in particular were anxious to make a renewed attack on the problems of Stonehenge: Professor Stuart Piggott, who already in 1938 had defined the Wessex culture of which the site was recognized to be the leading monument; Dr J. F. S. Stone, who had for long been the leading archaeologist of the district; and my-self, at that time engaged on a detailed study of the British henge monuments, of which Stonehenge is the most notable example.

Accordingly it was agreed with the Society of Antiquaries that the three of us should become jointly responsible for the production of a full and definitive report on Stonehenge, to be published as a Research Report of the Society, and for the direction of a limited programme of fresh excavations, de-signed to elucidate specific points which had been left obscure by previous workers. Permission for this work was readily granted by the Ministry of Works, the custodians of the monu-ment, and by the National Trust.

The first of these excavations took place at Easter 1950, and was confined to two Aubrey Holes (31 and 32). In June and July 1953 the first turning of the Avenue was examined, north-east of Stonehenge, and two Y and Z Holes were excavated (Y16, Z16). It was during this work that the pre-historic carvings were discovered in the course of a photo-graphic survey. In 1954 two sections were cut across the ditch and bank, and a segment of the bluestone circle was excavated on the east side of the site, yielding the first evi-dence for the existence of the double bluestone circle of Stonehenge II, though this, or something like it, had already been suspected as a result of the previous season's work.

As a result of this work, combined with a consequent re-interpretation of the evidence collected by Colonel Hawley, it is now possible to obtain a fairly coherent picture of at least the main outlines of the history of Stonehenge and the sequence of its construction, a picture which has been pre-sented in the earlier chapters of this book. No one, least of all myself, will pretend that this picture is complete, and it may well be modified, at any rate in detail, by further excavation.

The Development of Archaeological Thought

The history of public interest and inquiry concerning Stone-henge deserves some consideration by anyone who professes a more than casual interest in the monument, if only because it provides the historical background for the most recent views and researches, against which they can be seen not as revolutionary and immutable conclusions but merely as the latest products of a long process of search and interpretation, and no less liable to subsequent change and falsification than their antecedents. But apart from this, the history of research at Stonehenge may also serve, as it were, as a diminishing mirror in which is reflected in miniature the whole current of British antiquarian thought and archaeological method, from the Middle Ages to the present day.

The attitude of the Middle Ages to the remains of pre-historic and classical antiquity is something which it is very difficult to comprehend today, without a profound study of the habits of thought revealed (and to the layman only too often concealed) by medieval literature. Whatever we may think today of Geoffrey of Monmouth's account of Stone-henge, we must not forget that in his own day it was regarded as authoritative, and indeed unquestionable. To dismiss it as a mere fairy-story is to fall into the error of applying our own standards of appraisal to a universe of discourse in which they have no relevance whatever. We ourselves are so habitu-ated to the notions of temporal sequence, of technological progress, and of the possibility (and desirability) of recon-structing the past from its surviving remains in the present, that we can only too easily forget that such notions have not always been commonplaces. Indeed, probably the only reason why Stonehenge, almost alone among British prehistoric monuments, achieved notice in the Middle Ages is its mani-festly man-made character. Other more rugged but not less grandiose structures, such as Avebury, were then almost cer-tainly regarded not as the work of man at all, but as the capricious products of nature itself; and as such, they neither attracted particular notice nor required comment.

The rising tide of the renaissance of learning was at first slow to demolish this passive and indeed largely negative atti-tude towards the remains of antiquity. But by the time it reached its full flood in the dawn of the seventeenth century, it had swept away the medieval notions of the past, and had replaced them with a concept of history and of historical inquiry which is at least readily comprehensible to us today, even if we regard it as curiously restricted.

One of the chief characteristics of the renaissance was the achievement of a historical perspective, the realization that while the present slides imperceptibly into the recent past, survivals from a past much more remote stand around us and accompany us into the future as mute witnesses of our origins. To this extent the past was knowable, and its surviving remains were accordingly a fit subject for record and conjecture. This belief is reflected in the growing volume of topographical and archaeological works which appeared in the seventeenth and eighteenth centuries, in which prehistoric antiquities in general, and Stonehenge in particular, occupied a position of increasing importance.

Nevertheless the contemporary notions of the limitations of historical evidence were, to modern minds, curiously narrow and restricted. Stonehenge and other less spectacular remains were recognized as tangible survivals from the past, but no more. The idea that they were themselves potential documents, through the reading of which the dry bones of the past could be clothed in flesh, was still to come. The attitude towards such things, even in the Age of Reason, is nowhere better illustrated than by the opinion of one of its most characteristic figures, Dr Samuel Johnson, that 'all that is really known of the ancient state of Britain is contained in a few pages. We can know no more than what old writers have told us.' It is this persistent reverence for written authority which accounts for the essential dullness and insipidity, for the modern reader, of the antiquarian publications of the time. For apart from the descriptions and illustrations, which do admittedly provide invaluable evidence for things since obliterated by time or by human vandalism, most of these works resemble nothing so much as an interminable game of cards, in which the opinions and statements of classical and later authors are played one against the other, without hope of conclusion or result.

This purely literary approach to the reconstruction of the past was affected only superficially, if indeed at all, by the beginnings and growth of excavation after 1800. Until the very end of the century excavation remained a means simply of extending the activities of antiquarian collectors. It was consequently practised almost exclusively upon a single class of antiquities, namely barrows, since these alone afforded a consistent expectation of spoil. Other kinds of monument, Stonehenge among them, were ignored, and there was no general realization that the *structure* of ancient sites, no less than the objects found in them, might be made to yield a picture of the remote past no less valuable historically than that given for later periods by documentary sources.

The notion that excavation could be a means of gathering information for the writing of history or prehistory, was introduced in Britain, at least, by General Pitt-Rivers, only in the last two decades of the nineteenth century, and even then was slow to be generally accepted. It is thus hardly surprising (though perhaps fortunate) that no organized excavation took place at Stonehenge until 1901, and that even then it was confined to what was necessary for the erection of the leaning stone.

When excavation did finally begin seriously at Stonehenge in 1919 it was, as we have seen, on a large scale in the tradition of complete stripping originally established by Pitt-Rivers and already conspicuously practised elsewhere, notably at the Glastonbury Lake Village and the Romano-British town of Silchester. Indeed, Stonehenge, no less than these two sites, was dug up 'like potatoes' (a graphic phrase of Sir Mortimer Wheeler's). But whereas at Silchester and Glastonbury the very scale of the work enabled a broad, even if a blurred, picture to be painted of the life of their inhabitants, a result which could not have been obtained by any digging, however meticulous, on a smaller scale, at Stonehenge unfortunately no overall picture emerged.

Such large-scale undertakings are not likely to be repeated in the future, even if anyone could be found to finance them, for in the meantime a notable change has taken place in the archaeologist's concept of the purpose and limitations of excavation. It is now no longer considered sufficient, or even justifiable, to excavate a site in a repetitive and mechanical manner, merely waiting like Mr Micawber for something to turn up. On the contrary, every excavation and every part of one must be planned to answer a limited number of quite definite questions.

This new approach, which we owe largely to the precept and practice of the late Professor R. G. Collingwood, has certainly been justified by its results. And it has the additional advantage that by limiting the scale of excavation it ensures that as much as possible of the site remains intact for the excavators of the future, who may thus check independently the results of their predecessors. For excavation is necessarily destructive not only of the evidence which it reveals but also of other latent evidence, for whose detection the necessary techniques have yet to be developed. This has always been so, though it is only recently that it has begun to trouble the consciences of archaeologists, and is still ignored, let it be confessed, by far too many.

The recent excavations at Stonehenge have been planned and carried out with these principles in mind; and indeed not the least of our difficulties has been to organize them so that sufficient areas are spared for the same questions to be answered by renewed excavations at least once more in the future. To my mind (if I may be forgiven the impropriety of commenting upon work for which I have myself been in part responsible) the contrast between the earlier and the present excavations is extremely instructive, and illustrates most strikingly the value of questioning the evidence specifically. But it must not be forgotten that the recent work could not have been so fruitful, had we not the results of the earlier work, confused and inadequate though they may be, as a foundation on which to build. Moreover, however much we may be convinced of the superiority of modern methods and modern attitudes to those of the past, we can be sure that the archaeologists of the future will not hold us blameless. To hope otherwise would be to deny the possibility of further progress, whether at Stonehenge or elsewhere.

Appendix I

Recent Work on Stonehenge

Since the original edition of this book was published, we have undertaken two further seasons of excavation at Stonehenge. The first took place in the summer of 1956, and was designed to solve a number of outstanding problems, chiefly through the re-excavation of certain areas within the area in which the stones stand, which had already been examined by Colonel Hawley thirty years before. The second campaign, in the spring of 1958, formed an integral part of the programme of restoration so successfully carried out by the Ministry of Works. The results of this new work are described below within the framework of the five phases of construction already established.

Stonehenge I

For this period our recent work has been confined to the cutting of one additional trench on the West side of the Heel Stone, with the purpose of clearing up some uncertainties in Colonel Hawley's account of his digging in the same area.

In 1923 he dug out the filling of part of the ditch which surrounds the stone (p. 30), and in so doing he came upon an extensive disturbance on the west side. This started outside the ditch, and appeared to deepen in the direction of the stone. He interpreted it, tentatively, as the remains of a hole dug, but never used, in order to remove the Heel Stone at some time after its erection.

Our small trench here showed beyond doubt that the disturbance was earlier than the cutting of the Heel Stone's ditch. Since the ditch itself belongs to period II (p. 75), the disturbance must by inference belong to period I, that is, the period of the erection of the Heel Stone, and is thus very probably the ramp used in the setting up of the stone.

Near the bottom of the filling of this disturbance we found

a small fragment of Windmill Hill pottery (pp. 148–51), the
first example of this variety to have been recorded from
Stonehenge. It is worth noting in this connection that the
other Late Neolithic sanctuaries in Britain which form the
best parallels to Stonehenge I (p. 156) have also yielded
pottery of this kind.

One more fact concerning the Heel Stone deserves mention
here. A search in the literature of Stonehenge for the earliest
use of the name 'Friar's Heel' (p. 29n.) has shown that the
legend was first recorded by John Aubrey in his unpublished
manuscript *Monumenta Britannica*, compiled about 1660. He
says quite unequivocally that the legend then attached to
'one of the great stones that lies down, on the west side', on
which was 'a cavity something resembling the print of a man's
foot'. This cannot be the present Heel Stone, which cannot
by any stretch of the imagination be said to lie on the west
side of the monument. It is in fact a clear reference to stone
14, a recumbent stone of the outer circle on the south-west
side of the site, on which just such a natural 'footprint' can
still be seen. A trial fitting suggests that the Friar's right foot
was considerably larger than my own!

This reference in Aubrey's manuscript shows quite clearly
that between 1660, the date when he was writing, and 1771,
the year of the publication of *Choir Gaur; The Grand Orrery of
the Ancient Druids, commonly called Stonehenge* by Dr John Smith,
Inoculator of the Small-Pox, the name Friar's Heel and the
legend associated with it were transferred from stone 14 to
the present Heel Stone. This effectively disposes of any suggestion that the 'Heel' element in the name to is be derived
from the Greek *helios*, the sun.

Stonehenge II

The recent excavations have thrown a great deal more light
on the earliest bluestone structure (pp. 58–61), and in particular have shown that it was never completed.

Our work in 1954 had revealed the presence of the Q and
R Holes, spanning the line of the present bluestone circle
within stones 3, 4, 5, and 6 of the outer circle (fig. 3); and it

was then assumed that the elongated holes found by Colonel
Hawley within stones 47, 48, 49, and 31 were a continuation
of the same series of bluestones in a double setting, and represented additional in-lying stones flanking the axis and marking
the entrance of the circle.

In 1956 the whole of the area here examined by Colonel
Hawley was re-excavated, and it was at once clear that this
tentative interpretation of Hawley's discoveries was basically
correct, though it needed some modification in detail.

On either side of the axis separate in-lying holes had been
dug (fig. 3, R1 and R38), each of which had held three bluestones in line. The impressions of the bases of these stones
could still be seen in the chalk. To the right and left of these
holes, at R2 and R37, there was again a separate additional
hole inside the main circle of 'dumb-bell' trenches; but in this
case neither hole had been finished, and no stone had ever
stood in them.

The reconstruction of the entrance area of the double bluestone circle, shown in fig. 3, thus requires alteration. On
either side of the axis there should be *five* stones in line,
the inner three in a separate hole; and outside these, at R2 and
R37, there should be two stones in the main circle and an
unfinished hole inside them.

These two unfinished holes suggested that Stonehenge II
was never completed before it was dismantled; and this was
amply confirmed by the examination of a further arc of the
circle in 1956 and 1958, running clockwise from stone 15 to a
point midway between stones 42 and 43 (fig. 2). Within this
arc, almost exactly a quarter of the circle, it was clear that
hardly any of the Q and R Holes had been dug. We may thus
conclude that at the time Stonehenge II was dismantled at
least a quarter of its circumference was incomplete. The gap
may well have been even larger, since between stones 43 and
46 there is an unexcavated portion of the circle, in which further Q and R Holes may or may not exist.

The last complete pair of Q and R Holes to be dug lies just
to the west of the axis, some 10 ft inside stone 16 of the outer
circle. Beyond this in a clockwise direction there was only a
single hole, on the line of the remainder of the R Holes, and

this was clearly unfinished. It was filled with clean chalk rubble, tightly rammed; and on the bottom was the discarded antler pick which had been used in its excavation. It looks very much as if the construction of Stonehenge II was abandoned while this hole was actually being dug.

On the axis itself, just to the west of stone 15, the arc of the Q and R Holes was broken by a large circular pit, which probably held a single bluestone of exceptional size. It is naturally tempting to suggest that the present Altar Stone stood here in the earliest bluestone structure, directly opposite the entrance of the double circle. The filling of this pit had been greatly disturbed in modern times; but right at the bottom we were lucky to find a stone axe-head with the cutting edge battered away. This axe has been identified petrologically as the product of one of the Cornish axe-factories which flourished in Late Neolithic times.

The unfinished state of Stonehenge II presents an insoluble problem. All we can say is that it was not necessarily due to a shortage of the required stones, since it is clear that even in its modified form, as known from the most recent excavations, it would if complete have contained about 80 stones; and we know that in the later settings of bluestones (phases IIIb and IIIc) something very close to this number of stones was either envisaged or indeed actually used. It may well be that the erection of Stonehenge II was a slow and gradual process, carried out over a long period; and that it was still unfinished when the decision was taken to re-model the site in the most drastic manner, by the erection of the sarsen stones of period IIIa. If this interpretation is correct, it means that period II at Stonehenge should be brought down to somewhere in the sixteenth century B.C. (which would allow it to be still unfinished around 1500 B.C., the probable date of the erection of the sarsen stones), instead of between 1700 and 1600 B.C., as I originally suggested (p. 101).

Stonehenge IIIa

The excavations of 1958, associated with the re-erection of some of the fallen stones (Plate 2b), have yielded more information about the way in which the sarsens were originally put up.

The stone-holes of the fallen trilithon (stones 57 and 58) were both found to be very shallow. Indeed, it is remarkable that these two stones had not already fallen long before 1797, so insecurely were they rooted in the ground. This shallow depth doubtless accounts for the absence of any well-defined ramp leading down into the holes. In both cases, however, it was clear that the stones had been raised from the outside, that is, from the north-west, or indeed approximately from the positions in which they lay after they fell. In both holes, on the inner side, were traces of the decayed anti-friction stakes which had served to protect the back of the hole from being crushed by the toe of the stone, as it was being raised.

To the west of the fallen trilithon, and partly buried beneath the fallen stone 57, we found an immense sloping ramp, cut in the chalk and filled with tightly-packed chalk rubble, running inwards and downwards directly towards the base of stone 56, the surviving upright of the central trilithon. There can be no doubt that this ramp was used in the erection of stone 56. And for this purpose a ramp would indeed be very necessary, since the bottom of the stone-hole lies about 8 ft below the present ground surface, far deeper than in the case of any of the other sarsen stones of which we have details. The position of this ramp makes it clear that stone 56 was either put up sideways, lying initially on its narrower western edge; or else, if it originally lay flat on its broad face, must have been turned through ninety degrees after it was upright.

Either of these proceedings must have been more than ordinarily hazardous, and we can only assume that there was some very compelling reason for departing from more straightforward methods of erection.

In the outer circle of sarsens the stone-hole of stone 22 was also examined before the stone was re-erected in it. Here too there was clear evidence that the stone had been erected from the outside. But when the adjoining stone 21 was investigated, as a preliminary to straightening it, the back of the hole, set with anti-friction stakes, was found to be on the *outer* side of the circle, and the ramp correspondingly on the *inner* side.

This is the only stone which is so far known to have been raised from within the circle, and the reason for this departure from the usual method is not at all clear.

When the broken lintel (Plate 2b) belonging to these two stones (122) was being repaired, two sets of mortices were found on its under surface. The deeper and wider pair were set symmetrically, at equal distances from the ends of the lintel. The shallower pair, on the other hand, though separated by the same distance from each other, were offset by about twelve inches towards stone 21, so that at this end the mortice was very close to the end of the lintel.

It was also observed that the flat bed at the top of stone 21 was very much shorter than on any other upright of the outer circle; and indeed the shape of the top of the stone in profile suggests that at some stage in the work, perhaps while the top of the upright was being dressed and the tenons formed, the whole of the top edge of the stone nearest stone 22 was broken off, leaving an upper surface little more than a foot in length.

From these observations we may conclude that the mortices in this lintel (and very probably in all the lintels) were prefabricated while the lintel was still on the ground, and that the corresponding tenons on adjacent uprights were then worked at the correct distance apart. In this instance, however, the accidental breaking away of part of the top of stone 21 increased the span to be bridged between this stone and stone 22, and also drastically reduced the bearing-surface on stone 21, on which the ends of two lintels had still to be supported.

Under the changed circumstances resulting from this accident, it was impossible to set the lintel in the position originally intended. Instead, it had to be moved about a foot anticlockwise; and this meant that the original pair of mortices could no longer be used, so that a new pair had to be made.

The only other fresh discoveries relating to this period concern the carvings (pp. 43-7). In 1956 rubber latex moulds were taken of all the principal groups of carvings, and these have enabled us to reject several of the more doubtful representations of axes on stone 4 as the products of natural weathering, though at least a dozen genuine carvings on this stone still remain. A new axe has been found on stone 5, and what seems to have been a trellis or lattice pattern has been identified low down on stone 3, of a kind similar to some of the geometric patterns executed on the kerb-stones of the great chambered tomb of New Grange in Ireland. During the restoration in 1958 a new carving was also noticed on stone 120 by Mr Brian Hope-Taylor, F.S.A. This stone is a fallen and fragmentary lintel of the outer circle. The carving is much weathered, but seems to have been a smaller version of the sub-rectangular figure already known on stone 57 (p. 44). In its original position it would have been on the underside of the lintel, framed between the two supporting uprights, and would have been difficult to discern against the glare of the sky above it.

Stonehenge IIIb

It is in this period that the recent excavations have produced the most striking confirmation of earlier theories. Already in 1955 it was possible to guess that the dressed bluestone structure had been in the form of an oval or horseshoe, approximately on the line of the present bluestone horseshoe; and that the holes found by Colonel Hawley across the open end of the horseshoe (fig. 3, J, K, L) belonged to this hypothetical setting (p. 82).

The re-excavation of this area in 1956 showed that all three of these holes were certainly stone-holes. The central one, K, had held a single stone, and not two posts as Hawley had supposed. Hole J could also be seen to have been cut through a filled-up post-hole, which was almost certainly connected with the raising of the sarsens of period IIIa. The date of this hole was thus fixed as later than period IIIa; and it seemed improbable that it could belong to period IIIc, the period of the present bluestone horseshoe, since its position did not fit in with the known spacing of the surviving stones in the horseshoe.

Moreover, within stones 31 and 49, at the inner ends of the two in-lying stone-holes of period II (p. 205), and cutting into their filling were two more stone-holes. These, together with holes J and L, formed the end of an oval setting of which the remainder lay on the line of the present bluestone horse-shoe.

The spacing of these four holes averages 11 ft centre to centre, or just twice the spacing of the stones in the present horseshoe. It was estimated that if this spacing was continued round the oval, another hole in the same series should lie some 5 ft north-east of stone 70, between it and stone 59a. A small cutting was made here to test this hypothesis in 1956, and the hole was duly discovered exactly where it was expected with an impression of the stone on the soft chalk at the bottom. Further confirmation came during the restoration in 1958, when yet another hole in the same series was found close be-low the southern side of stone 69, again exactly in the pre-dicted position.

We have thus been able to identify the position of at least six holes for the stones of the dressed bluestone structure of period IIIb. These stones were evidently set in an oval, follow-ing and completing the circuit of the present bluestone horse-shoe, with an interval of about 11 ft between one stone and the next. The hole K on the axis probably belongs to the same setting, and there is reason to believe (p. 212) that there was a pair of stones in a corresponding position at the other end of the oval, immediately behind the present position of the Altar Stone.

Stonehenge IIIc

Since 1955 further areas of the present bluestone circle and horseshoe have been examined, with interesting results.

On the west side, between stones 15 and 43, the course of the bluestone circle has been traced, and four new stumps of stones have been found beneath the surface (fig. 2, 40c, 40g, 41d, and 42c). One of these (41d) is of volcanic ash, a rock also represented on the site by three other stumps already identified (p. 48). The stump near it (42c) was found in the autumn of 1958, during the levelling of the turf after the restoration. It has not so far been examined petrologically, but the description given by the workmen who uncovered it suggests that it is of the same rock as stone 40g.

This latter stone, and the stump to the east of it, 40c, were both found by Colonel Hawley in 1924, and were then wrongly described as being of volcanic ash. The first is in fact of Cosheston sandstone, a micaceous rock superficially similar to the Altar Stone, and like it derived, in all probability, from outcrops on the shores of Milford Haven. The second stump is a grey-blue calcareous ash, for which a precise origin has yet to be found. Both these varieties of rock were previously known at Stonehenge from among the numerous chips in the surface soil, but this is the first time that either has been identified among the stones surviving *in situ*.

In the bluestone horseshoe the holes for two missing pillars were found in 1958. Both lay in the gap between stone 70 and the fallen base of stone 59. Hole 70b had been greatly disturbed, but still contained a large fragment of spotted dolerite, though not in its original position. The adjacent hole 70a was dug directly over an earlier stone-hole of the IIIb setting already found at this point (p. 210). Indeed, the evidence suggested that after the IIIb stone had been extracted, the lower part of the empty hole was immediately filled with rammed chalk to about half its depth. On this foundation the bluestone pillar of the horseshoe setting was then erected. Its base was found still in position. It had evidently been damaged shortly before its erection, and the fractured end was used, lying on its side, as a kind of rough plinth for the base of the main pillar. The evidence here confirms the suggestion already made (pp. 85, 99) that the final reconstruction of the bluestones followed closely on the dismantling of the dressed bluestone structure of the previous phase.

The Altar Stone

During the work of restoration in 1958 a small excavation was made round the Altar Stone in order to settle its exact shape, and thus to decide, if possible, whether it had ever formerly stood upright on one end.

The north-western end of the stone was found to have been heavily battered and defaced by former souvenir-hunters; but enough remained to suggest that in its original form it had been squared off at right-angles to the length of the stone.

The other end, however, was better preserved, and had clearly been dressed to an oblique bevelled outline, very much like the bases of some of the sarsens (e.g. stones 57 and 58).

The purpose of these obliquely pointed bases seems to have been to facilitate the final adjustment of the stone after it had been raised to a vertical position. The occurrence of the same form, deliberately worked, at one end of the Altar Stone suggests that it too was a pillar, and one which, in view of its exceptional size among the bluestones, probably stood on the axial line. We were not able to dig beneath the stone, because it now supports the weight of two fallen sarsens (55b and 156) and is itself broken into two pieces. But it is at least possible that the Altar Stone has fallen over its own stone-hole, just as have several of the sarsens (e.g. 55, 57, 58).

Underneath stone 55b, immediately behind the Altar Stone and just to the south-east of the axis, we found a large hole which seemed to have been a stone-hole. It was hardly deep enough to have held the Altar Stone itself; and its position suggests that it is one of a pair, set symmetrically on either side of the axis. It was unfortunately not possible to verify this by further digging. Tentatively, however, we may conclude that a pair of stones stood here within the oval setting of dressed bluestones (phase IIIb). This pair of adjacent stones would thus serve, as it were, as a back sight for the observation of the midsummer sunrise, the single stone in the hole K at the other end of the oval acting as the fore sight.

Appendix II

The Chronology of Stonehenge and the Avenue

After the Pelican edition of this book went to press there were two further seasons of work at Stonehenge. In 1959 stones 4, 5 and 60 were straightened and set in concrete. In 1964 stone 23, blown over in the previous year by a gale, was re-erected and stones 28, 53 and 54 were also set in concrete.

This additional work has not altered the sequence of construction (chap. 3); but it has provided new evidence. A sample of the 'Stonehenge layer' (pp. 63–5) yielded at its base a clay pipe-bowl made by Jeffry Hunt in Bristol between about 1650 and 1670. This find makes it certain that the layer was laid down, presumably as a deliberate metalling of flints collected from nearby ploughed fields, not later than A.D. 1700. This, if frequently trodden, would take a long time to become grass-grown and buried out of sight. The numerous fragments of the stones now incorporated in its upper levels are almost certainly the product of the increasing demand during the eighteenth century for keepsakes broken off with a hammer.

Excavation around stone 60 showed that during its erection a large piece of its base broke off, leaving the stone too short to reach the height required. The builders adopted the bold expedient of supporting the stone on an improvised foundation of piled sarsen boulders. It is a tribute to their skill and courage that it was only some four thousand years later that the stone began to lean inwards and had to be consolidated.

During recent years it is the chronology of Stonehenge which has seen the greatest change. When this book was first written in 1955 there was only one radiocarbon date (p. 89). There are now five for Stonehenge itself and four for the Avenue, of which details are given below.

Moreover, it has meanwhile become clear that radiocarbon dates cannot be taken at their face value, and have to be corrected to give an estimate of the real date. This has been shown by the radiocarbon dating of tree-rings. Every year a living tree forms a new ring of wood beneath the bark, so that the mean date of a small sequence of rings can be found by counting backwards from the outside. The trees mainly used for this purpose belong to a very long-lived species, the bristle-cone pine of the White Mountains of California, whose environment is so cold and dry that trees long dead do not decay. In this way it has been possible to build up a table for converting radiocarbon dates to true dates which covers the last seven thousand years. For Stonehenge and the Avenue the corrected dates have two consequences.

First, it has previously been assumed (pp. 105–16) that the bluestones were transported directly from Pembrokeshire to Stonehenge by the builders of Stonehenge II. Now, however, there are seven radiocarbon dates for the building of long barrows within thirty miles of Stonehenge. These suggest that the bluestone boulder in Boles Barrow (p. 110) cannot have been deposited there much later than about 2900 B.C., which is about six centuries earlier than the first likely date for the use of the bluestones at Stonehenge itself. It may happen, of course, that further dates for Wessex long barrows will reduce the size of this gap in time; but meanwhile it looks as if the bluestones were first transported to Wessex during the earlier part of period I, or even before, to a site and for a purpose which are still unknown. For their re-use in the abortive double circle of period II they were probably transported from no great distance. The excavations of 1956 and 1964 now provide some slight and tantalizing evidence that the double circle of bluestones enclosed an inner setting; but its original plan must remain a problem to be solved by the excavators of the future.

The radiocarbon dates for the Avenue suggest that it is of two periods of construction, the first straight stretch from Stonehenge being built in period II, as far as the nearer margin of Stonehenge Bottom, about a third of a mile from its beginning outside the entrance of the surrounding earthwork. The remainder, from Stonehenge Bottom to West Amesbury, seems to have been added much later, about 1100 B.C. This implies that after the final rearrangement of the bluestones in period IIIc the use of Stonehenge continued for at least five centuries and perhaps more. The latest period of use, from 1100 B.C. onwards, must thus be defined as period IV.

I formerly ascribed the Station Stones, though tentatively, to period IIIa (p. 79). A reassessment of the evidence now suggests that they may date from the end of period I, but more probably from period II. Stone 93, however, is partially dressed like the sarsens in the centre, and may be a replacement in period IIIa.

In April 1978 a re-cutting of a section across the ditch first made in 1954 (p. 74) revealed a burial of Beaker age, accompanied by three flint arrowheads and an archer's wrist-guard of polished stone, just to the west of the original line of the section. This showed that the fragment of bluestone just above the thin earthy layer (p. 74) was in the filling of this grave, and does *not* mark the level of the silting when the bluestones first arrived at Stonehenge. This is much higher up, towards the top of the chalky rainwash.

In 1979 a new stonehole (97) was found 12 ft north-west of the centre of the Heel Stone (*Proc. Prehist. Soc.*, XLVIII (1982), 75–132). This stone was probably erected and dismantled before the Heel Stone was set up.

The revised sequence below replaces the table on p. 101. The radiocarbon dates, preceded by their laboratory numbers, are given in uncorrected form (b.c.) and in corrected form (B.C.).

2800–   *Stonehenge I.* Construction of the bank, ditch and
2100 B.C.   Aubrey Holes (antler from bottom of ditch,
             I-2328, 2180±105 b.c., 2810±120 B.C.). Erection
             of the Heel Stone, stones D and E, and of the
             timber structure at A. Inception and use of the
             cremation cemetery (charcoal, Aubrey Hole 32,
             C-602, 1848±275 b.c., 2305±280 B.C.). Station
             Stones perhaps erected near the end of this
             period.

2100– 2000 B.C.	*Stonehenge II.* Widening of the entrance causeway and transfer of stones D and E to holes B and C. Digging and filling of the Heel Stone ditch. Construction of the first part of the Avenue (antler from NW. ditch near Heel Stone, BM-1164, 1728±68 b.c., 2135±110 B.C.; antler from SE. ditch, ENE. of Heel Stone, HAR-2013, 1770± 100 b.c., 2190±115 B.C.). Erection of the double circle of bluestones in the Q and R Holes, unfinished (antler abandoned on bottom of R Hole, I-2384, 1620±110 b.c., 2000±125 B.C.).
2000 B.C.	*Stonehenge IIIa.* Transport of the sarsens from near Marlborough. Dismantling of the double circle of bluestones. Erection of the sarsen trilithons, circle, and of the Slaughter Stone and its companion (antler sealed in the erection ramp of stone 56, BM-46, 1720±150 b.c., 2120±160 B.C.). Carvings made after erection.
2000 (?)– 1550 B.C.	*Stonehenge IIIb.* Tooling and erection of stones of the dressed bluestone setting. At the end, digging and abandonment, unfinished, of the Y and Z Holes (antler from bottom of Y Hole 30, I-2445, 1240±105 b.c., 1540±120 B.C.).
1550– 1100 B.C.	*Stonehenge IIIc.* Dismantling of the dressed bluestone structure. Re-erection of all the bluestones in the present circle and horseshoe.
1100 B.C.	*Stonehenge IV.* Extension of the Avenue from Stonehenge Bottom to West Amesbury (bone and antler from both ditches beneath Amesbury bypass, I-3216, 800±100 b.c., 975±115 B.C.; antler from NE. ditch at West Amesbury, BM-1079, 1070±180 b.c., 1345±190 B.C.). The weighted mean of these two dates is 1075±100 B.C.
A.D. 50– 400	Possibly some deliberate destruction of the stones.

Select Bibliography

This list, arranged alphabetically by author, includes only the major articles and books on Stonehenge written since 1900. All the important publications before that date are listed in Harrison's Bibliography cited below. The bibliographical sections of the Wiltshire Archaeological Magazine, *from vol.* XXXII *(1902) to vol.* XLIX *(1942), contain additional references to minor publications, including letters and articles in the daily and weekly press.*

ATKINSON, R. J. C. 'Stonehenge in the light of recent research', *Nature*, 176 (1954), 474–5.
Stonehenge and Avebury, H.M.S.O., 1959.
What is Stonehenge?, H.M.S.O., 1962.
'Moonshine on Stonehenge', *Antiquity*, XL (1966), 212–16.
'Stonehenge in darkness', *New York Review of Books*, VI (23 June 1966), 14–16.
'The Stonehenge bluestones', XLVIII (1974), 62–3.
'Megalithic Astronomy: a prehistorian's comments', *Journ. Hist. Astron.*, VI (1975), 42–52.
'The Stonehenge Stations', *Journ. Hist. Astron.*, VII (1976), 142–4.
'Interpreting Stonehenge,' *Nature*, 265 (1977), 11.
'Some new measurements on Stonehenge', *Nature*, 275 (1978), 50–52.
Stonehenge and Neighbouring Monuments, H.M.S.O., 1978.
ATKINSON, R. J. C. and EVANS, J. G. 'Recent excavations at Stonehenge', *Antiquity*, LII (1978), 235–6.
ATKINSON, R. J. C. *et al.* 'The excavation of two additional holes at Stonehenge', *Antiquaries Journal*, XXXII (1952), 14–20.
BARCLAY, E. *The Ruined Temple, Stonehenge*, London, 1911.
BERGSTROM, T. and VATCHER, L. *Stonehenge*, London, 1974.
BURL, A. *The Stone Circles of the British Isles*, New Haven and London, 1976, 302–16.
CHARRIÈRE, G. 'Stonehenge: rythmes architecturaux et orientation', *Bull. Soc. Préhistorique Française*, LVIII (1961), 276–9.
CHRISTIE, P. M. 'The Stonehenge Cursus', *Wilts. Archaeological Magazine*, LVIII (1963), 370–82.
COLTON, R. and MARTIN, R. L. 'Eclipse cycles and eclipses at Stonehenge', *Nature*, 213 (1967), 476–8.
'Eclipse prediction at Stonehenge', *Nature*, 221 (1969), 1011–12.

CRAWFORD, O. G. S. 'The Stonehenge Avenue', *Antiquaries Journal*, IV (1924), 57–9.

'The symbols carved at Stonehenge', *Antiquity*, XXVIII (1954), 221–4.

CUNNINGTON, R. H. *Stonehenge and its date*, London, 1935.

DIBBLE, W. E. 'A possible Pythagorean triangle at Stonehenge', *Journ. Hist. Astron.*, VII (1976), 141–2.

GOWLAND, W. 'Recent excavations at Stonehenge', *Archaeologia*, LVIII (1902), 38–119.

GRINSELL, L. V. *The Archaeology of Wessex*, London, 1958, 59–66.

Legendary History and Folklore of Stonehenge (West Country Folklore, no. 9), Guernsey, 1975.

HARRISON, W. J. 'Bibliography of Stonehenge and Avebury', *Wilts. Archaeological Magazine*, XXXII (1902), 1–169.

HAWKES, J. 'God in the machine', *Antiquity*, XLI (1967), 174–80.

HAWKINS, G. S. *Stonehenge Decoded*, London, 1966.

Astro-archaeology (Smithsonian Institution Special Report 226), Cambridge, Mass., 1966.

Beyond Stonehenge, London, 1973, 9–70.

HAWKINS, G. S. *et al.* 'Hoyle on Stonehenge: some comments', *Antiquity*, XLI (1967), 91–8.

HAWLEY, W. 'Excavations at Stonehenge', *Antiquaries Journal*, I (1921), 19–41; II (1922), 36–52; III (1923), 13–20; IV (1924), 30–39; V (1925), 39–50; VI (1926), 1–16; VIII (1928), 149–76.

HOYLE, F. 'Speculations on Stonehenge', *Antiquity*, XL (1966), 262–76.

From Stonehenge to Modern Cosmology, San Francisco, 1973, 19–54.

On Stonehenge, London, 1977.

KELLAWAY, G. A. 'Glaciation and the stones of Stonehenge', *Nature*, 232 (1971), 30–35.

LOCKYER, N. *Stonehenge and other British Stone Monuments Astronomically Considered*, London, 1906; 2nd ed., revised, 1909.

MACKIE, E. W. *Science and Society in Prehistoric Britain*, London, 1977, 106–31.

NEWALL, R. S. 'Stonehenge', *Antiquity*, III (1929), 75–88.

'Stonehenge: a review', *Antiquity*, XXX (1956), 137–41.

Stonehenge, H.M.S.O., 1959.

'Megaliths once near Stonehenge', *Wilts. Archaeological Magazine*, LXI (1966), 93.

NEWMAN, C. A. *The Enigma of Stonehenge*, Tadcaster, 1964.

'Stonehenge: a neolithic "observatory"', *Nature*, 211 (1968), 456–8.

Supplement to the Enigma of Stonehenge, Leeds, 1970.

The Astronomical Significance of Stonehenge, Leeds, 1972.

PIGGOTT, S. 'Stonehenge Reviewed' in *Aspects of Archaeology in Britain and Beyond*, ed. W. F. Grimes, London, 1951, 274–92.

'Recent work at Stonehenge', *Antiquity*, XXVIII (1954), 221–4.

'Stonehenge Restored', *Antiquity*, XXXIII (1959), 50–51.

RICE HOLMES, T. *Ancient Britain and the Invasions of Julius Caesar*, Oxford, 1907, 213–17, 468–82.

ROBINSON, J. H. 'Sunrise and Moonrise at Stonehenge', *Nature*, 225 (1907), 1236–7.

SMITH, G. 'Excavation of the Stonehenge Avenue at West Amesbury, Wiltshire', *Wilts. Archaeological Magazine*, LXVIII (1973), 42–56.

STEVENS, F. *Stonehenge, Today and Yesterday*, London, 1916.

STONE, E. H. *The Stones of Stonehenge*, London, 1924.

STONE, J. F. S. 'The Stonehenge Cursus and its affinities', *Archaeological Journal*, CIV (1948), 7–19.

Wessex before the Celts, London, 1958, 74–83, 94–104.

THATCHER, A. R. 'The Station Stones at Stonehenge', *Antiquity*, L (1976), 144–6.

THOM, A. *et al.* 'Stonehenge', *Journ. Hist. Astron.*, V (1974), 71–90.

'Stonehenge as a possible lunar observatory', *Journ. Hist. Astron.*, VI (1975), 19–30.

THOMAS, H. H. 'The Source of the Stones of Stonehenge', *Antiquaries Journal*, III (1923), 239–60.

VATCHER, F. and L. 'Excavation and Fieldwork in Wiltshire, 1967', *Wilts. Archaeological Magazine*, LXIII (1968), 108.

'Excavation and Fieldwork in Wiltshire, 1968', *Wilts. Archaeological Magazine*, LXIV (1969), 123.

'Excavations of three postholes in Stonehenge car park', *Wilts. Archaeological Magazine*, LXVIII (1973), 57–63.

Index

A CHOICE OF
PELICANS AND PEREGRINES

☐ **The Knight, the Lady and the Priest**
Georges Duby £6.95

The acclaimed study of the making of modern marriage in medieval France. 'He has traced this story – sometimes amusing, often horrifying, always startling – in a series of brilliant vignettes' – *Observer*

☐ **The Limits of Soviet Power** **Jonathan Steele** £3.95

The Kremlin's foreign policy – Brezhnev to Chernenko, is discussed in this informed, informative 'wholly invaluable and extraordinarily timely study' – *Guardian*

☐ **Understanding Organizations** **Charles B. Handy** £4.95

Third Edition. Designed as a practical source-book for managers, this Pelican looks at the concepts, key issues and current fashions in tackling organizational problems.

☐ **The Pelican Freud Library: Volume 12** £5.95

Containing the major essays: *Civilization, Society and Religion, Group Psychology* and *Civilization and Its Discontents*, plus other works.

☐ **Windows on the Mind** **Erich Harth** £4.95

Is there a physical explanation for the various phenomena that we call 'mind'? Professor Harth takes in age-old philosophers as well as the latest neuroscientific theories in his masterly study of memory, perception, free will, selfhood, sensation and other richly controversial fields.

☐ **The Pelican History of the World**
J. M. Roberts £5.95

'A stupendous achievement . . . This is the unrivalled World History for our day' – A. J. P. Taylor

A CHOICE OF
PELICANS AND PEREGRINES

☐ *A Question of Economics* **Peter Donaldson** £4.95

Twenty key issues – from the City and big business to trades unions – clarified and discussed by Peter Donaldson, author of *10 × Economics* and one of our greatest popularizers of economics.

☐ *Inside the Inner City* **Paul Harrison** £4.95

A report on urban poverty and conflict by the author of *Inside the Third World*. 'A major piece of evidence' – *Sunday Times*. 'A classic: it tells us what it is really like to be poor, and why' – *Time Out*

☐ *What Philosophy Is* **Anthony O'Hear** £4.95

What are human beings? How should people act? How do our thoughts and words relate to reality? Contemporary attitudes to these age-old questions are discussed in this new study, an eloquent and brilliant introduction to philosophy today.

☐ *The Arabs* **Peter Mansfield** £4.95

New Edition. 'Should be studied by anyone who wants to know about the Arab world and how the Arabs have become what they are today' – *Sunday Times*

☐ *Religion and the Rise of Capitalism*
R. H. Tawney £3.95

The classic study of religious thought of social and economic issues from the later middle ages to the early eighteenth century.

☐ *The Mathematical Experience*
Philip J. Davis and Reuben Hersh £7.95

Not since *Gödel, Escher, Bach* has such an entertaining book been written on the relationship of mathematics to the arts and sciences. 'It deserves to be read by everyone ... an instant classic' – *New Scientist*

A CHOICE OF PENGUINS

☐ **The Complete Penguin Stereo Record and Cassette Guide**
Greenfield, Layton and March £7.95

A new edition, now including information on compact discs. 'One of the few indispensables on the record collector's bookshelf' – *Gramophone*

☐ **Selected Letters of Malcolm Lowry**
Edited by Harvey Breit and Margerie Bonner Lowry £5.95

'Lowry emerges from these letters not only as an extremely interesting man, but also a lovable one' – Philip Toynbee

☐ **The First Day on the Somme**
Martin Middlebrook £3.95

1 July 1916 was the blackest day of slaughter in the history of the British Army. 'The soldiers receive the best service a historian can provide: their story told in their own words' – *Guardian*

☐ **A Better Class of Person** **John Osborne** £2.50

The playwright's autobiography, 1929–56. 'Splendidly enjoyable' – John Mortimer. 'One of the best, richest and most bitterly truthful autobiographies that I have ever read' – Melvyn Bragg

☐ **The Winning Streak** **Goldsmith and Clutterbuck** £2.95

Marks & Spencer, Saatchi & Saatchi, United Biscuits, GEC . . . The UK's top companies reveal their formulas for success, in an important and stimulating book that no British manager can afford to ignore.

☐ **The First World War** **A. J. P. Taylor** £4.95

'He manages in some 200 illustrated pages to say almost everything that is important . . . A special text . . . a remarkable collection of photographs' – *Observer*

A CHOICE OF PENGUINS

☐ **Man and the Natural World** Keith Thomas £4.95

Changing attitudes in England, 1500–1800. 'An encyclopedic study of man's relationship to animals and plants . . . a book to read again and again' – Paul Theroux, *Sunday Times* Books of the Year

☐ **Jean Rhys: Letters 1931–66**
Edited by Francis Wyndham and Diana Melly £4.95

'Eloquent and invaluable . . . her life emerges, and with it a portrait of an unexpectedly indomitable figure' – Marina Warner in the *Sunday Times*

☐ **The French Revolution** Christopher Hibbert £4.95

'One of the best accounts of the Revolution that I know . . . Mr Hibbert is outstanding' – J. H. Plumb in the *Sunday Telegraph*

☐ **Isak Dinesen** Judith Thurman £4.95

The acclaimed life of Karen Blixen, 'beautiful bride, disappointed wife, radiant lover, bereft and widowed woman, writer, sibyl, Scheherazade, child of Lucifer, Baroness; always a unique human being . . . an assiduously researched and finely narrated biography' – *Books & Bookmen*

☐ **The Amateur Naturalist**
Gerald Durrell with Lee Durrell £4.95

'Delight . . . on every page . . . packed with authoritative writing, learning without pomposity . . . it represents a real bargain' – *The Times Educational Supplement.* 'What treats are in store for the average British household' – *Daily Express*

☐ **When the Wind Blows** Raymond Briggs £2.95

'A visual parable against nuclear war: all the more chilling for being in the form of a strip cartoon' – *Sunday Times.* 'The most eloquent anti-Bomb statement you are likely to read' – *Daily Mail*

PENGUIN TRAVEL BOOKS

☐ *Arabian Sands* **Wilfred Thesiger** £3.95

'In the tradition of Burton, Doughty, Lawrence, Philby and Thomas, it is, very likely, the book about Arabia to end all books about Arabia' – *Daily Telegraph*

☐ *The Flight of Ikaros* **Kevin Andrews** £3.50

'He also is in love with the country . . . but he sees the other side of that dazzling medal or moon . . . If you want some truth about Greece, here it is' – Louis MacNeice in the *Observer*

☐ *D. H. Lawrence and Italy* £4.95

In *Twilight in Italy, Sea and Sardinia* and *Etruscan Places,* Lawrence recorded his impressions while living, writing and travelling in 'one of the most beautiful countries in the world'.

☐ *Maiden Voyage* **Denton Welch** £3.95

Opening during his last term at public school, from which the author absconded, *Maiden Voyage* turns into a brilliantly idiosyncratic account of China in the 1930s.

☐ *The Grand Irish Tour* **Peter Somerville-Large** £4.95

The account of a year's journey round Ireland. 'Marvellous . . . describes to me afresh a landscape I thought I knew' – Edna O'Brien in the *Observer*

☐ *Slow Boats to China* **Gavin Young** £3.95

On an ancient steamer, a cargo dhow, a Filipino kumpit and twenty more agreeably cranky boats, Gavin Young sailed from Piraeus to Canton in seven crowded and colourful months. 'A pleasure to read' – Paul Theroux

PENGUIN TRAVEL BOOKS

☐ *The Kingdom by the Sea* **Paul Theroux**   £2.50

1982, the year of the Falklands War and the Royal Baby, was the ideal time, Theroux found, to travel round the coast of Britain and surprise the British into talking about themselves. 'He describes it all brilliantly and honestly' – Anthony Burgess

☐ *One's Company* **Peter Fleming**   £3.50

His journey to China as special correspondent to *The Times* in 1933. 'One reads him for literary delight . . . But, he is also an observer of penetrating intellect' – Vita Sackville West

☐ *The Traveller's Tree* **Patrick Leigh Fermor**   £3.95

'A picture of the Indies more penetrating and original than any that has been presented before' – *Observer*

☐ *The Path to Rome* **Hilaire Belloc**   £3.95

'The only book I ever wrote for love,' is how Belloc described the wonderful blend of anecdote, humour and reflection that makes up the story of his pilgrimage to Rome.

☐ *The Light Garden of the Angel King* **Peter Levi**   £2.95

Afghanistan has been a wild rocky highway for nomads and merchants, Alexander the Great, Buddhist monks, great Moghul conquerors and the armies of the Raj. Here, quite brilliantly, Levi writes about their journeys and his own.

☐ *Among the Russians* **Colin Thubron**   £3.95

'The Thubron approach to travelling has an integrity that belongs to another age' – Dervla Murphy in the *Irish Times*. 'A magnificent achievement' – Nikolai Tolstoy

PENGUIN REFERENCE BOOKS

☐ **The Penguin Map of the World**   £2.95

Clear, colourful, crammed with information and fully up-to-date, this is a useful map to stick on your wall at home, at school or in the office.

☐ **The Penguin Map of Europe**   £2.95

Covers all land eastwards to the Urals, southwards to North Africa and up to Syria, Iraq and Iran * Scale = 1:5,500,000 * 4-colour artwork * Features main roads, railways, oil and gas pipelines, plus extra information including national flags, currencies and populations.

☐ **The Penguin Map of the British Isles**   £2.95

Including the Orkneys, the Shetlands, the Channel Islands and much of Normandy, this excellent map is ideal for planning routes and touring holidays, or as a study aid.

☐ **The Penguin Dictionary of Quotations**   £3.95

A treasure-trove of over 12,000 new gems and old favourites, from Aesop and Matthew Arnold to Xenophon and Zola.

☐ **The Penguin Dictionary of Art and Artists**   £3.95

Fifth Edition. 'A vast amount of information intelligently presented, carefully detailed, abreast of current thought and scholarship and easy to read' – *The Times Literary Supplement*

☐ **The Penguin Pocket Thesaurus**   £2.50

A pocket-sized version of Roget's classic, and an essential companion for all commuters, crossword addicts, students, journalists and the stuck-for-words.